Political Theory and the Ecological Challenge

In recent years the engagement between the environmental 'agenda' and mainstream political theory has become increasingly widespread and profound. Each has affected the other in palpable and important ways, and it makes increasing sense for political theorists in each camp to engage with one another. This book draws together the threads of this interconnecting enquiry in order to assess its status and meaning. Andrew Dobson and Robyn Eckersley have gathered together a team of renowned scholars to think through the challenge that political ecology presents to political theory. Looking at fourteen familiar political ideologies and concepts such as liberalism, conservatism, justice and democracy, the contributors question how they are reshaped, distorted or transformed from an environmental perspective. Lively, accessible and authoritative, this book will appeal to scholars and students alike.

ANDREW DOBSON is Professor of Politics in the School of Politics, International Relations and Philosophy at Keele University, UK. He is the author of a number of books including *Citizenship and the Environment* (2003), *Green Political Thought* (2000) and *Justice and the Environment* (1998).

ROBYN ECKERSLEY is a Reader and Associate Professor in the Department of Political Science at the University of Melbourne. Her most recent books include *The Green State: Rethinking Democracy and Sovereignty* (2004) and *The State and the Global Ecological Crisis* (2005, co-edited with John Barry).

Political Theory and the Ecological Challenge

edited by

Andrew Dobson
and
Robyn Eckersley

CAMBRIDGE
UNIVERSITY PRESS

CAMBRIDGE UNIVERSITY PRESS
Cambridge, New York, Melbourne, Madrid, Cape Town, Singapore, São Paulo

Cambridge University Press
The Edinburgh Building, Cambridge CB2 2RU, UK

Published in the United States of America by Cambridge University Press,
New York

www.cambridge.org
Information on this title: www.cambridge.org/9780521546980

© Cambridge University Press 2006

First published 2006

Printed in the United Kingdom at the University Press, Cambridge

A catalogue record for this book is available from the British Library

Library of Congress Cataloguing in Publication Data

Political theory and the ecological challenge / edited by Andrew Dobson and
Robyn Eckersley.
      p. cm.
   Includes bibliographical references and index.
ISBN-13: 978-0-521-83810-8 (hardback)
ISBN-10: 0-521-83810-X (hardback)
ISBN-13: 978-0-521-54698-0 (pbk.)
ISBN-10: 0-521-54698-2 (pbk.)
   1. Political science – Philosophy. 2. Political ecology. I. Dobson,
Andrew. II. Eckersley, Robyn, 1958– III. Title.

JA75.8.P645 2006
320.01 – dc22
2006001738

ISBN-13 978-0-521-83810-8 hardback
ISBN-10 0-521-83810-X hardback
ISBN-13 978-0-521-54698-0 paperback
ISBN-10 0-521-54698-2 paperback

Contents

List of Contributors   *page vii*

Introduction
Andrew Dobson and Robyn Eckersley   I

Part I: Modern political ideologies and the ecological challenge   5

1   Conservatism
    Roger Scruton   7

2   Liberalism
    Marcel Wissenburg   20

3   Socialism
    Mary Mellor   35

4   Feminism
    Val Plumwood   51

5   Nationalism
    Avner de-Shalit   75

6   Communitarianism
    Robyn Eckersley   91

7   Cosmopolitanism
    Andrew Linklater   109

Part II: Political concepts and the ecological challenge   129

8   Democracy
    Terence Ball   131

 9 Justice
    James P. Sterba   148

10 The state
    Andrew Hurrell   165

11 Representation
    Michael Saward   183

12 Freedom and rights
    Richard Dagger   200

13 Citizenship
    Andrew Dobson   216

14 Security
    Daniel Deudney   232

    Index   253

Contributors

Terence Ball, Department of Political Science, Arizona State University

Richard Dagger, Department of Political Science, Arizona State University

Avner de-Shalit, Department of Political Science, The Hebrew University of Jerusalem

Daniel Deudney, Political Science Department, Johns Hopkins University

Andrew Dobson, School of Politics, International Relations and Philosophy (SPIRE), Keele University, UK

Robyn Eckersley, Department of Political Science, The University of Melbourne

Andrew Hurrell, Politics Group, Nuffield College, Oxford

Andrew Linklater, Department of International Politics, The University of Wales, Aberystwyth

Mary Mellor, Department of Sociology and Criminology, Northumbria University

Val Plumwood, University of Sydney

Michael Saward, Department of Politics and International Studies, The Open University

Roger Scruton, The University of Buckingham

James P. Sterba, The Joan B. Kroc Institute for International Peace Studies, Notre Dame University

Marcel Wissenburg, Nijmegen University

Introduction

Andrew Dobson and Robyn Eckersley

Over the past two decades, the landscape of political theory has been transformed by the ecological challenge. A growing number of political theorists have chosen to engage systematically with the moral, political and institutional challenges raised by the environmental agenda. This specialised engagement has seen the emergence of green political theory (or environmental political theory, as it is known in North America) as a distinct sub-field of political theory. At the same time, many 'mainstream' political theorists have found it increasingly difficult to quarantine their enquiry from the various challenges raised by this new sub-discipline and by ecological problems in general. This book seeks to draw together the threads of this interconnecting enquiry and to assess its status and meaning.

The encounter between mainstream and 'green' theory has taken two principal forms. First, there has been a discussion and analysis of the role of environmental politics in the context of modern political ideologies. Thus there have been reflections on (for example) the relationship between liberalism, conservatism, socialism, feminism and the environment – sometimes organised around a debate as to whether 'ecologism' is parasitic on other ideologies or whether it is an ideology in its own right, and sometimes in terms of potential compatibilities between 'green' ideology and other ideologies. There are now very few textbooks on political ideologies that do not contain a chapter on ecologism (usually the last chapter – the position formerly occupied by feminism). The first part of this book reflects this ideological engagement, while also adding fresh perspectives and new layers to this ongoing debate. The addition of nationalism, and the more overarching approaches or 'meta-' ideologies of cosmopolitanism and communitarianism, to the standard list of political ideologies are further evidence of the increasing infiltration of ecological ideas into the various ways in which we orient ourselves politically.

Second, there has been an interrogation of traditional political concepts from an environmental point of view. Sophisticated reflections on (for example) democracy, freedom and rights, on distributive justice, on the state and political space, on security and citizenship have enriched these concepts by demonstrating unexpected possibilities within them. Related to this is the rereading of canonical political theorists from an environmental point of view: Locke (his 'proviso'), Marx ('nature as man's inorganic body'), Hobbes and others (states of 'nature'), Burke (his intergenerationalism) – the list could go on – all these take on a fresh look from an environmental point of view. The second part of this book reflects this conceptual engagement and provides a more general illustration of the exciting ways in which old political concepts can be reinterpreted or refashioned to serve new purposes. It is our intention that this part of the book, in particular, should contribute forcefully to the growing realisation that mainstream theory is not – at this historical juncture – complete without taking account of its ecological counterpart.

Students and teachers of political theory will be aware, of course, that the distinction between 'ideologies' and 'concepts' drawn here is often one of organisational convenience rather than intellectual substance. They cannot be so easily kept apart, and there will be debates about which ideologies might be better regarded as concepts (communitarianism?), and which concepts are in fact ideologies (democracy?). More prosaically but no less importantly, political ideologies – the subject of the first part of this book – are often 'spoken' in terms of the concepts that populate the second part. So one of the issues that distinguishes liberalism from socialism, for example, is its particular understanding of the content, meaning and relevance of freedom and rights for political society. The contestation that is political theory therefore builds in a fluid way on debates between the ideologies that are explored in Part I, and the language of that debate is often conducted through arguments over the meaning of the concepts in the second part. This implies, too, that concepts themselves are ideological, at the very least to the extent that the way we think about them is inflected (or infected?) by ideological considerations. This might be deliberate and self-conscious, as part of a project to appropriate a certain understanding of social justice on behalf of socialism, for instance. Or it might be a result of a process of historical sedimentation and ideological hegemony, in which the sway of a given ideology is so great that its articulation of a given concept comes to be the horizon within which practically all thinking about that concept takes place. Something like this might have happened with liberalism and (liberal) democracy.

Thus we have chosen to divide the book up into ideologies and concepts not because we have an intellectual stake in doing so, but to give it a look that we hope will be recognised by those for whom political theory is a relatively new area of enquiry – students, in particular. We have seen undergraduate courses in political theory divided up in this kind of way, and the textbooks used on these courses often follow a similar path. We say a little more about the implications of this, below.

One of the effects of the irruption of 'the environment' on to the political scene has been a palpable rise in interest in environmental political theory among mainstream political theorists – in part for what it might mean in itself, but also for the challenges and opportunities to which it gives rise within mainstream specialisms. Thus, for example, writers on social justice find it increasingly necessary to reflect on the issue of intergenerational justice – prompted in part by the way in which environmental 'goods' and 'bads' are self-evidently distributed across time as well as space. Theorists of democracy have found that a fresh take on 'representation' is required if the principle of affected interests is to take in future generations and even other species, as well as the usual category of 'present generation humans'. Communitarian thinkers criticise liberal thinkers for dealing in the currency of apparently context-less individuals, but it might be that the embeddedness of which they talk should itself have an ecological as well as a cultural-historical dimension. Similar examples could be offered from other conceptual and ideological specialisms.

There are clear parallels here with the effect feminism had (and still has) on mainstream theory. Feminism has had a profound impact on the study of modern political ideologies, and there is hardly a corner of political theory that has not been affected by its questioning of the public – private divide, or by the assertion that the 'personal is political'. Similarly, environmental themes such as intergenerationalism, anti-anthropocentrism, cross-boundary pollution, limits to growth, and ecological embeddedness all impact upon enduring topics in political theory and make us think about them in different ways. So the aim here is not so much to try to outline a 'green political theory' that might be used by activists, for example, but rather to examine the effect that thinking from the point of view of the environment has on these enduring themes. Of course, this thinking may eventually lead to a turning of the tables insofar as certain environmental ideas may be found wanting from the perspective of other traditions of political enquiry. So, for example, while the chapters in this volume use ecology as the cutting tool, the chapter on feminism also suggests why ecology needs feminism.

Environmentalism is a little behind feminism in terms of both its own development and its wider impact, and this makes it possible to aim the present book at two types of audience. On the one hand, it is a textbook aimed at students of either political theory or environmental politics. Students will be familiar enough with the structure of the book for it to provide the landmarks they need for effective orientation, and they will be able to make the comparisons and contrasts that they are used to making in mainstream political theory courses – between conservatism and nationalism, for example. As we remarked above, the structure here is therefore deliberately traditional, and the surprises will come from the content – indeed the surprises should be all the more noticeable precisely for having been generated within a traditional context. For example, concepts that were originally developed in the domestic context have been reinterpreted to perform 'ecological work' across traditional state boundaries. Indeed, one of the hallmarks of the ecological challenge is the way it has prompted political theorists to re-examine the boundaries between inside and outside, and domestic and international. On the other hand, the material presented here is so relatively new, and the advances made are still so relatively original, that professional researchers in political theory will also benefit from it. There is no distinction here between 'state of play' and 'cutting edge'.

We have been fortunate indeed to recruit a high quality group of authors to this project. Each contributor has an international reputation – either in mainstream or in 'green' theory, and in some cases in both. We asked them to write authoritative chapters, but lightly referenced. The priority was to draw out the effect that the environmental point of view has on the ideology or concept under consideration. How is it reshaped, distorted, transformed, even, from this new perspective? What was in the background may come to the foreground, and entire new lines of enquiry may open up. Authors were given no checklist as to what constitutes the 'environmental point of view', since different aspects of environmentalism/ecologism are relevant to different chapters. Our concern has been to draw out and showcase the diverse and creative ways in which political ideologies and political concepts have been re-examined, including the diverse ecological vantage points from which this re-examination has taken place. Our belief is that each chapter speaks eloquently for itself, so we have not felt the need to paraphrase and comment on them here. The general aim has been to encourage not merely critical overviews, but individual, spirited and creative contributions that may be provocative. We believe that is what we – and you – have got.

Part 1

Modern political ideologies and the ecological challenge

1   Conservatism

Roger Scruton

Environmentalism has recently tended to recruit from people on the left, offering ecological rectitude as part of a comprehensive call for 'social justice'. However, concern for the environment is shared by people of quite the opposite temperament, for whom constitutions and procedures are more important than social goals, and who regard the egalitarian project with scepticism. The appropriation of the environmental movement by the left is in fact a relatively new phenomenon. In Britain, the movement has its roots in the nineteenth-century reaction to the industrial revolution, in which Tories and radicals played an equal part; and the early opposition to industrial farming joins guild socialists like H.J. Massingham, Tories like Lady Eve Balfour, and eccentric radicals like Rolf Gardiner, who borrowed ideas from left and right and who has even been identified (by Patrick Wright) as a kind of fascist. Moreover, contemporary environmentalists are aware of the ecological damage done by revolutionary socialism – as in the forced collectivisation, frenzied industrialisation and gargantuan plans to shift populations, rivers and whole landscapes that we have witnessed in the Soviet Union and China. Left-wing thinkers will not regard those abuses as the inevitable result of their ideas. Nevertheless, they will recognise that more work is needed if the normal conscience is to be persuaded that socialism contains the answer to the growing ecological problem. At the same time, they seldom recognise any affinity with 'the right', and often seem to regard 'conservatism' as a dirty word, with no semantic connection to the 'conservation' that they favour.

The explanation, I believe, is that environmentalists have been habituated to see conservatism as the ideology of free enterprise, and free enterprise as an assault on the earth's resources, with no motive beyond the short-term gains that animate the market. Those who have called themselves conservatives in the political context are in part responsible for this misperception. For they have tended to see modern politics in terms of a simple dichotomy between individual freedom on the one hand, and state control on the other. Individual freedom means economic freedom, and this, in turn, means the freedom to exploit natural resources for financial gain. The timber merchant who cuts down a rainforest, the mining corporation that ransacks the subsoil, the motor manufacturer who churns out an unending stream of cars, the cola merchant who sends out a million plastic bottles each day – all are obeying the laws of the market, and all, unless checked, are destroying some part of our collective environment. And because, in a market economy, the biggest actors do the most damage, environmentalists turn their hostility on big businesses, and on the free economies that produce them.

Abolish the market economy, however, and the normal result is enterprises that are just as large and just as destructive but which, because they are in the hands of the state, are usually answerable to no sovereign power that can limit their predations. It is a plausible conservative response, therefore, not to advocate economic freedom at all costs, but to recognise the costs of economic freedom, and to take all steps to reduce them, for example by legislation. We need free enterprise, but we also need the rule of law that limits it. When enterprise is the prerogative of the state, the entity that controls the law is identical with the entity that has the most powerful motive to evade it – a sufficient explanation, it seems to me, for the ecological catastrophe of socialist economies.

However, there is another and better reason for thinking that conservatism and environmentalism are natural bedfellows. Conservatism, as I understand it, means maintenance of the social ecology. It is true that individual freedom is a part of that ecology, since without it social organisms cannot adapt. But freedom is not the sole or the true goal of politics. Conservatism and conservation are in fact two aspects of a single long-term policy, which is that of husbanding resources. These resources include the social capital embodied in laws, customs and institutions; they also include the material capital contained in the environment, and the economic capital contained in a free but law-governed economy. The purpose of politics, on this view, is not to rearrange society in the interests of some overarching vision or ideal, such as equality, liberty or fraternity. It is to maintain a vigilant resistance to the entropic forces that erode our social and ecological inheritance. The goal is to pass on to future generations, and if possible to enhance, the order and equilibrium of which we are the temporary trustees.

This means that conservatism, in the eyes of its critics, will always seem to be doomed to failure, being no more than an attempt to escape the Second Law of Thermodynamics. Entropy is always increasing, and every system, every organism, every spontaneous order will, in the long term, be randomised. However, even if true, that does not make conservatism futile as a political practice, any more than medicine is futile simply because 'in the long run we are all dead', as Keynes famously put it. Rather, we should recognise the wisdom of Lord Salisbury's terse summary of his philosophy, and accept that 'delay is life'. Conservatism is the politics of delay, the purpose of which is to maintain in being, for as long as possible, the life and health of a social organism.

Moreover, as thermodynamics also teaches us, entropy can be countered indefinitely at the local level by injecting energy and exporting randomness. Conservatism emphasises historical loyalties, local identities and the kind of long-term commitment that arises among people by virtue of their localised and limited affections. While socialism and liberalism are inherently global in their aims, conservatism is inherently local: a defence of some pocket of social capital against the forces of anarchic change.

The conservative understanding of political action is therefore formulated, as a rule, in terms of trusteeship rather than enterprise, of conversation rather than command, of friendship rather than solidarity.[1] Those ideas lend themselves readily to the environmental project, and it always surprises me that so few environmentalists seem to see this. It is as obvious to a conservative that our reckless pursuit of individual gratification jeopardises the social order as that it jeopardises the planet. And it is obvious, too, that the wisest policies are those that strive to protect and keep in place the institutions that place a brake on our appetites and that renew the sources of social contentment.

The major difficulty, from the environmental point of view, is that social equilibrium and ecological equilibrium are not the same idea, and not necessarily in harmony. Two examples illustrate the problem. Democracies seem to achieve equilibrium only in a condition of economic growth. Periods of stagnation, rapid inflation or impoverishment are also periods of radical discontent, in which envy, resentment and anger lead to instability. Hence the first concern of democratic governments is to encourage economic growth, regardless of the environmental costs of it. We see this in the present British government's attitude to airports, business parks and roads, the environmental impact of which is put out of mind once these things are seen as economic assets. We see it, too, in the American response to the Kyoto accords. It is not big business that puts the real pressure on the American House of Representatives not to ratify such agreements, but the desire of its members to be re-elected.

---

[1] Trusteeship is associated with Burke, Moser and Gierke; conversation with Oakeshott; friendship with Aristotle. All are trying to reconstruct political authority as something intrinsically welcome to those who are subject to it.

Nor is democracy the only problematic case. Other forms of social equilibrium may equally pose a threat to the environment, not because they depend on economic growth, but because they depend on population growth, or on the consumption of some finite resource like a rainforest. Consider traditional Islamic societies, of the kind to be observed in North Africa and Saudi Arabia. These achieve equilibrium only when families enjoy spheres of private sovereignty, under the tutelage of a patriarch whose social standing is constantly enhanced by his reproductive powers. Each family must be forever adding to its retinue of sons if it is to retain its position. The result, in modern conditions, is a population explosion that is rapidly destroying the environment of Muslim Arabia, and spilling over into a Europe whose institutions and traditions are profoundly incompatible with the Muslim conception of the moral life.

The conservative response to this kind of problem is to recognise that environmental equilibrium is a part of any durable social order. The conception put before us by Burke is in fact one that ought to appeal to environmentalists. Burke's response to Rousseau's theory of the social contract was to acknowledge that political order is like a contract, but to add that it is not a contract between the living only, but between the living, the unborn and the dead (Burke 1987). In other words, to speak plainly, not a contract at all, but a relation of trusteeship, in which inherited benefits are conserved and passed on. The living may have an interest in consuming the earth's resources, but it was not for this that the dead laboured. And the unborn depend upon our restraint. Long-term social equilibrium, therefore, must include ecological equilibrium.

This thesis, which environmentalists are apt to express in terms of 'sustainability', is better expressed in Burke's way. For Burke reminds us of a motive that arises naturally in human beings, and which can be exploited for the wider purpose of environmental and institutional conservation: namely, love. This motive leads people both to create good things and to destroy them. But it turns of its own accord in a direction that favours conservation, since human love extends to the dead and the unborn: we mourn the one and plan for the other out of a natural superfluity of gratitude and good will. True social equilibrium arises when the institutions are in place that encourage that superfluity and channel it towards the maintenance of the social organism. The principal danger is that those institutions might be destroyed in the name of present emergencies, present appetites and the egregious needs of the merely living.

This emphasis on small-scale, observable and believable human motives is one of the strong points of conservative political thinking. Socialists place before us ideals of equality and social justice. But they seldom trouble to ask whether anyone – still less whether everyone – is motivated to pursue those things. The same problem arises with the environmentalists' goal of sustainability. It may be my goal and yours: but what about Jill, John and Marianne? Liberals are on safer ground with their ruling concept of liberty: it can be assumed that rational beings will aim for liberty, since liberty is the precondition of aiming for anything. On the other hand, people often surrender part of their liberty, and the principal cause of their doing so is the emotion – namely love – on which durable societies are founded.

It seems to me that the greatest weakness in radical environmentalism has been its failure to explore the question of human motivation. There is one overwhelming reason for the degradation of the environment, and that is human appetite. In the wealthier parts of the world people are too many, too mobile, too keen to gratify their every desire, too unconcerned about the waste that builds up in their wake, too eager, in the jargon of economics, to externalise their costs. Most of our environmental problems are special cases of this general problem. And the problem can be more simply described as the triumph of desire over restraint. It can be solved only when restraint prevails over desire, in other words, only when people have relearned the habit of sacrifice. For what do people make sacrifices? For the things that they love. And when do these sacrifices benefit the unborn? When they are made for the dead. Such was the core sentiment to which Burke and de Maistre made appeal.

There is a tendency on the left to single out the big players in the market as the principal culprits: to pin environmental crime on those – like oil companies, motor manufacturers, logging corporations, agribusinesses, supermarkets – who make their profits by exporting their costs to future generations. But this is to mistake the effect for the cause. In a free market these ways of making money emerge by an invisible hand from choices made by all of us. It is the demand for cars, oil, cheap food and expendable luxuries that is the real cause of the industries that provide these things. Of course it is true that the big players externalise their costs whenever they can. But so do we. Whenever we travel by air, whenever we visit the supermarket, whenever we consume fossil fuels, we are exporting our costs to future generations. A free economy is one that is driven by individual demand. The solution is not the socialist one of abolishing the free economy, since this merely places massive economic power in the hands of unaccountable bureaucrats, who are equally in the business of exporting their costs. The solution is to rectify our demands so as to bear the costs of them ourselves. In short, we must change our lives. And we can change our lives only if we have a motive to do so – a motive that is strong enough to constrain our appetites.

When Burke invoked our feelings towards the dead he was placing in the centre of political order a universal emotion which, he believed, could safeguard the long-term interests of society. But this motive extends no further than our local and contingent attachments. Through institutions of membership and the 'little platoons' that shape our allegiances we can extend our social concern beyond our immediate family. Nevertheless, the sense of a shared inheritance does not extend to all mankind, and the respect for the dead – which is a respect for *our* dead, for those who have made sacrifices on *our* behalf – peters out at the social horizon, where 'we' shades into 'they'.[2] Modern societies are societies of strangers. And one of the underlying conservative projects in our times has been to discover the kind of affection that can bind such a society together across generations, without risking fragmentation along family, tribal or mafia lines. Hence the importance in conservative thinking of the nation and the nation state – a point to which I shall return.

Conservatives are not in the business of conserving just any law, institution or custom. Their desire is to conserve the institutions that embody collective solutions to recurring problems, and which pass on socially generated knowledge. In Burke's view (and mine), the common law is such an institution; so are political institutions like representative government, and social institutions like marriage and the family. These are institutions that foster the habit of sacrifice, and which therefore generate the motive on which the husbanding of resources depends.

Now there is a real cost involved in upholding such institutions and defending them from predation – a cost that imbues Burke's *Reflections on the French Revolution* with its air of solemn melancholy. For entropy can beset even the most settled form of human engagement. The social conservative who, for example, defends the family in modern conditions attracts the anger of those who have liberated themselves from this particular institutional constraint. It does no good to follow Charles Murray and James Q. Wilson in pointing out the social costs of single parenthood and divorce. For that is simply to speak for future generations, people who don't yet exist, and who have been dropped from the equation.

Something similar happens when we consider questions of ecology. To defend slow food, slow transport and low energy consumption in a

---

[2] This theme is beginning to enter the environmental literature, thanks to writers like Avner de-Shalit (1995) and John O'Neill (1993).

society addicted to fast food, tourism, luxury and waste is to risk the anger of those who need to be converted. Not only are there no votes to be won by seeking to close airports, to narrow roads or to return to a local food economy. There is the serious risk of making matters worse, by representing environmental protection as the cause of nostalgic cranks. All environmental activists are familiar with this reaction. But I am surprised that they do not see that it is a version of the very same reaction that is directed towards social conservatives, when they defend the beleagured moral order that was – until a few decades ago – passed from generation to generation as a matter of course. Environmentalists and conservatives are both in search of the motive that will defend a shared but threatened legacy from predation by its current trustees.

Rational self-interest is not, I think, the motive that we are seeking. For rational self-interest is subject to the well-known free-rider and prisoner's dilemma syndromes, and cannot avert, but on the contrary will always promote, 'the tragedy of the commons'. Social contract theorists, from Hobbes to Rawls, have attempted to overcome this problem, but always they come up against some version of the original difficulty: why is it more reasonable to bide by the contract than to pretend to bide by it?

What is needed is a non-egotistic motive that can be elicited in ordinary members of society and relied upon to serve the long-term ecological goal. Burke proposed the 'hereditary principle', as protecting important institutions from pillage or decay, and believed that people have a natural tendency to accept the limits that this principle places on their desires. Hegel argued for the priority of non-contractual obligations, of the kind that sustain the family, and believed that similar obligations could be recuperated and exercised at the political level. In similar vein, de Maistre gave a central place to piety, as a motive that puts divinely ordained traditions and constitutions above the temptations of self-interest.

None of those suggestions is likely to carry complete conviction today, though each tries to frame a picture of human motivation that does not make rational self-interest the sole ground for collective decision-making. Burke's invocation of the hereditary principle is of particular interest, since it engages directly with what he predicted (rightly as it happened) would be the outcome of the French Revolution – namely, a squandering of inherited resources and a wholesale loss of what we would now call 'social capital', including law, educational institutions and public or quasi-public endowments.

Burke's model of inheritance was the English hereditary estate, which removed assets from the market, protected them from pillage, and erected in the place of absolute ownership a kind of trusteeship, with the life tenant as beneficiary. This institution, protected by law, withheld land and natural resources from exploitation and endowed tenants for life with a kind of sovereignty on condition that they passed the land unencumbered to their heirs. No environmentalist can be insensible of the enormous ecological benefit of 'settled land', so conceived. This was a resource that could not be exploited for all it was worth. It had to be used for the benefit of the 'successors in title' – in other words, sustainably. Modern environmentalists are likely to be sensible too of the social inequalities and hierarchies that this form of ownership perpetuated. And those of a leftist persuasion will no doubt share the passionate distaste expressed by Raymond Williams, in *The Country and the City*, for a social order that (according to Williams at least) kept the real producers unrewarded and the idlers forever in clover. The Settled Land Acts, passed and amended at various times during the nineteenth and early twentieth centuries, gave tenants for life the right to convert landed estates into monetary capital, by selling the land to someone who would be free to develop it and retaining the proceeds in trust for the successors in title. In no time the industrialists and the mining corporations had moved in. The result was a vast increase in the wealth of Britain, the first steps towards social equality, and a century of environmental destruction.

Burke saw the hereditary principle as a psychological obstacle before those who had wished to lay their hands on the estates, the endowments, the church-owned and institution-owned buildings and treasuries, that had safeguarded national assets of France from generation to generation. And he foresaw that, once the principle was rejected, restraint would have no motive, and the assets would be seized and squandered. But to respect the hereditary principle means to accept unequal holdings, hereditary status and the influence of family over individual fortunes. It is impossible to combine this state of mind with the modern demand for equality, which loudly affirms the rights of the living over the paper claims of the dead.

We cannot return to the kind of social motivations that Burke called upon: people don't think that way any more. But we should take a lesson from Burke, Hegel and de Maistre. We should recognise that environmental protection is a lost cause if we cannot find the human motive that would lead people in general, and not merely their self-appointed representatives, to advance it. And here, I think, is where environmentalists and conservatives can and should make common cause. And that common cause is local – specifically national – loyalty (and see de-Shalit, chapter 5).

Many environmentalists on the left will acknowledge that local loyalties and local concerns must be given a proper place in our decision-making if we are to counter the adverse effects of the global economy. But they will tend to baulk at the suggestion that local loyalty should be seen in national, rather than communitarian, terms. However, there is a very good reason for emphasising nationality. For nations are communities with a political shape. They are predisposed to assert their sovereignty by translating the common sentiment of belonging into collective decisions and self-imposed laws. Nationality is a form of territorial attachment. But it is also a proto-legislative arrangement. And it is through developing this idea of a territorial sentiment that contains the seeds of sovereignty within itself, that conservatives make their distinctive contribution to ecological thinking.

A useful contrast is provided by George Monbiot, who has trenchantly argued the case for some kind of global politics, through which ordinary people can fend off the disasters that are being concocted within the global economy and give voice to their desire for a safe, equitable and sustainable economic order. And I suspect that this would be the preferred way forward for those who have retained some vestige of the old socialist agenda, and who still wish to combine environmental rectitude with social justice. However, this approach is premised on two highly questionable assumptions: first, that sustainability and social justice can be combined, and secondly, that ordinary people, given the choice, would opt for sustainability rather than instant gratification. In some circumstances they would, of course. But it is precisely those circumstances that the global economy destroys.

The conservative approach, it seems to me, is more reasonable, even if it is also less ambitious. Rather than attempt to rectify environmental and social problems on the global level, conservatives seek local controls and a reassertion of local sovereignty over known and managed environments. This means affirming the right of nations to self-government and to the adoption of policies that will chime with local loyalties and sentiments of national pride. The attachment to territory and the desire to protect that territory from erosion and waste remain a powerful motive, and one that is presupposed in all demands for sacrifice that issue from the mouths of politicians (Scruton 2004). For this motive is the simple and powerful one, of love for one's home.

Take the example of Great Britain. Our environment has been a preoccupation of political decision-making for a very long time. Landscape, agriculture and climate have been iconised in our art and literature and have become foundational for our sentiments of national identity. Our planning laws, immigration laws and transport strategies until recently reflected this. However, we also know that our country is overcrowded, that its environment is being eroded by urban sprawl, commuter traffic and non-biodegradable waste, that its agriculture is under threat from European edicts and that – largely on account of the recent surge in immigration – our population is growing beyond our capacity to absorb the environmental costs. Sentiments of national loyalty can be called upon to gain support for policies that would control these entropic effects, and which would reflect the longstanding conservative goal of maintaining an inherited body politic in being, as an autonomous and self-reproducing unit. At this local, national, level, coherent environmental policies and coherent conservative policies seem to me to coincide.

And it is only at this local level that I believe it is realistic to hope for improvement. For there is no evidence that global political institutions have done anything to limit global entropy – on the contrary, by encouraging communication around the world, and by eroding national sovereignty and legislative barriers, they have fed into that global entropy and weakened the only true sources of resistance to it. I know many environmentalists who seem to agree with me that the WTO is now a threat to the environment, not merely by breaking down self-sufficient and self-reproducing peasant economies, but also by eroding national sovereignty wherever this places an obstacle before the goals of multinational investors. And many seem to agree with me that traditional communities deserve protection from sudden and externally engineered change, not merely for the sake of their sustainable economies, but also because of the values and loyalties that constitute the sum of their social capital. The odd thing is that so few environmentalists follow the logic of this argument to its conclusion, and recognise that we, too, deserve protection from global entropy; that we, too, must retain national sovereignty as our greatest political asset in the face of it; and that we, too, must retain what we can of the loyalties that attach us to our territory, and make of that territory a home. Yet, insofar as we have seen any successful attempts to reverse the tide of ecological destruction, these have issued from national or local schemes to protect territory recognised as 'ours' – defined, in other words, through some inherited entitlement. I am thinking of the recycling initiatives that are gradually freeing Germany from the plague of plastic bottles, the legislation that freed much of the United States from polythene bags, the clean energy initiatives in Sweden and Norway, the Swiss planning laws that have enabled local communities to retain control over their environments and to think of those environments as a shared possession, and so on. These are small-scale achievements, but they are better than nothing. Moreover, they are successful because they make appeal to a natural motive – which is love of country, love of territory and love of that territory as home.

That, it seems to me, is the goal towards which serious environmentalism and serious conservatism both point – namely, home, the place where we are, the place that defines us, that we hold in trust for our descendents, and that we don't want to spoil. Many of those who have seen this connection between conservatism and environmentalism have also – like Patrick Wright – been suspicious of it (Wright 1998). And local environmentalism between the wars – especially in Germany – was undeniably part of the collectivist turn, even if only circumstantially connected to the Nazi and Communist frenzy. However, I think it is time to take on a more open-minded and imaginative vision of what conservatism and environmentalism have to offer each other. For nobody seems to have identified a motive more likely to serve the environmentalist cause than this one, of the shared love for our home. It is a motive in ordinary people. It can provide a foundation both for a conservative approach to institutions and a conservationist approach to the land. It is a motive that might permit us to reconcile the demand for democratic participation with the respect for absent generations and the duty of trusteeship. It is, in my view, the only serious recourse that we have in our fight to maintain local order in the face of globally stimulated decay. And it is worth adding that, insofar as thermodynamics has a story to tell, it is this one.

This is why I think conservatives are likely to dissociate themselves from currently fashionable forms of environmental activism. Radical environmentalists are heirs to the leftist suspicion of nations and nationhood. They repudiate old hierarchies, and strive to remove the dead from their agenda, being largely unmoved by Burke's thought that, in doing so, they also remove the unborn. They define their goals in global and international terms, and support NGOs and pressure groups which they believe will fight the multinational predators on their own territory and with weapons that make no use of national sovereignty.

Conservatives dislike this approach for two reasons. First, the NGOs and pressure groups that are favoured by the activists are as unaccountable and unrepresentative as the predators they oppose. Secondly, they recruit their following through hatred and demonisation – hatred of the big businesses, the big polluters, the apologists for capitalism and so on, against whom they see themselves pitted as David against Goliath. In other words, they put politics on a war footing, in the manner of St Just and Lenin. This runs totally counter to the conservative desire to found politics in friendship and conversation, and to resolve conflicts wherever possible through dialogue. Conservatives tend to see the environmental NGOs like Greenpeace as threats to social equilibrium, on account of their desire to pin on the big actors blame which should in fact be distributed across us all. And by casting the conflict in the form of a zero-sum game between themselves and the enemy, they obscure what it is really about, which is the accountability of both.

The point can be illustrated in the remarkable case of Greenpeace versus Shell, over the matter of the Brent Spar oil rig, which Shell had proposed to dispose of by sinking it in the sea. Greenpeace weighed in with a massively orchestrated hate campaign against Shell, involving boycotts, advertising, leaflets and pressure on shareholders, in order to prevent the sinking of the oil rig. The reason given was that the rig contains many thousand tonnes of oil and would be an environmental hazard for years to come: a reason that turned out to be false. No suggestion was made that Greenpeace and Shell should sit down together and discuss the problem. This was a fight to the death, between the forces of light and the forces of darkness. Greenpeace won, and the rig is now rusting in a Norwegian fjord, an unsightly wreck costing many millions to dismantle, a process that will certainly be far more polluting than the one originally proposed by the corporation. Having cost Shell millions of dollars, and unjustly damaged its reputation, Greenpeace, on proof that the rig after all contained no oil, offered an airy apology and went on to its next campaign.

In such examples we see how environmental activism, divorced from national sentiments that can carry the people with it, and expressed through unaccountable bodies that follow self-chosen global agendas, does nothing to further the environmental cause. And conservatives will see this as an inevitable result of the radical mindset. Radicals prefer global ideals to local loyalties, and rather than making bridges to their opponents, prefer to demonise them (as Bjørn Lomborg, for example, has been demonised in recent assaults on his work). Institutions like Greenpeace bypass national governments, while exerting force that need never account for its misuse. They exhibit the exultant self-righteousness that Burke discerned in the French Revolution, and which he believed would lead not merely to the disenfranchising of ordinary citizens, but to the squandering of their inheritance.

A conservative who reads the ecological press will constantly encounter this self-righteousness, in the form of 'two-minute hates' directed against corporate executives, in the form of anti-American and anti-capitalist rhetoric of a Pilgerish kind, and in the form of conspiracy theories in which conservatives are identified as the principal culprits. And the conservative response is often to lump the ecological movement with other 'anti-' campaigns – anti-racism, anti-hunting, anti-animal experiments, anti-nuclear and so on – in which the punishment without trial of imagined criminals cancels the desire for reasoned argument. Conservatives then wrongly dismiss the whole environmental movement as a socially divisive one, endorse Bjørn Lomborg on the grounds that someone hated by the environmentalists must be a Good Thing, and try to pretend that the environment is an exclusively left-wing concern, and one that has no place in conservative political thinking.

My own hope is that environmentalists will grow out of the witch-hunting mentality that has alienated conservatives, and that conservatives will cease to be defensive about their true agenda, which is the one implied in their name. I would like to see an *Ecologist* magazine that makes room, in its scheme of things, for old Tory values of loyalty and allegiance. For it seems to me that the dominance of international decision-making by unaccountable bureaucracies, unaccountable NGOs and corporations accountable only to their shareholders (who may have no attachment to the environment which the corporations threaten) has made it more than ever necessary for us to follow the conservative path. We need to retreat from the global back to the local, so as to address the problems that we can collectively identify as ours, with means that we can control, from motives that we all feel. And that means being clear as to who *we* are, and why we are in it together and committed to our common survival. I respect George Monbiot's attempt to identify this first-person plural in planetary terms, just as I respect the Enlightenment conception of the human being as a rational agent motivated by universal principles. As a conservative, however, I bow to the evidence of history, which tells me that human beings are creatures of limited and local affections, the best of which is the territorial loyalty that leads them to live at peace with strangers, to honour their dead and to make provision for those who will one day replace them in their earthly tenancy.

References

Burke, E. (1987). *Reflections on the Revolution in France*. Indianapolis: Hackett.
de-Shalit, A. (1995). *Why Posterity Matters: Environmental Policies and Future Generations*. London: Routledge.
Hardin, G. (1968). 'The Tragedy of the Commons', *Science* **162**.1: 243–8.
Monbiot, G. (2002). *The Age of Consent*. London: HarperCollins.
O'Neill, J. (1993). *Ecology, Policy and Politics: Human Well-being and the Natural World*. London: Routledge.
Scruton, R. (2004). *The Need for Nations*. London: Civitas.
Wright, Patrick (1998). 'An Encroachment Too Far', in Anthony Barnett and Roger Scruton (eds.), *Town and Country*. London: Jonathan Cape.

2   Liberalism

Marcel Wissenburg

It is not uncommon to point to liberalism as the evil genius behind the ecological crisis. In this chapter, I shall argue that there were once good grounds to suspect liberalism of at the very least a certain indifference towards ecological challenges – yet this attitude is changing dramatically. Interest in environmental issues does not come naturally for liberalism, but its internal checks and balances are slowly yet perceptibly greening liberalism.

It is important in this context to distinguish between liberalism as a 'pure' political theory, and the practice of liberalism or the practices ascribed to liberalism, such as the free market and liberal democracy. Classical liberalism, especially, supports the *idea* of a free market, as it sees freedom of enterprise and freedom of trade as necessary conditions for the realisation of individuals' plans of life. Yet that does not necessarily mean that each and every existing free market system or each and every effect of free market enterprise is desirable or defensible from a liberal perspective – involuntary exploitation of humans through slavery or rape, for instance, never is.

Critique to the effect that liberalism is a threat to the world's ecology comes in many forms, and as it turns out, not all are appropriate. At the deepest philosophical level, critics argue that liberalism is a child of the Enlightenment from which it has inherited its parent's deficiencies (cf. Sagoff 1988). Primary among these defects are René Descartes' body/mind, mind/matter, human/nature and nature/culture dichotomies. Although these distinctions are supposedly neutral descriptions of 'how the world works', they would convey an implicit assumption of human superiority over everything else. Historically speaking, many philosophers and scientists did in fact confuse the descriptive and the prescriptive. Yet the argument is not as strong as it appears to be. Cartesian dichotomies are not a necessary condition for a superiority complex: the Bible, for instance, lends itself to similar interpretations. Nor are they necessarily part of what defines a liberal: for one of the greatest liberal philosophers, Spinoza, mind *is* matter.

Similar arguments and counter-arguments can be given for many other heirlooms of the Enlightenment. Its belief in progress, for instance, seems to be almost inevitably tied up with embracing growth, specifically material (economic) growth, and hence with thoughtless exploitation of nature – but 'almost inevitable' is not inevitable enough, and not every liberal confuses progress with economic growth. Thus, John Stuart Mill has in recent years become an icon in green political thought because of his defence of a steady state (or zero growth) economy a century before ecologists reinvented the idea (Mill 1999).

Yet there is one genetic defect that liberalism inherited from the Enlightenment that cannot so easily be discarded: its anthropocentrism (Eckersley 1992). As a *political* theory, liberalism is by definition focused on the welfare and wellbeing of humans, thus not just placing human interests, wants and desires above others but making them the exclusive measure of morality. As we shall see below, when liberals include non-humans (Kant's angels or Bentham's animals) they do so only because they are so like humans. The theory simply did not and could not take other interests or obligations into account; it could only see nature as resources with user value, as means to human ends. However broadly defined those ends may be, as a political theory liberalism is necessarily anthropocentric, therefore necessarily at odds with anti-anthropocentric ecologist theories, and from those perspectives necessarily a threat to the ecology.

In addition to its Enlightenment philosophical heritage, there is another cluster of reasons for believing liberalism and ecological concern to be incompatible. In part, these reasons concern the defining traits of liberalism itself, and in part, they signal the existence of a gap between liberal theory (its potential) and practice.

Democracy was the first defining trait of liberalism to be criticised in the 1970s (Ophuls 1976, cf. Holmes 1993). On the one hand, it would promote the expression of short-term individual (human) preferences, discouraging reflection on the formation and sensibility of those pre-ferences. On the other hand, democracy would limit the effectiveness and efficiency of government: the ecological crisis calls for drastic, unpopular measures, the good of which will only be visible in the long term.

Two responses are possible. First, democracy is not necessarily unre-flective or limited in temporal perspective – a position now widely accep-ted among green political thinkers, promoting 'deliberative democracy' and other improvements on Western democratic practice (Dryzek 1990; Barry 1999; Schlosberg 1999; Dobson 2003; Smith 2003). A second answer also addresses the concern that even ideal democratic procedures do not guarantee non-anthropocentric results: constitutionalism, special protection for fundamental rights and procedures against the democratic vogue of the day. Some rights and duties are deemed more important than others, and should thus be satisfied before others are; some rights may even be inviolable. Again, however, green critics have voiced reservations: the rights of liberalism are rights for humans, not rights for nature, and the rule of human law (or of human rights) is not necessarily good for the ecology.

One of the main liberal criteria for a good system of rights is that it be neutral. It should not only accept the fact of irreducible moral pluralism (the existence of multiple ethical theories, multiple theories of a good life, multiple plans of life and hence of lifestyles), but it should also promote pluralism. This means, depending on one's interpretation of liberal neutrality (cf. Bell 2002: 718), that it should either not unjustifiably exclude various theories of the good, or not unjustifiably inhibit their realisation in the form of plans of life and lifestyles. The operative word here is 'unjustifiably': moral pluralism has to respect human dignity and further the emancipation of the individual. One of the implications neutrality has for the ecology is that ecologically destructive lifestyles cannot be excluded on grounds of principle: neutrality prohibits judgements on the ethical worth of different lifestyles. Another implication is that there is little room for ecological lifestyles – ecologists who would want to live in a world of harmony between humanity and nature, cannot as long as they have to accept the lifestyle of others who do not share their ideals. In more abstract terms, liberalism is open-ended, a collection of procedural ideals for society, whereas ecologism defends a substantive ideal, demanding definite results (Dobson 2001).

As for specific, typically liberal, rights that would inhibit sound ecological behaviour, the role of property and free trade rights are probably most noteworthy. Private property is seen as a symptom of a deeper problem within liberalism: its acceptance (neutrally put) of materialistic plans of life and lifestyles, i.e. the idea that a good life can be defined by the kinds of goods one owns and consumes. One might argue that this is not a specifically liberal problem – the quest for property, consumption and luxury is eternal; all liberalism aimed to do was to bring this ideal within the reach of all of humanity rather than professional elites or an elite of the blood. However, there are also two problems associated with property rights that are typically liberal.

Private property, or more precisely legitimate ownership, implies that owners are free to use their property in any way they like, even to destroy it or use it to their own advantage, to the disadvantage of the community. Thus nature, landscapes, animals and natural resources are prima facie unprotected; the onus of proof is on those who would argue for a need to restrict property rights.

Private property rights also imply a right to transfer goods at will, and to produce them at will: the foundations of the free market and of capitalism, both of which can be argued to have contributed immensely to ecological problems. In historical and practical terms it is absolutely true that classical liberalism and capitalism were often close allies (for reasons on which we do not need to expand here) – and yet 'modern' social liberalism's critique of the unrestrained free market also *predates* e.g. Marxism. Property rights are not sacrosanct for liberals: particularly the Millian tradition of social liberalism has embraced the notion of a welfare state.

In this section we have discussed the green critique of liberalism, and have tried to establish what exactly 'the ecological challenge' is that liberalism would have to meet. We have in fact identified several challenges. First, as a *political* theory, liberalism has always ignored the non-political, and thus never developed any other notion of nature than as the other of humanity. It also seems to be *incurably* anthropocentric: unable to appreciate nature as anything but resources. Its ethical neutrality and in particular its insistence on the importance of property rights works to the disadvantage of ecologically minded theories of the good life.

The greening of liberalism

Although liberalism has not been fundamentally changed by its contact with green political thought, it has developed in many important respects. To be more precise, *some* liberals have taken on a shade of green. While liberals are united by an at times flimsy basic consensus on the importance of freedom, equality, individual responsibility and emancipation, it would be wrong to treat liberalism as a monolithic theory (as its green critics tend to do). Thus, *some* liberals have developed a variety of responses, and *some* strands of liberalism are capable of more. In the context of this brief text, a rough outline focusing on neutrality, anthropocentrism and economic freedom is all we can offer. Where appropriate, the different strands are distinguished, but most of the time we shall refer to generalised notions of social and classical liberalism.

Neutrality

Liberalism's neutrality may not be absolute: it is still in principle biased against green political thought, inasmuch as the latter demands more than a greening at the level of individual preferences. Neutrality of process and neutrality of outcome both seem incompatible with substantive green policies aimed at the realisation of a unique ecologically desirable society and way of life.

Nonetheless, the fact that liberal neutrality is never absolute allows it to come a long way towards answering green challenges – both in practice (pollution, global warming, etc.) and in theory. It all depends on the *kind* of solution one wants, and on whether that solution is compatible with neutrality. At least two factors limit neutrality: the liberal theory of the good, and its conception of reality as limiting the desirable.

No liberal political theory can do without a conception of the human good. For one, without at least some shared interests, both the existence of conflict over scarce resources and the presence of motives for co-operation and mutual benefit would be inexplicable – there would be no need for politics. Hence liberals have to make certain assumptions about what it is that makes individuals feel life is worth living and worth maintaining. In addition, liberal criteria for a desirable social order necessarily presume a foundational idea of the good life: if, for instance, liberty were a morally neutral or even amoral concept, there could be no grounds for promoting it. John Rawls' theory (1972, 1993), which has become the defining statement of liberalism relative to which all other versions of liberalism are understood, illustrates these points. Rawls presumes that individuals share an interest in so-called primary social goods, that is, properties of the physical world like wealth and income, rights and freedoms and self-respect, that all humans require to successfully pursue a plan of life – and all individuals will want more rather than less of these primary goods. This so-called 'thin theory of the good' explains both why social co-operation is required, and why liberty and equality are desirable.

In addition, all political theories including liberalism necessarily contain ontological hypotheses, that is, assumptions about how the real world works and how it restricts political and ethical desires. These hypotheses may concern human psychology (such as Rawls' idea that humans want to realise plans of life), but they can also include environmental factors – such as the notion that some resources really can be scarce. Together, these ethical and ontological assumptions necessarily limit neutrality. Neutrality is not absolute and was never meant to be absolute; its aim is to minimise the moral prerequisites for social co-operation and at the same time maximise social consensus (which comes down to a balancing act).

The fact that liberalism presumes rather than rejects ethical and ontological limitations to neutrality has allowed it, over the past decades, to absorb ecological ideas on the scarcity of natural resources in a multitude of forms. John Rawls' original theory of justice (1972), for instance, contained a so-called just savings principle demanding present generations to save some of their resources and achievements for future generations. After critics pointed out that this seemed to *oblige* us to guarantee infinite growth, Rawls (1993) adapted not the principle (its formulation was ambiguous enough to allow for shrinking economies) but its defence, turning it into a principle that requires present generations to take the welfare of future generations into account under any circumstances. Donald VanDeVeer and others (VanDeVeer 1979; Singer 1988; Garner 2003) accused Rawls and liberals in general of being biased in favour of humans, ignoring the good or interests of animals. This resulted among others in an ongoing debate on animal-friendly amendments to Rawls' theory, for example by including animals in the setting of the Rawlsian social contract. Other critics amended liberal conceptions of property rights, for instance by arguing that the right to ownership of a good does not include an absolute right to destroy the good in question – thus making room for a restraint principle demanding that no goods be destroyed unless necessary and unless proper compensation is offered (Wissenburg 1998: 123), or for a minimum harm principle that further limits the possibilities of justifying 'necessary' destruction (Wallack 2004).

Finally, several liberals have also moved beyond formulating public (political) limits to the neutral or impartial satisfaction of individual preferences into the realm of preference formation itself. In line with Immanuel Kant and John Stuart Mill, many liberals admit that ideals like emancipation and autonomy are not served by taking preferences as given. This has given rise, first of all, to a rapidly growing literature on public deliberation regarding private preferences, an example of which is the debate on whether ecological principles can be included in the so-called Rawlsian basic consensus, the set of values on which reasonable individuals should agree, values that make social co-operation possible and at the same time limit the areas in which individuals may disagree on the good life (Achterberg 1993; Bell 2002). Thus, allowing a government to a priori *prescribe* a moderate and quiet lifestyle (a life most green authors argue is a necessary condition for ecological and human survival; cf. De Geus 2003) and thereby impose a substantive ideal of the good life is definitely incompatible with liberal neutrality – but allowing ecological concerns for ethical or ontological reasons to *limit* the range of admissible lifestyles is an entirely different thing. In the end, the bottle that greens consider half empty (liberalism being unwilling to prescribe a substantively 'correct' way of life) may well be half full.

To direct the process of individual preference formation, some authors also point to Mill's harm principle (Mill 1998) as a forceful instrument for the protection of natural resources: if one may do what one wishes as long as one harms no one (as Mill interprets liberty), and if depriving others of resources they need constitutes harm, then there are again clearly limits to how one may use nature. Of course, there are weak spots in the argument. The strength of the harm principle depends on how one interprets harm, and the principle presumes that Pareto-optimality is actually possible, that is, that when one person benefits from an action, no one else is disadvantaged. If resources should indeed be considered finite, then Pareto-optimality is always impossible, regardless of the definition of harm.

All of these amendments to liberalism's neutrality have two things in common: they still perceive nature in terms of natural resources, and they limit neutrality only on ontological grounds. Even when animals are taken into consideration, the animals are still mere consumers of nature. Nature, it seems, is still nothing but resources.

Anthropocentrism

The distinguishing feature of deep-green or ecologist political thought is that it sees more in nature than resources for humans, unlike environmentalism – regardless of how broadly one defines resources. This ecologist critique of liberal anthropocentrism has two dimensions: on the one hand, it is a critique of the liberal subject (individual humans), on the other, a critique of its conception of the value of nature. Technicalities aside, liberalism can easily meet the environmental challenge, as we just saw – but it has had more difficulty with ecologism.

Until quite recently, liberals had no incentive or reason to worry about scarcity of the supply of natural resources – scarcity was not a matter of supply, nature being an eternally renewable horn of plenty, but of demand. The time factor was irrelevant: a liberally just political order today would be as just tomorrow or any day after. The ecological crisis changed this: suddenly, future generations came into the picture. Moreover, as long as the supply side of the equation could be ignored, there was no practical reason to question the ethical assumption that only humans matter, that only humans have interests and can be harmed, that only humans are moral subjects.

Future generations consist of future individual humans: the one difference with normal liberal subjects is that they do not yet exist – for the rest they fit perfectly within liberalism. It is now widely recognised within liberalism that present generations have obligations towards future generations – but the reasons given vary considerably (Carter 2001). Rawls originally argued that humans 'naturally' care for their own offspring, a concern that an impartially governed society should universalise and translate into solidarity between generations. His critics rejected the naturalness of procreation in the first place, and of natural care secondly, forcing Rawls later to argue for solidarity between generations on the basis of mutual advantage (Rawls 1993). Others argue that no one deserves to be born into this generation rather than another, hence that no generation deserves natural resources more than any other, leading to the conclusion that resources should be shared impartially by all generations (Barry 1989, 1995). Still, some liberals have voiced reservations: if procreation is not natural, and if (as many liberals would assume) it is or should be an individual *choice*, then how can I be held responsible for the fate of other people's children (including my own grandchildren), when others cause their existence (Wissenburg 1998)? Worries like these tie in with the debate on population policy (de-Shalit 2000), where liberals argue against compulsory birth control but in favour of information, emancipation, the availability of contraceptives, etc.

The introduction of animals into the liberal matrix has been at least as difficult. Although liberals like Kant and Bentham already addressed the moral concern owed to animals, it was not until Robert Nozick (1974) put the issue in a political context that it became salient. Nozick asked by virtue of which properties or qualities human interests should take precedence over those of animals, and concluded that whatever those properties might be, liberal moral theory's answer would always remain inconclusive since – if a hierarchy of qualities makes the difference – a race of alien space invaders could always claim superiority to humans by virtue of a quality unknown and unknowable to humans. The problem of inconclusiveness aside, the important thing is that liberals distinguish between humans and animals on the basis of a hierarchy of objective qualities, such as consciousness, a sense of self, of time, of morality, and other qualities that make it possible to have a plan of life and a theory of the good. The alternative (Wenz 1988) is to base priorities on the subjective recognition of responsibilities or relations of care – an alternative that is obviously incompatible with warranting liberty and equality for all humans.

The apparent inevitability of a hierarchy of moral concern does not imply that animals necessarily always draw the short straw. For one, 'typically human' qualities overrule qualities shared with other animals only when human needs (understood as what is vital to the execution of a plan of life) are at stake; in other cases, the interests of animals may be more important than those of humans (e.g. where the interest in not being painfully slaughtered meets a sadistic interest in seeing pain). Secondly, a hierarchy of moral concern means that some creatures may be morally less important than others, but not that their interests do not matter at all. Liberalism's giving precedence to human interests is therefore even compatible with the idea that MPs should not be asses only, but should actively represent the interests of all animals: it is simply a matter of proportion in representation.

The fact that liberalism and proper concern for animals are compatible as a matter of principle does not, of course, answer the question what we owe exactly to which animals when and where. Nor is it important how we refer to these obligations – greens and liberals have wasted countless pages on the smell-of-a-rose issue of whether animals are subjects of justice or 'merely' of 'less strong' moral obligations. What is important is that neither including animals nor including future generations will really satisfy ecologists because the obligations involved are still predicated on individualism (Devall and Sessions 1985; Naess 1989).

Ecologists defend communities and species and their distinct ways of life, landscapes and ecosystems, and not only individual humans or animals. Liberals cannot but argue that one cannot prick an ecosystem or tickle a stone: moral concern is owed only to what has an interest in being benefited or harmed, and that is individual beings, not collectives or senseless entities. This brings us to the second dimension of the ecologist critique of liberal anthropocentrism: if its conception of morally relevant subjects cannot be extended to include non-individuals, then perhaps it can meet the critique by valuing nature differently.

There have been three responses to this particular challenge. One has been for liberals to straightforwardly deny the possibility of valuing nature intrinsically or 'for its own sake'. The concept of intrinsic value, they argue, can only be sensibly applied to humans (or a more extended circle of morally relevant subjects), whereas all else that is valued must by definition be instrumentally valuable in some way, that is, it must be valued because of the purposes it can serve (Wissenburg 1998). Although this approach allows a very wide interpretation of the instrumental value of nature – from direct utility as economic resources to the pleasing, possibly purely aesthetic consciousness that somewhere some bit of pristine nature remains untouched by human hands – it is also an obvious refusal to accept one of the fundamental tenets of ecologism.

Recognising that the green agenda is not served by scholastic debates on the nature of value, various liberal and ecologist authors defended a second, more tactical response: accommodation. Thus Bryan Norton has argued that greens do not need to accept or reject, for instance, liberal *reasons* for acting as long as liberal *policies* are green enough – which they can be (Norton 1991; Barry 1999; Wissenburg 2004).

Recently, a third possible response – for which a name has not yet been coined – has been developed. Andrew Dobson (2003) argues that if liberals value choice for the sake of autonomy, then they should value the existence of as wide a range of 'life environments' as possible. Simon Hailwood (2004), using the term 'landscapes' since no part of nature is or can be untouched by human hands anymore, makes a similar point when he argues that liberals can and should appreciate the 'otherness' of nature (cf. DiZerega 1996). The crucial difference between this third and the other two responses is that it does not presume that nature (or the life environment or landscape) is always already imbued with value – rather, it is valuable because it *is there* as an option, to be appreciated or not. Although valuing a range of ecological options implies that non-individual entities like ecosystems and species are still in a way valued 'instrumentally' (as necessary conditions for the existence of a life environment or landscape), it would seem as if this answer finally takes the sting out of the green objections to liberal anthropocentrism and – ultimately – individualism. The reasons motivating ecologists and liberals may differ, but the results would be the same: maximised protection of ecological diversity combined with maximum freedom for humans to pursue a green life.

Economic freedom

There have been two quite distinct responses within liberal thought to ecologism's critical assessment of the free market and liberal conceptions of property rights: a reaffirmation of elements of classical liberalism, and an extension of social liberalism to ecological issues. Since the latter comes down to amending liberal conceptions of social or distributive justice, treated in another chapter in this book, I shall only discuss the former here.

Robert Nozick (1974) observed that John Locke's classic justification for 'original acquisition', that is, taking natural resources and calling them private property, was based on the flawed proviso that one cannot take anything from nature unless one leaves 'enough and as good' for others. The proviso is flawed because it assumes infinite resources: my taking the last breath of fresh air would be illegitimate because someone else took the last but one breath, leaving too little for me, and so on. The Lockean proviso actually makes the existence of legitimate property impossible. Nozick's solution involved the idea of adequate compensation; others in later years have tried to amend and refine Locke's proviso and the rest of his theory to make finite resources adequately available to future generations and animals (cf. Dobson 1998). One problem still facing the Lockean is that Locke's theory is distribution insensitive, i.e. it may give an account of legitimate property but not of the distribution of property. Natural resources may still end up benefiting some parties (e.g. the North) more than others (e.g. the South) – which is neither conducive to sustainable development nor to sustainable living.

For any free market advocate, the most natural but also most ambitious response to the accusation that the free market is a threat to the environment would be to argue that there is actually no better warrant for the environment than the free market. This is exactly what so-called free market environmentalism (Anderson and Leal 1991) argues: privatising natural resources makes individual owners directly responsible for the value of their property. A rational property owner will do anything necessary to maintain or even increase the value of her property over time, taking into account that resources may have different uses over time: a piece of land valued today merely as a potential second-rate business development area may tomorrow be appreciated as the most precious nature reserve ever.

Free market environmentalism is at best an environmentalist and at worst a nihilist answer to an ecological challenge (Stephens 1999). Consider a natural forest: if industrial forestry is (in the course of an owner's lifetime) more profitable than turning the forest into a nature reserve, the rational owner would be unwise not to start foresting – thereby destroying the forest's natural qualities. Moreover, the free market environmentalist confuses money with value: even if a strong preference exists somewhere in society for protecting the forest's naturalness, the nature lovers in question may simply not have sufficient resources to compensate the owner for lost economic opportunities.

Similar problems haunt most other attempts at reconciling classical liberalism and ecologism. Thus, green consumerism argues for environmental protection through changing consumer preferences, forcing producers to provide ecology-friendly products at the risk of losing clients and profit, but it too depends on contingent preferences and the financial power of consumers. Ecological modernisation (Weale 1992) argues that economic growth and ecological protection can be combined: producing in an ecologically sane way may well turn out to be a profitable growth market. Then again, it also may not. Finally, some authors offer a principled defence of ownership rights as a potentially strong instrument in the protection of the ecology: it may allow, for instance, large pharmaceutical companies to monopolise access to new medicines derived from ancient tribal practices, but it can also be used as an instrument by indigenous peoples to protect their 'local knowledge', not to mention their natural environment, against over-exploitation (Oksanen 1998). Note, however, that one must assume the indigenous property owners to be interested in maintaining their short, nasty and brutish way of life at all, and note that their property rights only protect nature because a worldwide system of property rights is already in existence – a system for which, as we saw above, only eco-logically suspicious justifications have been given.

An even greener liberalism?

Two conclusions can be drawn at this point. First, classical liberalism cannot meet the ecological challenge, however that challenge is defined, simply by insisting on negative liberty (and particularly on the free market) as the answer to all ecological problems. To ensure that those problems will be addressed, it has to accept limits to neutrality and rid itself of its anthropocentric bias. This requires at least a form of institutional representation and protection of non-human and non-present-human interests, and means and methods for accounting for the formation of individual preferences. The inevitable result is that negative liberty can no longer be seen as the supreme criterion of a good society.

Second, both a classical liberalism thus transformed (perhaps beyond recognition), and a social liberalism amended with ecological limits to neutrality and an ecological expansion of its original anthropocentrism, *can* be green, at least in theory. There is no fundamental contradiction between affirming human dignity through individual emancipation, and protecting nature as much as is humanly possible – indeed, the two may well mutually reinforce one another. There is room within liberalism for protecting the ecology rather than the environment and (behind that) for conceptions of nature's value that perhaps do not eliminate but at least pacify the conflict over intrinsic value. There is also room for appreciating animals as more than resources, for limits to neutrality and limits to the use of property rights on ecological grounds, and so on. There are and will at least for a long time be differences of opinion between liberal and ecologist political thinkers, yet most of these are no longer fundamental challenges – they no longer force us to ask *whether* but only *to what degree* liberalism can be green. The ball is back in the ecologist court: it is up to ecologism to indicate what kind of society can no longer count as ecologically sane.

Yet there are also, undeniably, a few topics on which fundamental agreement seems impossible. There will always be disagreement with those green thinkers who on principle reject the notions of property and ownership. Liberalism can go a long way in defending limits to the legitimate *use* and *acquisition* of property, and social liberalism offers ample opportunity to defend the *redistribution* of property even for green reasons – but at its heart remains the idea that individual beings matter, that their lives or plans of life matter, and that such lives cannot be lived without individually available material resources.

This ties in with another area of fundamental disagreement: there are deep-green thinkers for whom the only acceptable society is one where everyone leads an ecologically responsible, modest or even frugal life in a way and an environment that is as close to nature as possible – regardless of whether other lifestyles (like more efficient urbanisation) turn out to be better for all of non-human nature. Most liberals, on the other hand, can go no further than maximising the individual's opportunity to live a life like that alongside others living different lives; perfectionist liberals might even discourage 'unsustainable' lifestyles, but will never embrace the idea of a unique road to salvation. This contradiction is irresolvable for two reasons. First, it requires the prescription of a deep-green life and the explicit elimination and prohibition of all others, which is by definition incompatible with the liberal ideal of dignity and emancipation through freedom of lifestyle and equality of opportunity. Secondly, the deep-green life risks self-effacement by denying what liberalism seeks to regulate: the existence of rogue elements in society who willingly or unwillingly sabotage social harmony. In the case of deep-green 'naturalism', what is denied is the fear of the Four Horsemen from which humanity has fled throughout its existence, the fear that generated the quest for ever more safety and security through the acquisition of resources. To assume that humanity *should* conquer its fear and abandon the quest for material prosperity may (or may not) be reasonable; to expect that each and every individual *can* and *will* is suicidal.

It is here that we meet the final challenge. If liberalism can meet the theoretical challenges posed by green political thinkers (even if it is by rejecting some as unreasonable), the question remains why there is a gap between theory and practice. Why is there still a global ecological crisis? The intellectually honest answer is that this is an unfair question: it presumes a counterfactual situation in which the world could have been 'ruled' by 'true (green) liberalism', but where the ideal was betrayed by non-liberal politicians and political structures.

References

Achterberg, W. (1993). 'Can Liberal Democracy Survive the Environmental Crisis?', in A. Dobson and P. Lucardie (eds.), *The Politics of Nature: Explorations in Green Political Theory*. London: Routledge, 81–101.

Anderson, T., and Leal, D. (1991). *Free Market Environmentalism*. Boulder, Colo.: Westview Press.

Barry, B. (1989). *Democracy, Power and Justice*. Oxford: Clarendon Press.

(1995). *Justice as Impartiality*. Oxford: Clarendon Press.

Barry, J. (1999). *Rethinking Green Politics*. London: Sage.

Bell, D. (2002). 'How Can Political Liberals Be Environmentalists?', *Political Studies* **50**: 703–24.

Carter, A. (2001). 'Can We Harm Future People?', *Environmental Politics* **10**: 429–54.

De Geus, M. (2003). *The End of Overconsumption*. Utrecht: International Books.

de-Shalit, A. (2000). *The Environment Between Theory and Practice*. Oxford: Oxford University Press.

Devall, B. and Sessions, G. (1985). *Deep Ecology*. Layton, Ut.: Gibbs M. Smith.

DiZerega, G. (1996). 'Deep Ecology and Liberalism', *Review of Politics* **58**: 699–734.

Dobson, A. (1998). *Justice and the Environment*. Oxford: Oxford University Press.

(2001). 'Foreword', in J. Barry and M. Wissenburg (eds.), *Sustaining Liberal Democracy*. Houndmills: Palgrave, vii–ix.

(2003). *Citizenship and the Environment*. Oxford: Oxford University Press.

Dryzek, R. (1990). *Discursive Democracy: Politics, Policy, and Political Science*. New York: Cambridge University Press.

Eckersley, R. (1992). *Environmentalism and Political Theory*. London: UCL Press.

Garner, R. (2003). 'Animals, Politics and Justice: Rawlsian Liberalism and the Plight of Non-humans', *Environmental Politics* **12**: 3–22.

Hailwood, S. (2004). *How To Be a Green Liberal*. Chesham: Acumen.

Holmes, S. (1993). *The Anatomy of Anti-Liberalism*. Cambridge, Mass.: Harvard University Press.

Mill, J. S. (1998). *On Liberty and Other Essays*. Oxford: Oxford University Press.

(1999). *Principles of Political Economy*. Oxford: Oxford University Press.

Naess, A. (1989). *Ecology, Community, and Lifestyle*. Cambridge: Cambridge University Press.

Norton, B. (1991). *Towards Unity Among Environmentalists*. Oxford: Oxford University Press.

Nozick, R. (1974). *Anarchy, State, and Utopia*. New York: Basic Books.

Oksanen. M. (1998). 'Environmental Ethics and Concepts of Private Ownership', in D. Dallmeyer and A. Ike (eds.), *Environmental Ethics and the Global Marketplace*. Athens: University of Georgia Press, 114–39.

Ophuls, W. (1976). *Ecology and the Politics of Scarcity*. San Francisco: Freeman.

Rawls, J. (1972). *A Theory of Justice*. Oxford: Oxford University Press.

(1993). *Political Liberalism*. New York: Columbia University Press.

Sagoff, M. (1988). 'Can Environmentalists Be Liberals?', in M. Sagoff, *The Economy of the Earth*. Cambridge: Cambridge University Press, 146–70.

Schlosberg, D. (1999). *Environmental Justice and the New Pluralism*. Oxford: Oxford University Press.

Singer, B. (1988). 'An Extension of Rawls', Theory of Justice to Environmental Ethics', *Environmental Ethics* **10**: 217–31.

Smith, G. (2003). *Deliberative Democracy and the Environment*. London: Routledge.

Stephens, P. (1999). 'Picking at the Locke of Economic Reductionism', in N. Fairweather, S. Elsworthy, M. Stroh and P. Stephens (eds.), *Environmental Futures*. London: Macmillan, 3–23.

VanDeVeer, D. (1979). 'Interspecific Justice', *Enquiry* **22**: 55–79.

Wallack, M. (2004). 'The Minimum Irreversible Harm Principle', in M. Wissenburg and Y. Levy (eds.), *Liberal Democracy and Environmentalism*. London: Routledge, 167–78.

Weale, A. (1992). *The New Politics of Pollution*. Manchester: Manchester University Press.

Wenz, P. (1988). *Environmental Justice*. Albany: State University of New York Press.

Wissenburg, M. (1998). *Green Liberalism*. London: UCL Press.

(2004). 'Little Green Lies', in M. Wissenburg and Y. Levy (eds.), *Liberal Democracy and Environmentalism*. London: Routledge, 60–71.

3 Socialism

Mary Mellor

Introduction

Far from being a challenge, ecology greatly enhances the case for a redefined and refocused socialism. From its origins in the early nineteenth century, socialism has been a diverse and contested philosophy. Socialist principles and practice have been undermined and discredited through failures, atrocities and authoritarian activities undertaken in its name. By the late twentieth century, socialism had all but lost the ideological battle against a radical version of capitalism that rejected any political or social interference with 'free' market systems.

One of the most notorious clarion calls of capitalist market radicalism in Britain was that there was 'no such thing as society' and 'no alternative' to the market. State welfare systems were condemned as the 'nanny' state. Throughout the long, but ultimately unsustainable, boom of the late twentieth century, socialists were unable to mount an effective challenge to the inequalities and destructiveness of the globalised industrial capitalist system. Instead, variants of market socialists, social democrats and New Labourites tried to ally themselves to the 'new reality'. They accorded to capitalism the role of 'wealth creation' and waited patiently for taxable crumbs to fall from the capitalist table. At the beginning of the twenty-first century, confidence in the ability of globalised capitalism to achieve the worldwide freedom and prosperity it promised faltered. Even those at the heart of the project expressed their doubts, most notably the Nobel prize-winner and former Chief Economist at the World Bank, Joseph Stiglitz (2002). According to UN reports during the last two decades of the twentieth century, even while the number of millionaires increased, a quarter of the world became poorer (*New Internationalist* Jan./Feb. 2004: 32). Far from the success of liberal capitalism as peddled by Francis Fukuyama to great acclaim in the early 1990s, the global market was riven by scandals from gangster capitalism in Eastern Europe, to the criminality of Enron and Parmalat. The UK and US were at war, the Japanese economy remained stalled and the major economic success story was non-liberal China. People who had been sold the dream of endless riches through popular capitalism saw their life savings and pensions evaporate as the 'dot com' bubble burst. It was their debts, mainly as endowment mortgages, and their life savings, mainly as pension investment, which had fuelled the late-twentieth-century stock market boom. Like all get rich quick scams, the stock market boom was little different in essence from pyramid selling or a chain letter. The first people to invest made a lot of money and the last to join lost their shirts as the market dried up.

The traditional socialist movement in its various guises was unable to attract people to its cause as the promise of globalised capitalism faltered. Instead, a diverse opposition emerged which included the green movement, religious and spiritual movements, campaigning NGOs, indigenous people's movements, women's movements and many others (Fisher and Ponniah 2003). The core values of this movement did, however, chime with socialist, anti-capitalist and anti-militarist values, and with the goals of movements for global solidarity and economic and social justice. What has not emerged is a clear socioeconomic alternative, a social framework for the twenty-first century.

In order to mount an effective challenge to globalised capitalism, an understanding of its dynamics and weaknesses is required together with a clear vision of other possible socioeconomic frameworks. The political philosophy that has historically undertaken this task is socialism. A weakness of actually existing socialism in its various forms was that although socialism had emerged alongside, and often in reaction to, industrialisation, it became captured by the possibilities of industrial production. The Marxist and labourist focus on struggles around production tended to ignore struggles around reproduction, consumption or the environment and often did not question the 'economy' as defined by capital. This enabled the capitalist promise of growth and consumerism to gain the ideological and material high ground. Social democrats, democratic socialists and other left and centre-left groups argued about the relative unfairness of the system and sometimes challenged its racism and sexism, but rarely its ecological impact. A socialism for the twenty-first century must put at its heart the ecological challenge and escape from the limits of productivist thinking.

Socialism within limits

Most twentieth-century socialist movements shared one core ideological commitment with twentieth-century capitalism: the aim of progress through the industrialisation of production. The political focus was on the ownership and/or control of the means of production or the distribution/taxation of its output. Capitalism by the mid-twentieth century had won the efficiency argument. It appeared that its seemingly unlimited potential for growth and allocation through the market would eventually benefit all: everyone would have their share of 'people's capitalism'. Collective or co-operative systems were no longer relevant.

In the UK, the 'nanny' state, so hard-fought for in the early part of the twentieth century, was derided and mutual societies nurtured for more than a century by working class people were 'de-mutualised'. The state greatly reduced its responsibilities to its citizens as people were deemed to be 'free' to look after themselves. Employers also found themselves free to abandon hard-won benefits such as pensions and guaranteed jobs and wages. Countries that tried to build health, welfare or protected production systems were 'structurally adjusted' to be open to so-called market forces. State assets and 'commons' resources were privatised. All of this was done with the promise that the global efficiency of the market would in the long run enhance the 'wealth' of nations and individuals. Privatisation, harsh industrialised employment systems, rapid resource usage, destroyed environments, reduced social and welfare benefits, unemployment, huge boardroom payments, free movement of capital (but not people) were all justified on the basis of eventual benefit for all.

When socialists, feminists and other groups argued against inequality and injustice the answer always came back that capitalism would in the end incorporate everyone into its system of production/consumption. Women were promised equal opportunities ... eventually. The peoples of the South were promised 'modernisation', 'development', 'progress' even as their lands and resources were being stripped away. It is the ecological crisis that has shown these promises for the charade they always were. Where resources are limited, the question of who benefits and who loses cannot be passed off as a byproduct of the 'hidden hand of the market' or some personal failure of will, risk or effort. It is clearly revealed as a question of moral and political choices, of power relations and social justice.

At the high point of apparent capitalist hegemony, the main, and perhaps the only, effective challenge came from the green movement.[1] The early 1970s 'limits to growth' studies threatened to undermine the core justification for market capitalism (Meadows, Randers and Behrens 1972). Although this research was commissioned by industrialists for market reasons, and the findings were challenged, the question of resource limits and environmental damage was on the global agenda.

---

[1] Green is used very broadly here to mean the environmental movement in general.

Within a resource-limited system, even if those limits were far off, the cruelties and inequities of global capitalism and its rather coyly admitted 'market failures' could not be justified. In an unlimited system, capitalism could justify the coexistence of wealth and poverty as being the result of the personal inadequacy of those who failed to embrace opportunity. In a land of plenty, those who did not grab assets and exploit them for personal benefit were idle fools. In a non-zero-sum world, those who had resources and money deserved them and were benefiting the whole of society by exploiting them.

In a limited system, the case for the private ownership and control of resources is much more difficult to make. Where the distribution of resources is zero sum, whoever takes the resource automatically denies others the possibility of ownership or access. The argument must therefore move to issues of socioeconomic justice and how responsibly a resource is used. Market capitalism claimed the high ground on the latter. Its pseudo-scientific ideological support system, classical and neoclassical economic theory, claimed that the market system offered the most efficient use of resources. This was claimed on scientific grounds, the natural law of economics. While political and possibly social rights were on the political agenda, economic rights were not. It was socialism that put economic rights and justice at the heart of its project. These are even more vital in a limited system. Human wellbeing in this context cannot help but be a social and political question.

The green challenge to capitalism was accompanied by a flowering of movements that brought together the green, socialist and other radical agendas: ecofeminists, green socialists, socialist greens, green anarchists. Newspapers, books, magazines and academic journals such as *Capitalism, Nature, Socialism* reflected these new ideas and synergies.

At its most basic, socialism represents the view that human wellbeing is the collective responsibility of society as a whole. Green socialism would extend the notion of wellbeing to all other species and the ecosystems of the planet. The more difficult question is: how will this be achieved?

From green to red

A major difficulty for the green movement is that while it unites around a critique of the abuse of the natural environment, it does not have a common political position on which to base an alternative. Ideas range from a return to hunter-gathering through local economies to market solutions. From a socialist perspective, both market and premodern solutions would be unacceptable, the former because they still retain a capitalist system, the latter because they are unlikely to be suitable for large-scale populations. Non-capitalist solutions at the local or community level are more possible but suffer from a lack of clarity about how the 'local' would be defined. Geographically it is hard to say what is local (neighbourhood, city/town and hinterland, regional ecosystem, sub-national region, nation, sub-continent, continent?).

From a socialist perspective, the political meaning of local is vital. Socialism is about the solidarity of peoples across the globe. Much green thinking shares these values, but some leans towards a narrow parochialism and place orientation that would freeze current settlement patterns and the inequalities that go with them.

The economics of the local is also an issue for socialists. How would production be organised? Would there still be private ownership and waged labour? How industrialised would a local economy be? What would be the pattern of land ownership? Would there be a welfare system? Would there be a system of taxation? How would the market, if any, function? Would a green economy reform market capitalism, exist alongside it, spread through it like a virus or confront it directly? What is to happen to the millions of people now living in the cities? These are practical questions that have been asked many times before but they all seem to point to a wider socioeconomic solution than the green small scale.

Some green solutions may appear to challenge the status quo but mimic market solutions. For example, buying plots of land and aiming for self-sufficiency would seem to be a radical solution. However, buying land is an individualised response based on access to money or credit. In a limited system it is also highly unlikely there will be enough land for everyone. There is also the possibility that self-sufficient communities will include unacknowledged positive externalities such as the cultural and educational heritage of the members, national communications and transport systems, hospitals etc.

Socialists would also question whether the fairly widespread green view of 'community', the local, the regional, the human scale as having 'natural' virtue is justified. Historically human societies have shown a range of behaviours from benign to violent, open to restrictive, egalitarian to hierarchical, and most show evidence of male domination and a sexual division of labour if not outright repression of women. For these reasons, while the green perspective is a vital challenge to capitalism, it is not sufficient.

Green thinking focuses on two main areas: the existence of physical limits and the actions humans should take in the face of them. With regard to the existence of limits there are two possible approaches, the natural and the social. The natural position would say that there are givens in the physical conditions of existence that must be accom-modated rather than overcome. A social perspective would argue that physical conditions are a product of human decision-making past and present. Limits that are socially constructed can be socially unravelled. As might be expected, most greens and green socialists would take a natural stance while technological optimists from left and right would generally tend to lean towards a socially constructed view of limits.

While green socialists would share with greens a natural view of (ultimate) limits, they would not see possible solutions as emerging from 'Nature' (Soper 1995). Much green thinking, implicitly or explicitly, proposes a 'natural' basis for action. From the deeper green perspectives to some relatively shallow ones, there is an assumption that humans have strayed from a natural path of harmony and balance with Nature. In order to return to the true path it is necessary to draw lessons from natural systems, from indigenous peoples, from unpeopled wilderness or from some spiritual insight associated with natural conditions.

Ironically this naturalistic framework of balance and harmony is also reflected in the ideology of market economists, although in a very dif-ferent form. The market system is seen as automatically seeking equi-librium, with economic behaviour considered as an intrinsic part of human rationality. For market ideologues, social intervention in the market risks upsetting or distorting a natural process that can only be discovered by the 'science' of economics.

From a socialist perspective, any naturalistic approach to human actions must be questioned. Why should there be harmony and balance in nature any more than there should be harmony and balance within markets? It is perfectly possible to see humans as existing within con-strained physical limits without assuming that there is any natural answer to guide human solutions. To paraphrase Marx, humans must understand the dynamics of their condition in order to be able to change it. This is not to make the human-centred assumption that humans can ultimately change the conditions of their existence, but it is also not to assume there is a natural answer. Natural conditions are constraining but not determining.

Elsewhere I have suggested the approach of 'immanent realism' (Mellor 1997a). This sees humans as existing within an interconnected environmental framework that includes their own embodiment as phy-sical beings. The first task of all knowledge is therefore to recognise human embeddedness (immanence) in a physically constrained, but not immediately knowable, reality (realism). This immanent position denies human knowledge an Archimedes point from which to observe the whole; therefore the starting point is an acceptance of the limitations of both the natural world and human knowledge. Human action is always bounded by uncertainty. However, to say that there are limiting conditions to human action and knowledge does not imply that a ready solution can be found through either some appreciation of laws of natural balance or natural economic systems. If there is no natural answer to the human condition, there must be a socially constructed solution. The actions of humanity must be open to social debate and analysis, to a politics of human existence in nature.

This is the case for reclaiming a socialist perspective. If there are no natural answers in the market or in Nature then humans are free, within uncertain limits, to construct their own answer. What prevents humans being able to understand and control their own future is the illusion of (super)natural systems (God, Nature, the market). Within the context of uncertainty the task is to develop ways of acting that maximise the potential of life in all its forms. Socialism has historically been anthropocentric, but a green socialism would need to take responsibility for all life forms and all environments in its decision-making. This can be done for bio-egalitarian reasons (extending socialist principles to all nature) or human-centred reasons (it is in humanity's material or aesthetic interest to preserve nature).

As the issue of equality must be addressed in any limited system, the case for a socialist approach to building an ecologically sustainable society is very clear. As Marx and Engels put it in the *Communist Manifesto*, this aim is to build a society where the free development of each is the condition for the free development of all. For green socialists, this condition would be extended as far as possible to other species.

Combining a green and socialist perspective must therefore begin from a materialist ontology. Humanity is materially grounded in its embodiedness, that is, all the bodily needs that human existence requires and its embeddedness within its ecosystem. Humanity faces physical constraints, but these limitations provide no guidance for how humanity should meet these needs and restrictions. Human existence within the human condition therefore becomes a social and political question particularly around the democratic and equal control and allocation of resources. As unequal control and allocation of resources is at the heart of the capitalist system, it is on this basis that it must be challenged.

Money, wage labour and commodification in capitalist market systems

The capitalist market system is based on the private ownership of the means of production including natural resources. In the face of private ownership, the mass of the people have no direct access to their means of sustenance and must therefore work for a wage in order to access goods and services through a money-based market system. Production is only carried out where a profit can be achieved such that any capital invested will always expand in value. The means of expansion of value lies in the link between money (value), wage labour and the production of commodities. For greens, this system is destructive because it demands continual growth, while socialists point to its exploitation of wage labour and its inequality of ownership, control and distribution.

Feminists have added the critique that there is a convergence of the interests of (most) men in industrial society with capitalist definitions of the 'economy'. The market as the driving force of human society has historically mainly rewarded what men do ('skilled work' for 'the family wage') and what could be commodified to produce a profit. Although in Eastern European command economies the profit motive was eliminated, the economy was still dominated by similar priorities, in particular armaments and heavy engineering. Feminists argue that much of women's lives, particularly in non-industrial rural economies, lies outside the formal 'economy'. Work that is not traded, such as women's domestic and subsistence work as well as the ecological costs of production, is excluded from 'the economy' (Waring 1989, Mellor 1997b).

What is distinctive about capitalism is that it removes from people the means of meeting their own needs directly. Conventional economics justifies this on the basis of productivity and efficiency, but leaves fundamental issues unexamined. One is the lack of economic democracy; most people have no say in, or control over, their means of livelihood. Another is the fact that within a profit-driven economy there is no necessary link between production and need. The priorities of production in a capitalist society have only a loose relationship to the production of the means of sustenance, that is, the goods and services that are necessary to provision human existence. No distinction is made between needs and wants; both are subsumed under the notion of 'market forces' and 'effective' demand, i.e. through access to money. The need for money is the basis for wage labour.

For most of history, people produced most of their immediate needs in a subsistence economy and traded the surplus. These markets were generally aided by some kind of money system and follow the pattern identified by Marx: commodities traded through a money system (C–M–C). Such systems were not necessarily egalitarian or benign, but the economy as a whole would not have been distorted by the existence of a market. People could in theory (if not in practice because of other social distortions) determine what goods and services were produced and how much production was needed to meet particular levels of consumption. That is, they had the basis for determining sufficiency. Both of these are lost in the capitalist market system, with profound implications for socioeconomic justice and ecological sustainability.

Marx identified the origin of capitalist society when products were produced with only the aim of selling them for money at profit. Money is invested in commodity production and then sold at an increased money value (M–C–M+). Money has now been capitalised. It embodies enhanced value and is not just a medium of exchange. Goods and services are no longer primarily a means of sustenance and utility; they are commodities for exchange. Human labour and natural resources now have no value other than their ability to create profit. The destruction of the health of the worker or the ecosystem is of no concern to the capitalist unless it has an impact on profits (O'Connor 1996).

Production based on capitalised money following the priority of profit seeking owes no allegiance to the meeting of human needs or the sustainability of the planet. Those forced into waged labour must seek employment where they can, making guns to buy butter. 'The economy' that much of the world has come to accept as a determinant of human choices has no necessary relationship with human need, as market choices are based on access to money. With, by definition, little access to money, the poor do not make good market leaders. Equally, the planet cannot assert effective demand.

The failure of market systems to meet the needs of the poor is well known and was the basis of the demand for welfare states. The impact of market systems on natural resources is only just beginning to be addressed, mainly as the notion of externalities. However, the concept of externalities implies the desire to be 'brought in', and this is the main aim of environmental economics – to price the environment. From a socialist perspective the market can never solve the problem of environmental destruction. To understand this is it necessary to analyse the role of money within a capitalist market (Hutchinson, Mellor and Olsen 2002).

Making money – destroying life

As Marx pointed out, money value in capitalist exchange systems must destroy any use or intrinsic value within the original commodity. This is for two reasons: first, because commodities are produced and exchanged only for their money value, and second, because money is intrinsically valueless. The contradiction of capitalist money is that something of no value is taken to embody value. To turn anything into money is therefore to destroy its value. Even gold has no intrinsic value: its value must always be established in terms of another equivalent such as silver or paper money. Money therefore appears to be valuable and much sought after as a capital asset, but that value is never intrinsic, as is evidenced by the inability to maintain such concepts as a 'gold standard'.

Since money is essentially valueless, it gives those dependent on money systems no security no matter how rich they may appear. There is also no basis for sufficiency. For example, people being urged to 'save' for their pensions can have no way of knowing if what they save will be of any value in fifty years time. Recently there has been a temporary delusion that people could become rich through so-called capital growth. In this case, money was invested in money forms to create money (M–M–M+) without any relation to actual productive systems. The distortion of the economy had become complete and real goods and services had become irrelevant.

The response from a capitalist ideologue would be that investment through money systems is a way of efficiently allocating resources to the best use. Such claims have led to an exploration of how money is actually generated and circulated within capitalist market systems. As Marx noted, alongside the emergence of the capitalist wage system was a system of issuing credit through the banking system, both to governments as the national debt and to industrialists to enable capital accumulation (Marx 1954: 703–8). Under the fractional reserve banking system it is well known that banks issue more credit than they have reserves. Credit issue has been vitally important for capital accumulation: it has been estimated that 95–97 per cent of money currently circulating in the UK and the US was issued as debt, recently mainly for mortgages (Daly 1999). It might be questioned whether under present consumer credit issue, the concept of bank reserves against debt has any meaning at all.

The operation of the capitalist market and associated issue of money and credit raises questions about ecological sustainability and economic democracy (Hutchinson, Mellor and Olsen 2002). Many greens have questioned the ecological sustainability of the growth dynamic within capitalist systems. As debts have to be repaid at interest and profits are demanded, there is a constant growth dynamic built into the system. Marx pointed to the potential crisis of buying power within market economies, and in the current context this is represented by the constant need for new generations of people, companies or governments to take on debt. Only one of these has statutory limited liability. Personal indebtedness has achieved crisis levels in the UK particularly among the single young and the poor, echoing the indebtedness crisis of poor countries (Rowbotham 1998).

The issue of money/credit in a capitalist economy is becoming an increasingly important issue for democracy. Credit, which represents virtually all new money within the economy, is issued through the financial services sector (banks and credit companies). The vast majority of this debt-based money does not represent savings or reserves, i.e. it does not represent the savings of other people. It is created quite literally out of nothing. Since credit money is created out of nothing, should its creation and circulation not be a matter of public debate as to its use? At present the choice about credit money expenditure is predominantly private (companies and individuals), although a substantial part represents government spending which is arguably (although not practically) open to public influence. This means that the ownership and control of natural resources, property, companies, workers, can be achieved effectively out of 'nothing'.

Within a capitalised money economy, whoever activates the 'nothing' that is money debt chooses the direction of production. In many cases borrowings are put into a purely money investment, for example bidding up the value of a house that has already been built, or buying shares in a company from another investor, or gambling on a currency shift. This would not matter if resources were infinite, if people's needs had been met and no harmful investment was ever made. However, none of these is the case. Resources are not infinite; the rich are raising their levels of consumption on things such as sports utility vehicles while the poor are finding it harder to meet their needs.

Given the exploitative and harmful nature of the capitalist market, it is important that green socialists should ask questions about the democratic, social and ecological issues that the creation of money as debt raises. There is no logical reason why 'wealth' as money can only be created in the private sector. There is nothing natural about the market system, since all economic systems are social constructions. Arguably the so-called 'wealth-producing' private sector is parasitical on everything else including public services, women's communal work and the natural world. Social expenditure could as easily be the focus of money making/creation with no necessity of issuing money as debt except where it represents the savings of other individuals. Even then, money could be exchanged without interest. Democratisation of money issue would mean that governments, individuals and private for-profit companies (if they still existed) would have to make a public case for their priorities. Economic decision-making would no longer be depoliticised by the seeming neutrality of the market.

The capitalist economy was never built with the primary aim of meeting human needs; rather, it distorts human lives and choices through the private ownership and control of the means of sustenance. Its only aim is to make profits from commodities traded through a market based on capitalised money and waged labour. It has no mechanism to secure the future of humanity or the planet (Perelman 2003). It is not a natural system and it is not inevitable.

Socialism is the philosophy that sees the economy as a social question. That economy also exists within a limited natural environment. The goal for green socialism must be to find a way of maximising human potential in a democratic, egalitarian and ecologically sustainable way.

Socialism as sufficiency

The traditional aim of socialists was to attain the ownership and control of the means of production and overthrow the wage labour system. To this must be added the aim of living within the means of the planet, leaving space for the livelihood of other species. As has been argued above, the ecological challenge has made the case for socialism much stronger and undermines the case for capitalism's continued existence. The question is how can an egalitarian and sustainable economy be achieved: one that can provision society and enable human creativity? Provisioning in its widest sense is much broader than traded goods, and includes many activities and values including women's domestic work, which at present have no 'price' (Nelson 1993).

There are various possibilities for how a sufficiency provisioning economy could be achieved. Many green ideas flow towards a local economy or the rebirth of a subsistence sector. For socialists there is a tendency to look to collective or co-operative structures or a more democratised local or national state. The rest of the chapter will explore some of these possibilities.

The call for a subsistence perspective embraces examples from around the world that run from small-scale local initiatives in highly consumerist societies to large movements that exist beyond or resist the global market system. An example of the latter is the Nayakrishi Andolon (New Agricultural Movement) of 60,000 organic peasant farmers in Bangladesh (Bennholdt-Thomsen and von Werlhof 2001). The practicality of adopting a subsistence perspective as the basis of sufficiency depends upon what is meant by subsistence. This can range from a system based on a preindustrial, precommodified sector to the notion of minimal consumption within a more industrialised economy, what Elgin has called 'voluntary simplicity' (1981).

The subsistence perspective does not necessary imply an egalitarian society, and socialists certainly would not uncritically support the retention or (re)creation of a preindustrial, non-commodified socio-economic system. The idea of voluntary simplicity is also problematic in that it implies that one has the choice not to be 'simple' as against what Marx called the 'unnatural simplicity of the poor'. While the struggle to retain or re-establish the remnants of a subsistence sector and common lands is being made in the majority (South) world, the position in the minority (North) world is more problematic. Although women still do a large amount of unpaid domestic work, there is no clear distinction between subsistence needs and the 'market' in the North. The capitalist economy has incorporated both wants and needs in its search for capital accumulation. In many countries this has been made even worse by privatisation policies. To ask people to withdraw from destructive economic systems is asking them to abandon their livelihood.

Democratic control of the means of sustenance

For socialists, the issue must be raised of the collective ownership of the means of sustenance. There is no justification for private ownership of the global 'commons', that is, the resources necessary for the existence of humans and other species. A commons is not just the existence of a common resource, but a collective social mechanism for its use. Commons cannot be secured unless people are certain they can have equal access and that others will not take more than their share. This can only be achieved within a political framework based on equality and mutuality: that is, socialism.

For socialists and for many greens, provisioning structures would be based on social ownership and control. There are many forms of social ownership, from the public ownership of the state or municipality to community ownership, co-operatives or social enterprises (Pearce 2003). Recently new forms have emerged to build local not-for-profit provisioning systems, local money circulation, Time Banks or Local Employment and Trading Schemes (LETS) (Raddon 2003). While many of these initiatives are small, there are large-scale examples of social ownership.

The British consumer movement at the height of its development met the needs of twelve million households. People could live their entire lives within a co-operative framework (Mellor 1980). The co-operative movement is still the largest farmer in Britain and has committed itself to ecological aims. The co-operative movement also developed its own banking system and thereby solved the problem of money investment.

Most notable for the vital role of a co-operative investment bank are the Spanish Mondragon co-operatives, although their activities are directed towards the existing consumer market (Mellor, Hannah and Stirling 1988). The most important aspect of the development of co-operatives is not just their structure of ownership, but the kinds of goods and services they provide and the way they relate to the surrounding society and environment.

Arguably, different structures are relevant for different provisioning activities, and one of these levels is that of the state. After the collapse of the command economies of Eastern Europe, socialists are very wary of advancing a case for the state. This is understandable, but the attack on the democratic socialist welfare state was mainly led by an aggressive neoliberal market system that paid little attention to its own dependency on state-provided structures. Where there is a case for large-scale public provision, the local or national state has traditionally built and sustained the infrastructure for human sustenance. Green socialist economic democracy would then demand that such a state structure be responsive to democratic control, be committed to fundamental principles such as citizen's rights, socioeconomic equality and the defence of the natural world. The need for democratic control of public expenditure has been addressed by the development of participatory models to direct local state or city budgets, most notably in Brazil (Nylen 2003).

For the democratic operation of a sufficiency provisioning economy, real (and not artificial market) choice must be put in the hands of people as consumers/users and producers. An economic system that exists within limits would also need to prioritise needs. As poor people have the most immediate sustenance needs and women (who are over-represented among the poor) are the primary providers of basic care, this must mean a decisive move towards an economy dictated by the needs of women and the poor. Suggestions of ways this could be done have been to put purchasing power directly in the hands of citizens as a Basic Income or citizen's income; 'a social wage and a guaranteed income for all' (Hardt and Negri 2000: 403). Within the current economy this can be criticised for requiring too high a tax base. However, new thinking about money systems as outlined above is beginning to suggest ways in which a decentralised socialist economy could be achieved through a socialised issue and circulation of money (Mellor 2005). Public investment could also be organised through a local social investment bank responsive to democratically identified local priorities.

The capitalist market economy has denied economic democracy by defending private control of resources and production and imposing its view of social and public expenditure as wasteful. The task for green socialists is to reverse that definition. There are many non-market, not-for-profit provisioning activities even in the most commodified societies. Even on a small scale they can provide what Joel Kovel has described as 'prefigurative ensembles' for a future socialist society (2002).

Conclusion

The case made in this chapter is that the ecological challenge provides the basis for a new and invigorated socialism. The need to live within limits and organise a system that can provision the human community demands that the means of sustenance be a matter for democratic social organisation. The livelihood of human and animal communities can no longer be determined by the private ownership of the means of existence and by the structures and priorities of a profit-oriented market system.

However, proposals for egalitarian and ecologically sustainable mechanisms of provisioning human societies have to be realistic, starting from present economic, social and environmental conditions. There are many organisations looking for an answer and the exact form that a democratic socialist and ecologically sustainable human community will take is still open to debate.

What is clear is that there is no 'natural' way for humanity to relate to its environment. Socialism is about analysing the sources of inequality and ecological destruction humanity faces and looking for new ways of living that would enable people to control democratically their means of sustenance in a way that minimises human impact on the natural world and enables each individual to express their own creativity in peace.

References

Bennholdt-Thomsen, Veronika, and von Werlhof, Claudia, (2001). *There Is an Alternative: Subsistence and Worldwide Resistance to Corporate Globalisation.* London: Zed.

Daly, Hermann (1999). *Ecological Economics and the Ecology of Economics.* Cheltenham: Edward Elgar.

Elgin, D. (1981). *Voluntary Simplicity.* New York: William Morrow.

Fisher, William F., and Ponniah, Thomas (2003). *Another World Is Possible: Popular Alternatives to Globalization at the World Social Forum.* London: Zed.

Hardt, Michael, and Negri, Antonio, (2000). *Empire.* Cambridge, Mass.: Harvard University Press.

Hutchinson, Frances, Mellor, Mary, and Olsen, Wendy, (2002). *The Politics of Money: Towards Sustainability and Economic Democracy.* London: Pluto Press.

Kovel, Joel (2002). *The Enemy of Nature: The End of Capitalism or the End of the World*. London: Zed.

Marx, Karl (1954). *Capital, vol I*. London: Lawrence and Wishart.

Meadows, Donnella, Randers, J., and Behrens, W. W. (1972). *The Limits to Growth*. New York: Universe Books.

Mellor, Mary (1980). 'Motivation, Recruitment and Ideology: A Case Study of the Co-operative Movement in the North East of England', unpublished Ph.D. thesis, Newcastle University.

(1997a). *Feminism and Ecology*. Cambridge: Polity Press.

(1997b). 'Women, Nature and the Social Construction of "Economic Man" ', *Ecological Economics* **20**: 129–40.

(2005). '*The Politics of Money and Credit as a Route to Ecological Sustainability and Economic Democracy*', Capitalism, Nature, Socialism **16**.2 (June): 45–60.

Mellor, Mary, Hannah Janet, and Stirling John, (1988). *Worker Co-operatives in Theory and Practice*. Buckingham: Open University Press.

Nelson, J. A. (1993). *Beyond Economic Man: Feminist Theory and Economics*. Chicago: Chigago University Press.

Nylen, Willian R. (2003). *Participatory Democracy versus Elitist Democracy: Lessons from Brazil*. New York: Palgrave.

O'Connor, James (1996). 'The Second Contradiction of Capitalism', in Ted Benton (ed.), *The Greening of Marxism*. New York: Guilford, 197–221.

Pearce, John (2003). *Social Enterprise in Anytown*. London: Calouste Gulbenkian Foundation.

Perelman, Michael (2003). *The Perverse Economy: The Impact of Markets on People and the Environment*. New York: Palgrave.

Raddon, Mary-Beth (2003). *Community and Money: Men and Women Making Change*. Montreal: Black Rose Books.

Rowbotham, Michael (1998). *In the Grip of Death: A Study of Modern Money, Debt Slavery and Destructive Economics*. Charlburg: Black Rose Books.

Soper, Kate (1995). *What Is Nature?* Oxford: Blackwell.

Stiglitz, Joseph (2002). *Globalization and Its Discontents*. New York: Norton.

Waring, Marilyn (1989). *If Women Counted*. London: Macmillan.

4   Feminism

Val Plumwood

Hybridity shifts the focus

Feminist thought and environmental thought, feminist and ecological movements, have both emerged in recent times to challenge dominant worldviews and to acknowledge major aspects of the world that have been ignored, excluded or denied. They have much in common, and I write as a feminist who is also an environmental activist. But feminism and environmentalism have also challenged one another and come into conflict. The main forum for fruitful dialogue between them has been the hybrid area of ecofeminism, which aims at developing 'a feminism that is ecological and an ecology that is feminist'.[1]

Feminist and ecofeminist thinkers have applied feminist analyses to problems in environmental philosophy and theory. These have added significantly to the choices about how to theorise environmental issues. Some theorists from the environmental side express special suspicion and distrust of the 'hybrid' loyalties they discern here, contrasting these with the supposedly purer and 'ungendered' loyalties of predominantly male and white environmental theorists who have dominated the field.[2] Treating women's experience and theories as gendered, and dominant theories based on male experience as pure and ungendered, is the equivalent of seeing black as coloured or racially based but dominant theories based on white experience as neutral and pure, lacking in colour or racial bias.

Many 'pure' positions in environmental theory involve hybrid loyalties, which are the worse for being unexamined and unannounced – for example, unrevealed political loyalties, eurocentric and androcentric loyalties. Examination of the dominant versions of environmental thinking I discuss below that are based on coverture, expulsion of difference and stress on detachment, shows they are are not 'pure' and ungendered, as they claim. Contrasting these theorisations with others based

[1] King 1989.   [2] For example Hay 2002.

on feminist commitments can reveal implicit loyalties to masculinist worldviews and male-privileging life forms.

Hybridity should not be understood as an exception, an interruption to the main discourse, as conceding the centrality of dominant theories or as implying any kind of secondariness of discourse or perspective. Indeed, to the extent that 'the classic' theories and concepts occupying the central ground in environmental theory have evolved without the input of women, or in ways hostile to or suppressive of their lives and agency, hybridity based on re-envisioning the problems through a feminist perspective is crucial. Hybridity clarifies the range of theoretical options and can *shift the problem focus* in helpful ways that dislodge blockages. It could be argued that it is hybridity – and not purity – that is desirable at this early stage of environmental theorisation, to offer the best, politically focused development of environmentalism as a world-view that is distinctive but inevitably in dialogue with and informed by other critiques.

This welcoming of hybridity can go deeper still, to the view that what is distinctive about environmentalism is itself a certain kind of hybridity, a recognition of the links between human and non-human concerns. A study of environmental issues suggests that a distinctive, in the sense of ineliminable and non-subsumable, core of concern for environmental thought involves recognition of non-human elements of the world, and their relationship to the human. On this view, the critique of human-centredness should be as central to environmental thought as that of androcentrism is for feminist thought. I will argue that dominant androcentric forms of environmental theory have dealt rather poorly with the human/non-human connection. This does not mean that feminism is automatically a better foundation for an ecological world-view. I would make only the claim that some feminisms and ecofe-minisms provide better philosophical foundations for an ecological consciousness and alternatives to the human-centredness that disap-pears and distorts our connection with the non-human world.

For a feminism that is ecological

Critics of ecofeminism often take it as a major objection to such a hybrid that a feminist consciousness is no guarantee of an ecological worldview or consciousness. But such hybridity should not be seen as a claim to identity of interests between women and nature, or to automatic transfer of liberation consciousness. Such transfers are achievements, although much better fostered under some social conditions than others. Some forms of feminism have little ecological awareness, but feminist theory itself can provide an explanation of this as well as a basis for their critique. The dominant models and narratives that historically in Western culture have linked these two systems of oppression, for women and for nature, are often challenged only very partially in feminism, and in what are thought of as liberation positions generally. Socialism, postcolonial and anti-racist theory, as well as feminist theory, have all demonstrated that rejecting one form of oppression (and the centrism associated with it) does not ensure that other related forms will also be rejected.

For example, some very basic forms of feminism, which I have called feminisms of uncritical equality or Artemisian feminisms,[3] have aimed simply at having more women included in a privileged class previously reserved exclusively for elite white males. When the Greek goddess Artemis sought affirmation from her father Zeus by asking for equality with her brother Apollo and demanding all his stuff, including his weapons, she failed to challenge the model he represented for its androcentrism or its destructiveness. The individualised Artemisian strategy of extending the boundaries of male privilege lacks solidarity, aiming to escape the normal fate of woman rather than to improve it. But the strategy of Artemis in group form is also that of 'liberal' feminism, confusing terminology for a form of feminism that aims to extend the boundaries of privilege and achieve gender equality within an unquestioned androcentric ideal. More women professors, company directors or generals are what is needed, and women's likeness to men is the basis for equality as common participation in an androcentric model. Thus Simone de Beauvoir's classic text *The Second Sex* speaks tellingly in its concluding sentence of women and men 'unequivocally affirming their brotherhood'.[4] Artemisianism appealed in early articulations of feminism because it appeared to simplify demands and minimise the task of change.

Many later feminists have urged that women need to ask for much more than Artemis for real equality, because the androcentric ideals of humanity and culture Artemisians would join subtly presuppose and privilege maleness and its associated ideals and characteristics, real or assumed. Although a few women may succeed by shifting the boundary of privilege, Artemisian strategies are ineffective for most women, because most women will not do well or achieve equality under androcentric regimes – as shown in contemporary public life and in the workplace. In the same way, ecological feminists add, Artemisian strategies are anti-ecological; neither women nor men will do well in a

[3] See Plumwood 1993.   [4] Beauvoir 1965: 464.

regime which subtly denies the ecological basis of human life. An ecological form of feminism must be willing to mount a more thorough challenge to the dominant models of culture and humanity which define them against or in opposition to the non-human world, treating the truly human as excluding characteristics associated with the feminine, the animal and nature.

The project of all varieties of feminism is the recognition of women's equal humanity, but there are many different analyses of basic concepts and ideals of the human and of what equality involves. Feminist critiques of the gendered dualisms of Western culture suggests several requirements and problems for rethinking women's equal inclusion in humanity. Many feminists find objectionable women's traditional treatment as less than fully human and their consequent inclusion in the separate and inferior sphere of nature as opposed to culture. But there are two distinct ways to go about challenging this construction, corresponding to gynocentric and critical forms of feminism. One way would retain the traditional gender separation and the idea that women are part of nature, but reverse the traditional ordering to proclaim that women and nature are superior to men and culture, glorifying women because of their supposedly closer relationship to nature, especially through their position as mothers and nurturers.

This strategy, in which women rather than men represent the new ideals of humanity, replaces androcentrism by gynocentrism. This challenges androcentric models, but in a rather simplistic way via reversal, a strategy which subtly preserves via inversion what it seeks to escape. Gynocentric reversal strategies have drawn much criticism from other feminists, who see them as continuing women's imprisonment in the sphere of reproductivity and family and their exclusion from the true humanity of the public world of culture, work and public life. Gynocentrism challenges the traditional presumed inferiority of the sphere of nature and women, but does not challenge the idea that women (but not men) are part of it. Substitution of a traditional female for a traditional male model of the human does not challenge women's exclusion from culture, or the way these spheres of culture and nature are dualised – conceived as hyperseparated and highly exclusive of each other. Nor does it address the issue of distortion of the basic model of humanity by human-centredness and the ideal of humans as apart from nature and animals.

It takes a further development of feminism, hybrid ecological feminism, to question gendered traditions of nature/culture dualism and their associated models of humanity. Like gynocentric feminism, critical ecological feminism disputes the inferiority of the sphere of nature, but unlike gynocentric feminism, denies its exclusive link to women. Critical ecological feminism argues that women are no more 'part of nature' or 'closer to nature' than men are – both men and women reside in both nature and culture. Our hybrid form goes on to contest the idea that real human life proceeds in a hyperseparated sphere of culture, for which nature is inessential. These feminisms argue that the supposed creative transcendence of culture is built on the denial and subjection of those assigned to the sphere of reproduction or nature – both women and the non-human – whose supporting role is essential but invisible. Making visible our human dependency on this backgrounded sphere of nature is a key part of good ecological practice. The dominant commodity culture's distancing from and backgrounding of nature augments traditional apartness, leading to a sense of independence from nature that is dangerous and illusory.

The resulting hybrid program then is both feminist and ecological; with feminism, an ecological feminism rejects women's exclusion from culture, defined dualistically as the province of elite men who are seen as above the base material sphere of nature and daily life and able to transcend it (in creativity or production) through their supposedly greater share in reason, agency or enterprise. With ecology, a critical ecological feminism insists that such transcendence is an illusion. Humans of both sexes are as much a part of nature and as dependent on it as other living creatures. A truly human life is embedded in both nature and culture, which are not hyperseparated spheres as Artemisian feminism assumes. Concepts of woman *and of the human* must be rethought together in ecological terms that are respectful of non-human difference, sensitive to human continuity with non-human nature, and attentive to the embodiment of all life and the embedment of human culture in the material, ecological world.

Unravelling these layers and strategies, we can see that hybridity, far from introducing some suspect impurity, is a process of theoretical development and enrichment, a forward movement resulting from the testing, refinement and elaboration of a critical theory in dialogue with other critical theories. Here are opportunities for convergence of ecological feminisms with contemporary versions of socialist ecology and socialist ecofeminisms. These hybrids emerge from ecological revision of older Marxist and socialist feminisms that endorse dominant narratives of human superiority and hyperseparation from nature, and which laud progress as the progressive distancing of the human and of culture from the subjugated sphere of nature.

Also influential in this hybrid development have been socialist feminist critiques of productivism,[5] rejecting the exclusion and distancing of the 'ideal' human type, the 'productive' male worker, from the sphere of nature and reproduction to which women have been confined, and the typically Marxist idea that such hyperseparated concepts of production and culture mark the true home and distinctiveness of the human. Such hybrids also move beyond older, monological socialist forms that define value exclusively in terms of human labour and production, as the key characteristics of the human. The new hybrids, in contrast, see the production of value in more mutualistic terms that recognise the crucial contribution of the non-human to the production and reproduction of value.[6] They stress the category of reproduction that is denied and backgrounded in productivist frameworks. Both men and women participate in the sphere of reproduction, which includes the labour of the household, child rearing – and of course the ecological services of nature that make all production and reproduction possible.[7]

Anthropocentric feminisms

This process of feminist hybridisation seems very promising, but I am far from claiming that feminism in any form can provide good foundations for an ecological worldview. Many contemporary forms of both feminism and ecofeminism are human-centred, often in subtle ways. Contemporary ecofeminism, especially in the USA, is heavily committed to a vegan animal defence perspective that sees little need to try to accommodate ecological standpoints,[8] and is often based on a human-centred paradigm of care for private, 'cultural' animals as pets or companion species fitting into human lives.[9] An ecological consciousness should certainly, in my view, include respect and concern for animals, as both individuals and species – a respect which has often been absent in ecological thinking based on reductive science. In this regard the caring orientation of vegan ecofeminism is a corrective to the excesses of ecological rationalism, holism and scientism.

The dominant position that is deeply entrenched in Western culture constructs a great gulf or dualism between humans on one side and animals and nature generally on the other. Human/nature dualism conceives the human essence as mind or spirit, not body; they (humans) are inside culture but 'outside nature' – not conceived ecologically as

---

[5] See Benhabib and Cornell 1987.   [6] See Brennan 2000.
[7] See Shiva 1988, 1994; Plumwood 1993, 2002; Merchant 2003.
[8] See Adams 1990.   [9] See Haraway 2003.

part of a system of exchange of nutrition and never available as food, for example, to other animals. Non-humans are seen in polarised and reductive terms as outside ethics and culture, and as mere bodies, reducible to food. Feminist veganism offers a very incomplete challenge to this deep historical gulf, bringing animals into ethics by enlarging human/nature dualism to animal/nature dualism rather than rejecting dualist structure. To the extent that it fails to challenge this Christianised narrative of apartness, vegan ecofeminism becomes an Artemisian boundary-shifting exercise aiming to preserve human status and privilege but extend it to a bigger class of 'semi-humans' who, like humans themselves, are conceived as above the material ecosphere and 'outside nature', beyond ecology and beyond use, especially use in the food chain. In doing so, vegan ecofeminism stays within the system of human/nature dualism and denial that prevents the dominant culture from recognising its ecological embeddedness and places it increasingly at ecological risk.

But we can oppose the abuse of animals in factory farms and support animal defence within another, ecologically aware framework affirming continuity between life forms and without the Artemisian resort to privileging the human in the guise of the human-like or animal. We can celebrate and support animal lives through a dialogical ethics of negotiation or partnership between humans and animals, while undertaking a re-evaluation of human identity that affirms inclusion in animal and ecological spheres. An ecological consciousness gives a more thorough disruption of the dominant narrative which sets humans beyond ecology and apart from animals as commodifiable bodies by resituating humans in ecological terms at the same time as it resituates non-humans in ethical and cultural terms.[10]

Such a position would be semi-vegetarian, advocating an end to factory farming and great reductions in first-world meat-eating, but could still see a place for respectful and mutual forms of use in the food chain, rather than assuming the vegan dualism of no use at all for the human-like and unconstrained use for the rest of nature. (Because it is so indiscriminate in proscribing all forms of animal use as having the same negative moral status, vegan ecofeminism fails to provide philosophical guidance for environmental activism or even for animal activism that would prioritise action on factory farming over less abusive forms of farming.) To marry care for both animals and ecology with human liberation concerns, we must take account of context and acknowledge different cultures in widely differing ecological contexts,

[10] See Plumwood (2004).

nutritional situations and needs, rather than ignoring contexts other than contemporary Western urban ones, or treating them as minor, deviant 'exceptions' to the Western consumer perspective that is taken to be the ideal or norm.[11]

Feminist human-centredness is not confined to animalist theories. Some forms of postmodernist feminism that stress breaking down boundaries between culture and nature lead to a rejection of the otherness of nature that is subtly human-centred. Postmodern constructivisms suggest that nature is something illusory we can dispense with or dismiss, that nature is not really other at all but is entirely constructed by human agency. Generalising from particular cases of deceptive naturalness (where, for example, a countryside that embodies human labour is taken to be purely natural) to cast broader doubt on nature and nature's agency is a major basis for nature scepticism and for constructivism applied to nature. If we also, perhaps more often, indulge deceptive humanness, an over-emphasis on human elements in a landscape combining nature and culture, countering deception requires mixed strategies of making visible the hidden elements, human or non-human, not the wholesale abandonment of nature concepts.[12] Now, of all times, when we press so many natural limits, nature scepticism and constructivism of this highly generalized variety is immensely problematic, since we cannot come to terms with another whom we do not recognise as presenting to us any independent form of agency or limit on our projects.

Feminist and ecofeminist thought is diverse and evolving; testing theory against the requirements of ecological activism and criteria of human-centredness is an ongoing project. The fact that some feminisms fail in this area shows not that feminism is useless as a base for ecological thought, but that some forms have failed to consider the ecological question. As we will see, feminist thought also contains many elements that can be mobilised to give a more satisfactory basis for environmental thought than those currently on offer.

The inadequacy of dominant theories for environmental activism

The current crop of androcentric environmental theories in ethics and politics creates a number of false choices, disconnections and unnecessary polarisations that do not appear, or appear so strongly, at the level of environmental movement and activism. One major disconnection – a significant one for developing a rich politics of nature – appears

[11] For examples see Adams 1990.   [12] See Plumwood 2001.

between human and non-human issues. Some environment groups specialise in human or in non-human environmental issues, but many address both kinds of concern. In a small community, the people who demonstrate about penguins are often the same ones who demonstrate about traffic pollution. Many, perhaps most, environmental issues involve both humans and non-humans, often in connected ways that are hard to disentangle. Typical struggles are concerned both with situating human lives or living places ecologically and with winning more security for non-human life and places. Although mixing is the norm at the level of activism, at the level of theory, there is a puzzling segregation. Most theories fail to provide an integrated focus for environmental struggles that makes a good connection between human and non-human environmental struggles and takes both seriously. Many theories create a choice between human and non-human issues and forms of concern, or try to privilege one kind over the other in some universalising, context-insensitive way (for example, as 'deep' versus 'shallow').

We need a non-reductionist integration of human and non-human issues that takes both kinds of concerns seriously and explores their connections and political implications. Theorisations based in feminist thought promise better connections in two problem areas: first, integrating human and non-human aspects of environmental concerns and movements, and acknowledging the potentially radical character of both areas. Second, they enable positions with a non-human focus to move beyond personal consciousness change to develop a politics of human/non-human relations, expressed in human institutions, rationality and political structures.

In the long-running debate over instrumentalism and human-centredness (anthropocentrism), most environmental theories either offer us some environmental elaboration of concern for humans (to take account of environmental services for humans) or else focus exclusively on non-humans. Few theories offer us both, and those that do, such as utilitarianism or rights theories, operate with an extensionist and semi-reductionist approach that includes a few 'higher' non-humans ethically on the basis of their similarity to humans, for example their capacity to suffer (Singer 1990). The dominant instrumentalism takes in non-human concerns via a reduction to human concerns – non-human harm matters just when humans suffer too. Western environmental philosophy has been preoccupied with validating this reduction and with debating whether our environmental relationships are distorted, destructive and irrational because they are based on lack of prudence as care for self, or lack of altruism as care for the other – a choice of self or other. As we have seen, the issues are segregated on another level as well, splitting ethics from politics, for they have mostly been framed as ethical ones for non-humans and political ones for humans. Human or non-human, self or other, politics or ethics? These false choices have framed the conventional problem focus.

Deep ecology is the most prominent dissenter from the dominant human-centred, instrumentalist reduction of non-human to human issues and values, but instead of offering an alternative integrating the human and non-human, it often promotes a *reverse reduction to non-human issues*. Deep ecology promotes valuing non-humans for their own sake, but makes notably poor connections with human ecological issues. In the mind set of deep ecology, struggles concerned with situating human life in ecological terms are decried as 'shallow', while issues of wilderness and the defence of non-humans are treated as 'deep', and are set apart from human environmental justice and sustainability issues. Deep ecology identifies the environmental problematic with just one side of it, compassion for other life forms.

Thus in his first chapter introducing the 'ecological impulse' and motivating the movement, 'deep' environmental historian Peter Hay proceeds immediately to set up the paradigm of environmental activism as non-human and wilderness defence. 'The cornerstone of the environment movement', he writes (2002: 25), 'may well be the impulse to defend ... the existential interests of other life-forms.' The ethical and ecological failures involved in other kinds of environmental struggles emerge as peripheral, for example those concerned with nuclear power, herbicides and insecticides, overfishing, desertification, air pollution, land degradation, unsustainable farming and forestry, unliveable cities, and for environmental justice, to name just a few. These human concerns are assumed not to challenge major traditions or norms (to be 'shallow' or 'not radical'). Unsituated in any larger historical and social context, these struggles appear as semi-technical problems of sustainability that can be solved in terms of better political and economic organisation.[13] A feminist focus on the larger political and historical context of human/nature and self/other formation can give us a richer, more integrated and more coherent conception of the environmental problematic, broadening the narrow 'deep' focus on non-human and wilderness issues to represent more closely the full range of issues and concerns in real environmental struggles.

Feminist ethics discerns a major false dichotomy here in the implicit choice between human and non-human interests and needs, between

---

[13] Hay motivates the second, human set of concerns using the concept of 'ecocentrism'. On the problems of 'ecocentrism' see Weston 2004: 29.

prudence and altruism, care for self and care for the other, politics and ethics. Analyses drawing on the Self/Other dynamics of recognition problematise these kinds of choices, and see human and non-human interests in mutualistic terms as complementing each other rather than as primarily competing or conflicting. Many feminists have argued for a relational concept of the self[14] that breaks down the dualism of pure self or pure other, opening ethical space for and moving ethical emphasis to the question of how self and other are connected and can negotiate or mutually adjust – a focus important for addressing the environmental crisis. This kind of account moves the focus from disjunction to conjunction, from whether we should base relationship on self *or* on other, human *or* non-human, towards a focus on relationship between self *and* other, on self-in-relationship with other, and, only as *pathology*, on a *choice* of self or other, or self in failed relationship to other. Feminist focus on the gendered dualisms of self and other, mind and body, and its variant as human/nature dualism, can provide a more integrated way to understand the environmental problematic, as a problem for both the human and non-human sphere.

Who or what is 'deep'?

These choices implicit in the theoretical segregation of non-human from human issues reflect the network of dualisms feminist thought has identified as the key to many of the failings of Western culture. Human/nature dualism is a key, linking part of the network of culture/nature, spirit/matter, mind/body and reason/nature dualisms that have shaped Western culture, and is an active force in contemporary life. Human/nature dualism is a Western-based cultural formation going back thousands of years that sees the essentially human as part of a radically separate order of reason, mind or consciousness, set apart from the lower order that comprises the body, the woman, the animal and the pre-human.[15] Human/nature dualism conceives the human as not only superior to but as different in kind from the non-human, which is conceived as a lower non-conscious and non-communicative, purely physical sphere that exists as a mere resource or instrument for the higher human one. The human essence is not the ecologically embodied 'animal' side of self, which is best neglected, but the higher disembodied element of mind, reason, culture and soul or spirit.

[14] See for example Benjamin 1988; Benhabib 1992; Plumwood 1991, 1993.
[15] See especially Plumwood 1993; Spelman 1988; and Lloyd 1984.

This ideology of dualism and human apartness can be traced down through Western culture through Christianity and modern science. In the scientific fantasy of mastery, the new human task becomes that of remoulding nature to conform to the dictates of reason to achieve salvation – here on earth rather than in heaven – as freedom from death and bodily limitation. The idea of human apartness emphasised in culture, religion and science was, of course, shockingly challenged by Charles Darwin in his argument that humans evolved from non-human species. But these insights of continuity and kinship with other life forms (the real scandal of Darwin's thought) remain only superficially absorbed in the dominant culture, even by scientists. The traditional scientific project of technological control is justified by continuing to think of humans as a special superior species, set apart and entitled to manipulate and commodify the earth and other species for their own exclusive benefit. This ideology has been functional for Western culture in enabling it to colonise and exploit the non-human world and so-called 'primitive' cultures with less constraint, but it also creates dangerous illusions in denying human embeddedness in and dependency on nature, which we see in the generally poor response to the ecological crisis.

This feminist-inspired historical narrative (barely sketched here) helps to link the human and non-human sides of the problem and to give us a different perspective on what it is about environmentalism that is radical or challenging to the weight of cultural tradition. A feminist approach enables us to see what the dominant theories have obscured, that *the environmental problematic is double-sided*, with denial of our own embodiment, animality and inclusion in the natural order being the other side of our distancing from and devaluation of that order. Human hyperseparation from nature establishes a discontinuity based on denying both the human-like aspects of nature and the nature-like aspects of the human, as the denial of the sphere of 'nature' within the human matches the devaluation and denial of nature without. The key insight here, as Rachel Carson understood in the 1960s, and the work of Mary Midgley and Rosemary Ruether suggested in the 1970s, is that the resulting conception of ourselves as ecologically invulnerable, beyond animality and 'outside nature' (as a separate and pure sphere which exists 'somewhere else'), leads to the failure to understand our ecological identities and dependency on nature, a failure that lies behind so many environmental catastrophes, both human and non-human.

On the other side, the treatment of human concerns as 'shallow' has prevented a double-sided focus on anthropocentrism as a problem for humans too, as a factor which prevents us situating ourselves as ecological beings and makes us insensitive to ecological dependencies and interconnections. What is problematic about deep ecology, then, is not its challenge to the non-human side of this tradition, but the way it goes on to marginalise the human side, the many highly significant hybrid forms of environmental activism that are concerned with environmental justice and with situating human life ecologically.

This focus on the radical implications of both human and non-human sides of activism enables a feminist account to avoid the 'deep/shallow' divide as a way of marginalising human concerns, and to discern a degree of integration and radical challenge in the environment movement as a whole that both deep ecology and conventional environmental ethics miss. Because *both* human and nature sides of the dualism are thus affected by hyperseparation, resolving the dualism gives rise to two distinct but intertwined projects, the project of situating human life ecologically and the project of situating non-human life ethically and culturally. It is the first concern with situating human life itself in ecological terms that motivates the important and familiar range of environmental struggles for liveability and sustainability deep ecology neglects and disparages as 'shallow'. Both human and non-human projects involve cultural remaking at many levels, not a neat split into non-human ethics and human politics. And this kind of analysis, which notes the way the agency of the non-human world has been rendered invisible, can also help to explain our current mode of denial, which the framework of identification does not convincingly do. Because they challenge different aspects of a deeply entrenched conceptual structure of denial, both human and non-human struggles can be subversive and provoke resistance. If Aldo Leopold is 'deep', so is Rachel Carson.

The 'deep/shallow' distinction might still have some use in the reformulated problematic, but does not mark a dualistic division between human and non-human concerns, or automatic privileging of one type of concern over the other. Some non-human concerns can be decidedly 'shallow', for example those that automatically privilege human pets like cats or dogs over other animals, or which treat such pets as the paradigm of animality. A focus on situating human lives and settlements ecologically might be very challenging to accepted ways of thinking about both the human and the non-human. A combined human and non-human focus might become shallow if it limited excessively its political or ethical thinking. Should we automatically privilege as 'deep' the human over the non-human, or vice versa? We do sometimes have reason to privilege certain issues over others (although I think a minimal-ranking approach is the best way to go here), but if choices must be made, we can usually make them on the basis of contingent and contextual features of particular cases. The need for choice in limited contexts does not support any universal, context-invariant or automatic privileging of human over non-human issues – or vice versa.

A feminist approach can thus reformulate both human and non-human sides of the problem as an outcome or expression of the *human/nature dualism* that in Western culture deforms and hyperseparates *both sides* of what it splits apart.[16] This analysis escapes the false choices between human and non-human, instrumental and intrinsic, prudential and ethical, self and other, because it sees our failures in situating non-humans ethically and our prudential failures in failing to situate our own lives ecologically as closely and interactively linked. Countering the human/nature dualism that is a key part of human-centredness gives us two tasks: (re)situating humans in ecological terms and non-humans in ethical terms. The first is apparently the more urgent and self-evident, the task of sustainability, as prudence or care for self, while the other is presented as optional, the inessential sphere of ethics or care for the other. But this is an error; the two tasks are interconnected, and cannot be addressed properly in isolation from each other.

Human and non-human struggles and ethics are thoroughly inter-linked because when we hyperseparate ourselves from nature and reduce it conceptually (in order to justify domination), we not only lose the ability to empathise and to see the non-human sphere in ethical terms, but also get a false sense of our own character and location that includes an illusory sense of agency and autonomy. Is this failure to understand our embeddedness in and dependency on nature a failing concerning self or other? A conceptual reduction or devaluation of the Other that licences 'purely instrumental' relationships can distort our perceptions and enframings, impoverish our relations and make us insensitive to limits, dependencies and interconnections. These conceptual frame-works are a direct hazard to the Other, but are in turn often a prudential hazard to self. Is such a misunderstanding of self and Other a failure of politics or ethics? The refusal to recognise the way others contribute to or support our lives has many political and ethical aspects: political because it encourages us to dispossess the other and to starve them of resources rather than to share, justice aspects because we fail to give others their due, and ethical aspects because we fail in care, con-sideration and attention.

On this kind of account, environmental activism aiming to situate human life ecologically is not necessarily opposed to non-human defence, nor is it necessarily 'shallow', 'anthropocentric' or lacking in radical challenge. A feminist framework of analysis provides a basis for

---

[16] Plumwood 2002; Merchant 2003.

solidarity with humans similarly subject to the status of 'nature', such as women and so-called 'primitive' peoples (Plumwood 2002). It also foregrounds a cultural project or reconceptualisation. If the ideals and conceptions we use to distance ourselves as humans from the non-human world also explain our failure to understand ourselves as essentially ecologically embodied beings, and if they support the dangerous and tenacious illusions of autonomy and invulnerability to ecological failure that threaten our future, clearly we need new ones.

Unity, difference and coverture in ethics and politics

However, the potential for complementarity of human and non-human concerns this account reveals doesn't mean we can ignore the potential for human/non-human conflict, which is acute in human-centred contexts. If there are systemic, structural and cultural sources of conflict and delusion of this kind in our relationship with nature, the issue can't be properly dealt with just at a personal level of individual conversion to green uplift aimed at enlarging personal consciousness and identification.[17] We need a better politics, an environmental culture, and a good structural analysis at all levels. The hyperseparation deep ecology would seek a remedy for in a *personal 'state of being'*, one of identity or unity with nature, appears in feminist analysis as a major, historically situated deformation in the dominant culture that affects all areas of understanding, including ethics and politics. If human hyperseparation involves exaggerated human differentiation from nature, its opposite requires not a personal state of unity that erases boundaries but a just recognition of non-human kinship and difference that permeates culture.

For deep ecology, the solution to environmental problems is a personal 'state of being' or form of personal ecological enlightenment in overcoming human species bias – 'the construction of as wide a sense of self as possible through a process of identifying out and including an enlarged scope of life and living processes [*sic*] within one's sense of (S)self' (Hay 2002: 47). This 'unity interpretation' implies reduction to the personal, a dismissal of ethics, and a limitation of the political to the intra-human. Deep ecology's emphasis on personal psychological identification and unity as the basis for suitable relationship with the non-human precludes useful theorisations of human-centredness, interspecies conflict or political and structural failings. A position that negates difference is poorly equipped to correct the foundational

---

[17] Although these can have an important role to play in limited contexts.

delusion of human self-enclosure and make visible our dependency on the denied and backgrounded presence of nature.

The dominant liberal model treating nature as instrument that is naturalised in politics and property formation is at bottom a model of nature as slave. The dominant human-centred instrumentalism of the economic system erases nature or represents it in powerless and apolitical terms, as slave, as property, or as coverture wife, an emotional resource lacking separate interests. Under the institution of coverture,[18] women were in effect legally subsumed by their husbands, renouncing any claim to separate identity or separate property upon marriage. A wife's interests were 'covered' politically and legally by her husband, who, when in the properly harmonious 'state of being',[19] would come to have interests indistinguishable from hers. Coverture stepped up from slavery, since the slave had no sphere of presence or power. Coverture women had private presence but only the power of love within the family, conceived as a sphere of love but not of justice, and in the public sphere of justice women were denied both power and presence.[20]

The model of nature as slave or coverture wife underpins the dominant model of private property that is the foundation of contemporary global capitalism. As I and others have argued,[21] capitalism's nullification of non-human contributions and agency in production work appears in Locke's famous model of property formation, in which the colonist is entitled to appropriate that product into which he has mixed his labour, on condition that it falls under the category of 'nature', a class whose separate agency and deserts are entirely erased. If nature is seen instead as a field of distinct actors and agents who are accorded power and presence, such as land or place, Locke's entrepreneur appropriates entirely for himself (and unjustly) what is essentially a joint production between the human and various extra-human agents (or actors), including the land. The reasons for capitalism's colossal environmental destructiveness go right to the heart of liberal concepts of property and their original dispossession of nature.

The unity interpretation of deep ecology offers a poor corrective to liberal coverture, acknowledging non-humans as having interests, but continuing to represent these as subsumed or covered by the ecologically enlightened individual who is successful in identification. Under the unity account, nature is subsumed by the enlarged Self: the ecologically enlightened 'husband' of nature – in the right 'state of

---

[18] See Pateman 1989.
[19] The properly harmonious 'state of being' was one a good wife was responsible for bringing about in her husband.
[20] See Pateman 1989; Okin 1989.   [21] See Plumwood 2002; O'Neill 2002.

being' – will have interests identical with those of nature. Just as the coverture household is seen as a natural 'unity' or harmony of interests, so nature as 'wife' is included in the enlarged Self household, voiding recognition of multiple presences, boundaries and conflicting interests. Unity, like coverture, works for favourable cases, but fails for conflict cases. It does not acknowledge relations with nature as a sphere of justice, or recognise the subsumed party as a distinct political and economic actor whose interests require separate attention in conflict resolution and other social arrangements. Many oppressive projects have used the cover of unity for denying or violating boundaries – for example, assimilation projects in colonialism. Nature defence positions formulated in terms of unity need to consider the potential for abuse and impoverishment inherent in such approaches and look for alternative ways to articulate their ideals.

From coverture to politics and partnership

An analysis in terms of unity makes unavailable a richer range of analyses that take account of political, dialogical (communicative) and self/ Other dynamics, for these require recognition of difference and multiplicity. It reduces solidarity to sameness, and the defence of nature to the extension of the self through identification and self-realisation. In contrast, a feminist partnership conception would replace monological concepts, processes and rationalities based on unity by dialogical ones involving multiple parties, such as communication, mutuality, negotiation and accommodation, concepts suitable for theorising collaboration, conflict resolution and power relations between human and non-human. To make the field of nature available for dialogical and political concepts, we need to replace reductive vocabularies and develop representations that accord it presence and power. Thus a cultural project of reframing and dialogical development must necessarily accompany or precede the political one.

Such reframing opens human relationships with nature up to rich ethical and political discourses like feminism, positioning nature within political narratives of subsumption and colonisation, injustice and oppression, among others. What once seemed a peaceful bucolic landscape can now appear as a landscape of contest. Feminists can see non-human others as situated in a parallel way to women, hyperseparated, reduced and backgrounded or 'covered' as co-agents. Feminist analysis can treat human-centredness not in the apolitical terms of detachment from the human, but as a parallel 'political' distortion to androcentrism and eurocentrism, similarly justifying domination, colonisation and dispossession. These political narratives can now be applied to clarify the conceptual history of nature in particular cultures. Such discourses might tell of a dominant human class directing the instrumentalisation of others as throughput, and support basis in production, but remote from production processes and their adverse ecological consequences for others, both human and non-human. They tell of a non-human world conceptually reduced to slave or coverture wife, similarly represented as incapable of agency in self-determined projects, directions and unfoldings. When the other is reduced and instrumentalised, its consideration, contribution to and share of the world minimised, it presents no obstacles to monological projects, and can be nullified and dispossessed, harnessed and appropriated.

Feminist models suggest parallels to women's coverture in the denial and subsumption of nature's agency, especially in systems of property that erase subordinate contributions and award all credit for and benefits from joint production to the dominant party. The invisibility and erasure of agency on which this unjust appropriation is based provides an important further structural parallel between the situation of women and that of non-human nature. The modern equivalent of 'nature' is the category of 'maintenance labour', sometimes called 'reproduction', especially those forms involving bodily services. Feminists do not see production, associated with men's labour and privileged in both capitalist and Marxist frameworks, as the key category for understanding, but rather reproduction, associated with women's labour in the home, renewing the human and non-human household population, and various supporting activities of household and ecosystem maintenance. For ecofeminists there is a parallel erasure of this category of reproduction, understood as including both women's labour and the non-human ecological conditions and services that renew the ecological foundations upon which production depends.[22] This erasure, characteristic of wives, appears in the devaluation and disappearance of their contributions to joint productions and conceptual consignment to the background role of providing support for a foregrounded male superior to whom all agency is attributed and who appropriates the product.

The distorted view of the world enshrined in this erasure corresponds to the perspective of a dominant gender, class and species category, that of an appropriative human male elite who foreground their own claims and contributions as 'production' and background what others, human and non-human, do to make that possible. The agency of the world is theirs; they are the entrepreneurs, the ones who make things

---

[22] See Merchant 1980, 2003.

(commodities) happen, while others are mere instruments, back-grounded as wives, 'hired hands', secretaries and support staff – which includes, on a very lowly rung, the ecological systems of the biosphere. Both the anonymous commodity and highly recognised and rewarded creativity of the entrepreneur who 'produced' it are built on the denial, dispossession and silencing of those Others assigned to the background sphere of reproduction (or 'nature') – both women and the non-human – whose supporting role is essential but invisible.

Feminist models can again be useful in imagining alternatives here, seeing parallels to women's coverture in the denial and subsumption of nature's agency, especially in systems of property and representation that erase non-human contributions and award all the benefits from joint human–nature production to the human partner. Women moved beyond both slave and coverture models with the first women's move-ment, when the wife was recognised as a distinct political actor whose interests required equal acknowledgement in institutional arrangements – partially achieved with the arrival of women's franchise. Women moved further with the second women's movement, the development of solidarity between women, and the acknowledgement of the family as a sphere of justice rather than of unity. However, improved recognition of women as productive workers and economic actors[23] in the traditional areas of male labour has proved compatible with continued under-recognition of the role and agency of women and nature in the sphere of reproduction. The world remains under the economic control of elite white males, and women are denied power and presence.

Partnership concepts treat non-humans as distinct actors and stake-holders whose interests, efforts and agency, like those of the wife, require distinct recognition, visibility, consideration and justice. To defeat coverture, we need, at a minimum, to afford respect to nature's presence, needs and agency and to give not only personal but institu-tional recognition to its possibly conflicting interests in these spheres.[24] Coverture concepts of property award owners virtually unconstrained power over the land and its life. Partnership conceptions of property are more constrained, accommodating and respectful of the more-than-human world, requiring standards for the maintenance and thriving of both human and more-than-human partners.

---

[23] See Okin 1989; Pateman 1989.
[24] See Okin 1989 on women's comparable interests. For examples from biotechnology and intellectual property rights, see Shiva 1994 and Mies and Shiva 1993. Feminist expansions of ethics to include moral epistemology, place ethics and counter-hegemonic ethics are also helpful for environmental theory and activism.

A politics of solidarity and culture of negotiation

Our feminist replacement would not be complete without a dialogical reworking of identification as motivation for activism. For a feminist analysis, the key concept for understanding why people become active on behalf of the non-human world is not identification or unity but solidarity, the most fundamental of political relationships.[25] Environmental theory can learn much from feminist and anticolonial theory about developing a concept of solidarity with nature distinct from unity, one which at the same time allows us to affirm continuity and to respect non-human difference. There are multiple bases for critical solidarity with nature, as interpreted by feminist theorists like Sandra Harding (1991). One important critical basis for human solidarity can be an understanding that certain human societies position humans as oppressors of non-human nature, treating humans as a privileged group shaping non-human roles to parallel those of oppressed people within human dominance orders. The 'traitorous identities' that enable some men to be male feminists in active opposition to androcentric culture, some whites to be actively in opposition to white supremacism and ethnocentric culture, can also enable some humans to be critical of 'human supremacism' and in active opposition to anthropocentric culture.

What makes such traitorous identities possible is precisely the fact that the relationship between the oppressed and the 'traitor' is *not one of identity*, that the traitor is critical of his or her own 'oppressor' group as someone from within that group who has some knowledge of its workings and its effects on the life of the oppressed group. It depends on the traitor being someone with *a view from both sides*, able to adopt multiple perspectives and locations, understanding her relationship with the Other from the perspective of both kinds of lives. A dialogical articulation of interspecies solidarity avoids several potential hazards for unity positions, the arrogance of reading in your own location and perspective as that of the Other, and the arrogance of assuming that you can 'read as the Other', know their lives as they do, and in that sense speak or see as the Other.

Solidarity with nature is a key concept for both ethics and politics. Environmental movements can be seen as motivated by and acting in solidarity with the more-than-human, as well as with those (usually marginalised) humans who suffer with and as 'nature', such as poor women, indigenous people and others close to the ecological consequences from which the privileged are remote. Not only those

---

[25] See Plumwood 2002.

projects aimed at defending non-humans, but also the projects of sustainability, of ecologically situating human lives and communities, can be seen as projects of solidarity, partnership and negotiation with the land.

The ability to empower in deliberative systems those in solidarity with nature is clearly a desideratum for any environmentally satisfactory form of politics. Liberal democratic systems may seem initially to meet this test, until we notice that they treat environmental movements as just another special interest group and environmental interests as tradeable off against other kinds of benefits, a position that fails to reflect the intrinsic value of nature and the fundamental enabling services it provides. Deliberative and administrative systems must be structured to make non-human needs, contributions and impacts visible at all levels and empower representatives motivated by solidarity with nature (or contextually appropriate aspects of nature). In many situations, we can treat nature directly as a stakeholder – the river, for example, can be seen as a stakeholder in decisions about water use and diversion, whose maintenance imposes constraints on acceptable human projects.

The double-sidedness we identified in human and non-human ethics and ontology reappears in environmental politics. Political systems that recognise the non-human – in economic, distributive and political terms – as independent agent and co-producer of our basic life conditions must be supplemented on the human side by ecologically appropriate and accountable political systems that help humans to recognise their ecological identities and situate their lives ecologically. While there are probably a range of systems that can satisfy these requirements, we can draw some conclusions about what such appropriate political systems will *not* be like. They will not be systems of consumption based on the anonymous commodity and the global market, since these create remote, unimaginable and unmanageable ecological footprints. They will not be one- or two-party systems prioritising a maximising concept of economic good defined without reference to ecological conditions and allowing little choice or voice on issues of ecological adaptation. They will not be highly unequal societies where decision-making elites benefit from processes creating excessive ecological costs that can be passed on to politically inarticulate and powerless parties. Appropriate systems will be systems of equality and justice that empower those least remote from ecological damage. Systems that accord a high priority to ecological agendas and interests will consider these factors in determining political and administrative units and boundaries, aiming to create communities of shared ecological fate.

Environmental culture fosters a communicative politics, ethics and rationality as best suited to conflict resolution and mutual adaptation.[26] A feminist partnership ethic advocates communicative strategies of recognising, listening to and negotiating with the land and the systems that sustain all our lives, so as to allow for their renewal and flourishing. A dialogical form of rationality aimed at mutual benefit clearly cannot be one that aims at maximising outcomes, including economic outcomes, for just one party, the human party. A dialogical economics would replace monological economic maximisations by concepts of sufficiency or enough.

A partnership ethic supports institutional representation for nature in deliberative, rational and communicative systems, and similar recognition of its foundational and enabling character. Sensitivity to these should aid recognition of the forms of denial and coverture enshrined at the economic level in dominant systems of property and commodity. This is crucial, not because the economic level is always more basic than other levels (as economic reductionists assume), but because in the current global order of neoliberalism, the economic sphere is hyperseparated, fetishised and empowered to structure and dominate all other spheres. Political systems of social democracy that block the dominance of and provide effective political means to intervene in the economic sphere may thus avoid the worst excesses of global capitalism's destruction of nature (at least domestically), but can still be undermined by the forms of erasure naturalised in the global economic system, in dominant property formation systems and in the resulting regime of anonymous commodities.

Commodity culture's extreme reduction, distancing from and backgrounding of its denied and hidden partners fosters an exaggerated sense of self-enclosure and independence from nature that is dangerous and illusory. These illusions of autonomy are reinforced continually in commodity culture, and help to explain why there is so little sense of urgency about the environmental crisis. If the maintenance services of nature and women are erased, rendered invisible, 'taken for granted', their fundamental enabling character, as the precondition and foundation for other 'higher' activities, will not be understood or provided for. At worst, they will simply be ignored, and left to degrade under competitive market mechanisms like the cost-price squeeze; at best, they will be counted as amenities or factors of production that can be minimised or traded off against other benefits, rather than their maintenance being

---

[26] See Dryzek 1990a and 1990b; Plumwood 2002; Weston 2004.

treated as crucial constraints on production and economic activity.[27] Economics will remain a distorted form of reason that maximises the throughput of nature (in production) to maximise wealth and property formation, without allowing for nature's continuation and renewal (in the sphere of reproduction). Although we need to work at all levels to correct the erasure of nature, monological forms of economic rationality that assume but simultaneously deny their ecological foundations are rightly prioritised for change, as foremost among the factors that threaten our future.

References

Adams, C. (1990). *The Sexual Politics of Meat*. New York: Continuum.

Beauvoir, S. de (1965). *The Second Sex*. London: Foursquare Books.

Benhabib, S. (1992). *Situating the Self*. New York: Routledge.

Benhabib, S., and Cornell, D. (1987). *Feminism as Critique*. Cambridge: Polity Press.

Benjamin, J. (1988). *The Bonds of Love*. London: Virago.

Brennan, T. (2000). *Exhausting Modernity: Grounds for a New Economy*. London: Routledge.

Dryzek, J. (1990a). 'Green Reason: Communicative Ethics for the Biosphere', *Environmental Ethics* 12: 195–210.

(l990b). *Discursive Democracy: Politics, Policy and Political Science*. Cambridge: Cambridge University Press.

Haraway, D. (2003). *The Companion Species Manifesto*. Chicago: Prickly Paradigm Press.

Harding, S. (1991). *Whose Science? Whose Knowledge?* Ithaca, N.Y.: Cornell University Press.

Hay, P. (2002). *Main Currents of Environmental Thought*. Sydney: UNSW University Press.

Jacobs, M. (1999). 'Sustainable Development as a Contested Concept', in Andrew Dobson (ed.), *Fairness and Futurity: Essays on Environmental Sustainability and Social Justice*. Oxford: Oxford University Press, 21–45.

King, Y. (1981). 'Feminism and Revolt', *Heresies* **4**.1: 12–26.

Lloyd, G. (1984). *The Man of Reason*. London: Methuen.

Merchant, C. (1980). *The Death of Nature*. London: Wildwood House.

(2003). *Reinventing Eden: The Fate of Nature in Western Culture*. New York: Routledge.

Midgley, M. (1983). *Animals and Why They Matter*. Athens, Ga.: University of Georgia Press.

Mies, M., and Shiva, V. (1993). *Ecofeminism*. London: Zed Books.

Okin, S. M. (1989). *Gender, Justice and the Family*. New York: Basic Books.

---

[27] See Jacobs 1999. 'Trading off' nature corresponds in the economic sphere to the instrumental treatment of nature as the province of 'special interest groups' in the liberal democratic and deliberative sphere.

O'Neill, J. (2002). 'Wilderness, Cultivation, and Appropriation', *Philosophy and Geography* **5**.1: 35–50.

Pateman, C. (1989). 'The Civic Culture: a Philosophic Critique', in *The Disorder of Women*. Cambridge: Polity Press, 141–78.

Plumwood, V. (1991). 'Nature, Self and Gender: Feminism, Environmental Philosophy and the Critique of Rationalism', *Hypatia* **6**.1: 4–32.

  (1993). *Feminism and the Mastery of Nature*. London: Routledge.

  (2001). 'Nature as Agency and the Prospects for a Progressive Naturalism', *Capitalism, Nature, Socialism* **12**.4: 3–32.

  (2002). *Environmental Culture: The Ecological Crisis of Reason*. London: Routledge.

  (2004). 'Animals and Ecology: Towards a Better Integration', in S. Sapontzis (ed.), *Food for Thought*. New York: Prometheus Books, 344–58.

Ruether, R. (1975). *New Woman, New Earth*. Minneapolis: Seabury.

Singer, P. (1990). *Animal Liberation*, 2nd ed. New York: Avon Books.

Shiva, V. (1988). *Staying Alive: Women, Ecology and Development*. London: Zed Books.

  (ed.) (1994). *Close to Home: Women Reconnect Ecology, Health and Development*. London: Earthscan.

Spelman, E. (1988). *The Inessential Woman*. Boston, Mass.: Beacon.

Weston, A. (2004). 'Multi-Centrism: A Manifesto', *Environmental Ethics* **26**.1: 25–40.

5   Nationalism

Avner de-Shalit

It is widely accepted that the planet's ecosystems are under threat: there are unbearable levels of pollution, development often does not take account of environmental protection, a growing number of species are becoming extinct, and so on. Let us call the attempt to change or stop this tendency the 'ecological challenge'. In this chapter I ask two questions. To what extent do the ecological challenge and nationalism conflict? And if they do, is preventing environmental degradation a reason to restrict the quest for nationality? In order to discuss these questions I first define nationalism. I then discuss three reasons why nationalism might work in favour of protecting the environment. However, I also suggest four reasons why ecological protection and nationalism do not tie in with each other. I claim that these four reasons override the first three, and so if one accepts that the ecological challenge is urgent it should have priority over nationality. However, this should not imply that those who already enjoy national self-determination could restrict the quest for nationality among those who do not.

I should start, though, by clarifying my use of the term 'nationalism'. In general it is an ideology that puts forward both empirical and normative claims. The empirical ones are that people do regard themselves as members of communities that are defined as nations, based on some ethnic coherence, a shared history, customs and traditions, often a common language and shared values. These people are attached sentimentally, but also politically, to these communities as nations. I shall refer to this attachments as 'nationality'. The normative claim is that it is good that people have a sense of nationality. Why? Some nationalists offer psychological reasons, e.g. that only through belonging to a nation can people experience self-fulfilment, or that only through national attachments can individuals overcome alienation. Others advance ontological claims about nations as a good source of personal identity. Finally, nationalists of a liberal bent put forward economic and social arguments, e.g. that nationality – with its alternative values to the market and its self-interested behaviour – is a precondition for a stable system of distributive justice.

Obviously, the more psychological justifications for nationalism tend to be more right-wing in their implications, whereas the economic and social justifications that emphasise distributive justice tend to be more liberal and left-wing. However, when I refer here to nationalism I refer only to those ideologies which are *egalitarian* in the sense that they claim that if indeed nationality is a good, then *all* our planet's inhabitants should experience the sense, and that, therefore, if A deserves to experience national self-determination, so do B and C and so on (Beran 1984; Tamir 1993; Miller 1995; de-Shalit 1996a). In this chapter I do not refer to a form of chauvinistic nationalism that attributes superiority to one's own nation, since it not only poses a challenge to ecology but generates a challenge to every reasonable political standpoint and to many fundamental democratic values.[1]

Nationalism and ecology: can they go hand in hand?

Solidarity

I begin with three reasons why nationalism might work in favour of ecology. First, nationalism demands from its members solidarity and responsibility towards other members of the state, in particular when the latter contains large and anonymous populations (Miller 1995; Miller 2000: 31–2). For nationalists, the danger is that the members of the nation absorb attitudes of self-interest and consumerism from the economic sphere and apply them to the political arena. It is the sense of nationality that prompts them to think differently, at least in the political domain, and to switch from 'consumerism' to 'citizenship'. Nations need to foster such attitudes because otherwise it would be extremely difficult to mobilise individuals and to ensure that public goods are provided. Nationality therefore calls on us to care for the wellbeing of others, as if it were part of our own wellbeing. Since we are part of a community, we inevitably consider its other members and their wellbeing to be part of what constitutes our own 'selves'. Nationalists claim that this psychological need explains why citizens are ready to pay taxes to help the needy in their own nation while they are reluctant to assist

---

[1] Elsewhere I rejected Anna Bramwell's theory that connects Nazism with the rise of ecology movements by claiming that she fails to distinguish between the romantic glorification of rural life and modern, science-based environmentalism. See de-Shalit 1996b.

foreign individuals with similar (or even greater) needs and often regard with suspicion any foreign aid financed by their government.

But what does the wellbeing of compatriots consist of? The common answer is basic wealth, housing, health, education, perhaps access to work, and security. However, many environmental theorists have put forward the idea that a good life (or wellbeing) is also a life with a clean and natural environment, with open spaces, and so on. Leading a moral life includes experiencing these environmental goods because they are part of what makes one mentally healthy. In fact, reconnecting humans with their natural environment is a precondition for getting rid of alienation (Naess 1989). Taking part in restoration ecology is a way to educate citizens to become democratic and to get them involved in the nature around them and thus to foster their culture, and implementing environment-friendly policies is a precondition for forming a truly free society or a just one (Dobson 1998; Wissenburg 1998; Light 2002). Becoming environment-friendly offers a great opportunity for cultural renewal and emancipation, be it political or gender-based.[2] Finally, an Aristotelian account of wellbeing implies that there should be a close linkage between the wellbeing of humans and that of animals and nature. (O'Neill 1993)

To put aside, for the moment, the question whether this 'emancipation' includes overcoming national affiliation, if nationalism insists that one should care for one's compatriots and their wellbeing, and since wellbeing is closely related to nature and its integrity, then indeed nationalism implies that one should care for the environment. As a matter of fact, we don't need nationalism as such; what we need is a community-oriented attitude. However, since nationalism is very strongly communitarian, it is a good candidate for achieving and maintaining this communitarian attitude. As mentioned above, such an attitude claims that concern for the wellbeing of others enriches one and makes one's life much more meaningful.

In order to see why this premise about communal obligations is needed to protect the environment, perhaps we should first consider what would have happened if the citizens' behaviour were individualistic. Their normative behaviour would be borrowed from, guided and motivated by instrumental rationality, and possibly attracted to future benefits. Now, consider an individual who behaves according to this model and who has to reflect on whether to protect a piece of land which has remained untouched by humans for ages, and which is the habitat for a rare species of wolf. This person's instrumental rationality

---

[2] For the political emancipation see Eckersley 1992. For the gender based see Cuomo (1998).

combined with the attraction of future benefits leaves no room for sentimental attachment to this piece of land. The only environmental consideration that is allowed is instrumental: e.g. recreational value. Alas, if he believes that he will benefit from a project to, say, build houses on this land, he will have no hesitation in supporting it. He will weigh one instrumental value against another, and calculate which is greater. The historical value of this area, its role in the nation's past, or its value to fellow citizens would be irrelevant.

Now, the interesting point about nationalism is that it does not naively believe that this person will shed all these symptoms of economic behaviour once he sees himself as part of a nation. This would be far-fetched. However, nationalists do argue that, since we grow up in communities of nations, we learn to balance such tendencies (which obviously harm the environment) with other obligations, such as taking into account the wellbeing of others. The context of the nation will therefore weaken this instrumental rationality.

Thus, claim nationalists, if our individual were raised to have nationalist sentiments, he should have internalised considerations that go beyond his own instrumental interests. He should be concerned with the history of this piece of land, with its value for the nation, as well as with other citizens' wellbeing. So nationalism does form a positive obstacle to full instrumentalism and to the application solely of economic rationality to policies, and this may work in favour of environmental protection.

Heritage promotes policies of preservation

Nationalists argue that nationality nourishes the idea of heritage and is therefore likely to promote policies of preservation and conservation. Even if nationalism is not romantic and does not look backwards, it does assume some sense of common history or a shared tradition. However, while this could be seen as mere history, for nationalists it is a heritage. The difference is that heritage implies duties towards ancestors and their deeds. 'History' is a less demanding notion: for example, one can be critical of one's history. 'Heritage', though, one is expected to respect. It conveys the idea of a duty to be carried, transmitted and bequeathed to the next generation. Now, heritage does not have to be based on evidence (although it often is, with the support of scientific theories advanced by archaeologists, historians and sociologists). It might even be said that 'national identities typically contain a considerable element of myth' (Miller 1995: 35) or even deliberate inventions made for political purposes. The nation is a community rooted in the past, regardless of whether or not its understanding of its history is accurate. As Miller rightly argues, while some could conclude that nationality is therefore ridiculous or, rationally speaking, pointless, we could, alternatively, examine the social function of such beliefs or constructions, and be less critical of them. There are at least two such functions: national history provides a reassurance that the nation of which one is a member can be legitimised, and it serves as a reassurance of the nation's values and customs. These two functions are often referred to as 'heritage'. Thus heritage serves to sustain members' solidarity with and obligations to other members.

Heritage is often related to stories and myths about constitutive events that took place in certain places: the battle in Dunkirk, the life of Sibelius (the Finnish nationalist composer), the Boston tea party, the story of Daniel Boone (the great American frontiersman), Napoleon's defeat in Moscow, Mozart's birth in Salzburg and Shakespeare's theatre in London. From the point of view of the environment, these stories and myths are interesting because they intimately tie the nation's values and norms to locations, thereby sustaining an obligation to preserve those places and their atmosphere.

Notice that this is not the 'classic' argument in favour of preservation or conservation, about ecosystems, their balance or integrity. Nationalism, though, adds a different dimension and a further argument: we do not conserve the objects themselves, as monuments, lakes, forests or houses. Instead, we want to conserve ideas of the good, intentions, and human deeds in general, which we could call 'national stories' and which have to do with those lakes, forests or monuments. For nationalists any conservation or preservation is in fact a restoration, because often its goal is to breathe life into a forgotten story of national greatness or into a monument that has fallen into decay but that nationalists find meaningful, valid or significant. So nationalists call for the restoration, in fact, of ecosystems, lakes, parks, streets, houses and the like, in order to restore not only the objects themselves but also the national story, and thus to create heritage. The term 'heritage' or 'common inheritance' was, indeed, used by the British Conservative government in the late 1980s in its White Paper on the environment (Young 1993: 58–9), which might suggest that nationalists regard the term as an easy way to convince sceptics about the need for environmental policies.

Nationalism sustains a sense of obligations to future generations

While the idea of 'heritage' refers to obligations that living members of the nation have towards past generations, the idea of the nation also embodies a sense of obligation to future generations. Such an attitude may help to support environmental policies. It is likely to work against a common anti-environmental tendency for time preference.

Nationalism teaches the nation's members to extend their notion of identity into the future, including beyond their own deaths. This 'self-transcendence' is presented by nationalists as a claim both about psychological health and about moral integrity and duty. Members of the nation identify with, and seek to further the wellbeing, preservation and endurance of, communities, locations, causes, artefacts, institutions, ideals and so on, that are outside themselves and that they hope will flourish (even) beyond their lifetime. Now, if I want a certain project to be realised, then *this* is what I want, rather than the satisfaction of observing and witnessing its realisation.[3]

Nationalism thus overcomes our tendency for time preference, that is, for preferring a good that is likely to become available in the near future to an equivalent (or even greater) good that is likely to become available in the remote future. There is a considerable literature on whether time preference is rational. However, it is widely accepted that time preference is a great obstacle to sustaining environmental policies. This is because the fruits of environmental policies often lie only in the remote future. One example is investing a huge sum of money today to treat hazardous waste professionally rather than to bury it, so that remote future generations enjoy a safer environment and are not exposed to the risk of radioactive or chemical leakage from burial sites. Such policies might be unpopular for two reasons. First, many contemporaries could claim that these policies benefit people who do not yet exist, and who have done nothing to benefit us contemporaries. Second, applying time preference, such people will tend to devalue what happens many years from now, regardless of whether they or different people are likely to suffer.

At this point nationalism, with its idea of the nation as an ongoing chain of generations that is not only past- but also future-oriented, and which extends beyond one's lifetime into the future, may sustain an obligation to future generations that overrides any time preference. This obligation is a key to sustainable development. Nationalists argue that we contemporaries must not inflict harms on our descendants (e.g. destroying rare species of plants, depleting non-renewable resources) because it might risk the continuation of the nation. Nationalists are therefore likely to consider environmental issues as a matter of distribution of access to environmental goods across generations and rule out any policy that arbitrarily inflicts harm on future generations.

---

[3] See also Partridge 1981 and Barry 1983: 151–2.

Nationalism and ecology as foes

So far I have analysed why nationalism does work in favour of the ecology and may protect the environment. Now I turn to discuss why nationalism is, in fact, a threat to the ecological challenge.

Nationalism contradicts acting locally while thinking globally

Many environmentalists subscribe to the view that activism should be local, for various reasons: people find it easier to express themselves and participate in local matters, it sustains an affinity between inhabitants of a town, neighbourhood, or village and the ecosystem in which they live, and so on. Nevertheless, they claim, *thinking* about the environment should be global. Their slogan is 'think globally – act locally' (Searle 1997; Kemball-Cook et al. 1991; Lamb 1996: i). The Dutch and New Zealand governments, which have been more active in environmental protection than others, delegate the responsibility for managing local environmental problems to local authorities. However, they both have plans and strategies at the national level, and they both promote thinking regionally and globally about environmental issues (Johnson 1997). Indeed, international co-operation between states and within international organisations like the UN and in civil society (i.e. between NGOs and individual activists) is necessary to cope with ecological disasters and environmental protection. Without it, there is little hope for any significant change in states' policies. For example, while a group such as 'Reclaim the Streets' may act locally in a small town demanding a car-free zone in the town centre, they in fact have in mind the environmental impact of the use of private cars on the global level. Their demand is valid even if in their particular town there is rarely a problem of air pollution. Their demand is valid because they fight a culture and a world phenomenon which contributes heavily to air pollution and to respiratory illnesses.

However, it seems that nationalism contradicts this principle – that is, 'think globally – act locally' – in two ways. First, the nation often demands that a local group subordinate its interests and preferences to the national interest. Often nationalists would regard local activities as nothing but an expression of a NIMBY ('not in my back yard') preference, and would call upon the person or group involved to comply with the national perspective on the matter. Indeed, the term 'national interest' is sometimes used by politicians to support domestic policy objectives.

The tension between 'think globally – act locally' and the 'national interest' becomes stronger and clearer when the 'national interest' is defined by the state and its government, and is used in support of a particular course of action in foreign policy. In such cases, the 'national interest' is used to advance a self-interested perspective of the particular nation. The term invokes 'an image of the nation, or the nation state, defending its interests within the anarchic international system where dangers abound and the interests of the nation are always at risk' (McLean 1996: 333).

Such an attitude is hostile to any effort to reach international agreements on the environment. In a way, the Bush administration's negative reaction to the Kyoto protocol (1997) can be interpreted as deriving from a mentality of 'national interest'. The Bush administration claimed that global warming talks threatened the 'American way of life', which was described as a 'national interest', and global climate policies were judged a threat to national security (McCright and Dunlap 2003). In 1997 the Senate decided by a huge majority not to confirm the Kyoto protocol unless it were amended so as to protect the American national interest. It seems, then, that nationality, as projected in the idea of 'national interest', can work against thinking globally about environmental matters.

From soil to earth

Contrary to the widespread belief that nationalism includes a sense of 'place' and therefore nourishes an environmental attitude, I would like to argue that nationalism's sense of place is mystical, abstract and instrumental, and therefore may not work in favour of environmental protection. At most it would encourage a sense of 'ruralism' – the romantic glorification of rural life as superior to urban life; but it would not necessarily advance environmentalism, a philosophy based on scientific information, anti-speciesism and respect for all organisms.

For nationalists, the nation is associated with a territory. Therefore the question of this territory's boundaries becomes crucial, since whatever exists within those borders constitutes the members' identity, and what is outside the borders is not only less important but in fact not 'ours', and therefore is often alien, even the enemy itself. The nation is defined not only by reference to what *unites* or *characterises* 'us', who live within the territory, but also by what *distinguishes* 'us' from 'them', who live outside the borders. The 'other' becomes the antithesis by reference to which a nation defines itself. This can be seen both in popular feelings about the nation, e.g. in the way the French regard their culture and their cuisine as different from the 'other' fast-food culture, and in the rhetoric of ethnic groups and states about secession and independence: it is often based on the claim that a particular group is unmistakably distinguishable from another group. Often part of what distinguishes this group is the area in which they live or used to live, such as the claims put forward by the Basques, the Palestinians, the people of Kosovo. Such a claim is accompanied by stories and myths about the particular linkage between the nation's members and the earth on which they live or used to live. The attitude towards such land is therefore instrumental: it is used to emancipate the members. For example, when the Jews returned to the land they claimed, Zion, they regarded the reunion with it as a way of overcoming their degraded bourgeois character. They thought that cultivating and 'developing' this land would enable them to become a normal nation, not only with a land of its own but with a working class, industry and a normal economy. The same goes for many other nations, which regard their connection to a homeland as a healing and remedial relationship. So, according to nationalism, if, in order to emancipate or unite the members, a drastic (even anti-ecological) change in the environment is needed, it should be carried out. For nationalists, 'place', then, is never 'soil' or 'ecosystem', as in scientific–environmentalist discourse. Instead, it is 'earth', endowed with history, myths and symbolism. The latter can be used instrumentally to achieve national goals.

Political versus ecological definitions of borders

Following this, ecosystems and ecological problems have nothing to do with political definitions of geographical units (i.e. borders), whereas nationalism demands that nations be organised in sovereign states. So protecting ecosystems often implies harming national sovereignty, and environmental damage is frequently done in the name of national sovereignty (Gopal-Jayal 2003: 300–5).

Let me elaborate on what I mean by 'sovereignty', because many commentators argue that this is a rather elusive concept. Sovereignty here means simply the existence of a supreme authority whose powers cannot be restricted by other authorities, unless it breaks the rules or misbehaves in the political sphere. Many students of sovereignty distinguish between external and internal (or domestic) sovereignty. The latter is the state's supremacy with regard to affairs within the state's borders, whereas the former refers to the state's autonomy with regard to affairs taking place outside the state's borders. Of course, since there are many limitations on what states can do in the international arena, external sovereignty is mostly negative, e.g. immunity from outside interference. Now, needless to say, states do not exercise unlimited control over affairs taking place either within their borders or, especially, outside them. For example, states must not harm citizens' rights arbitrarily. It could be argued that at the beginning of the twenty-first century, states' sovereignty is restricted or threatened – whether states see their sovereignty as restricted or threatened is a normative decision – by international bodies such as the UN, NGOs, multinational corporations and so on. However, the case of environmental protection is yet another example of how states' sovereignty, especially the notion of it which relies on the idea of nationality and the nation's 'right' to be politically autonomous, is becoming less and less relevant.

Nature – as contemporary green and environmental activists claim – knows no boundaries. Indeed, environmental protection is related to two spheres of policy: policies for the protection of human beings from ecological instability, e.g. the build-up of carbon dioxide in the atmosphere, and policies that are meant to protect endangered species (e.g. whales), forests (for example, from road construction) and so on. In all such cases of environmental protection, what we do in practice is *protect ecosystems*. However, ecosystems' boundaries have nothing to do with political borders. Hence, when we protect an ecosystem or strive to secure its stability, we must cross political boundaries. This, of course, raises the question of what it means to talk about the British, Egyptian or Australian Minister of the Environment. Does it mean that, say, the Dutch minister is responsible for what happens to the environment in the Netherlands? But surely, s/he cannot be responsible for this unless s/he has some control over what happens to these ecosystems in the Netherlands. And in order for her/him to be able to do so, s/he should have control over the 'environment' and what is done to it in neighbouring countries such as Germany and Belgium. Which is why international agreements are so crucial for the environment.

However, many states regard environmental agreements such as the Kyoto protocol as public goods, and play the free rider. They seek to benefit from an international agreement without paying the cost. Interestingly, although the problem of free riders threatens to take the sting out of such international agreements, many international agreements have been signed in recent years. These include agreements on transboundary air pollution (acid rain) aimed at reducing emissions of sulphur dioxide and nitrogen oxide, which poison rivers and lakes, limitations on the use of CFCs, whaling, trade in ivory from African elephants (an agreement which drastically changed a trade worth an estimated US$5 billion annually), and so on.

However, while more and more agreements have been signed, their implementation has become an even more urgent and controversial problem. In many countries there is growing opposition to such agreements, since they dramatically limit the state's internal sovereignty. It was on such grounds that the US administration opposed the Kyoto agreement.

How, then, can such international agreements be enforced? Many environmental activists claim that it is time to think in terms of international intervention. Such intervention need not be implemented by militaristic means. It could be economic, that is to say, take the form of sanctions and voluntary or organised boycotts.

Such intervention involves deliberate action by a state or coalition of states, or by international bodies of citizens from different states, whose purpose is to bring about political, legal, economic or even ideological changes in another state, changes which are often imposed on this state, or on firms, organisations and individuals within the state (Krasner 1993). So even if the intervention, aimed at protecting ecosystems, is not military, it nevertheless limits the state's sovereignty. It does so by leaving the state or its citizens no other choice but to revise their policies on pain of damage to their wellbeing: in other words, the most reasonable option for this state is to revise its policies and co-operate with the intervening bodies.

Now, when foreign states or NGOs intervene in order to transform a state's political structure (as in the case of the Iraq war), this might be very controversial, morally speaking. However, when a state does not comply with international environmental agreements and by this threatens the wellbeing and health of citizens of other states, then foreign intervention by states and NGOs, using peaceful means such as economic sanctions and moral persuasion, and aiming at changing particular policies rather than a state's formal structure, is much more legitimate. And yet it does limit sovereignty and, if that sovereignty is based on the nation's right to be autonomous, it does make sense to maintain that nationality should be subordinated in such cases to higher considerations. No nation should have the right to harm other people's health and wellbeing just for the sake of being autonomous.

Moreover, at this point the distinction between internal and external sovereignty becomes crucially important. Internal sovereignty is not harmed by such intervention. Remember that a parliament or a people is sovereign internally if the people agree on the agencies that govern and legislate for their everyday life. In order to harm internal sovereignty, an invasive act must be involved – there must be some power invading a territory and trying to take away the sovereignty of its citizenry.

However, if state A imposes high taxes on goods imported from state B so as to punish it for its refusal to comply with international agreements, but has no such policies towards the import of goods from other states, then clearly state A is interfering in B's policies without committing an invasive act. Such policies limit state A's external rather than its internal sovereignty (Batty and Gray 1996).

Nationalists claim that this is still wrong because it harms a state's autonomy. If a state's agencies and its people are less autonomous, if they can choose how to act but their choices are limited by such manipulative policies of foreign states or NGOs, it is argued, then this is morally wrong. States and nations should be autonomous, just as individuals should be.

However, this seems to me incredibly naive and out of touch with contemporary reality. In a world that is a global village, in which people lose their jobs in London due to a collapse of the stock markets in Singapore or Bangkok, in which one country's information sources are freely accessible to people in other states, in which immigration is in practice often free despite laws which try to prohibit and limit it, in which regional agreements guarantee the free flow of money, goods and labour, and, of course, in which pollution moves from one country to another and from one continent to another, there is no scope for thinking in terms of state autonomy, terms which were dominant in the political and legal theory of the eighteenth and nineteenth centuries.

However, I want to claim that environmentalists should not oppose peaceful means of intervention even if this does harm sovereignty. The first reason is that many of the international agreements of the sort mentioned above fail to come into force because of the actions of a veto state. This is usually a monopoly; intervention is often necessary in order to break a monopoly. For example, there is an ongoing attempt to construct a global warming agreement, in particular with regard to the greenhouse effect. Needless to say, all nations are affected by greenhouse warming. Some might be affected more severely than others, such as the low-lying Pacific island nations. Still, most nations are more or less equally vulnerable to this ecological problem. The USA is the heaviest polluter when it comes to emissions of carbon dioxide. In the last forty years it has emitted fifteen times more carbon dioxide than India has. And yet, since this pollution is not local but rather global – what is at stake here is the build-up of the carbon dioxide in the atmosphere – the USA does not suffer more than other countries. The world needs the USA to consent to any agreement on reducing the use of greenhouse gases. The US administration has been promoting an agreement under which the USA will agree to reduce carbon dioxide emissions to 7 per cent below the level of the year 1990, on condition that the world agrees to completely free trade in polluting rights. This isn't innocent bargaining. Once the world agrees to completely free trade in pollution rights, American enterprises will buy pollution rights from firms in other countries. Since the trade will be completely free, poor countries' governments will not be allowed to control it and prevent firms from selling their rights to American firms. The price the latter will pay will be low in American terms. This will allow Americans to produce more, benefiting from full employment and from selling its products to the poor countries, which by then will be producing less because they will have sold their polluting rights. Since the sort of pollution we are talking about is not local, it will be distributed more or less evenly worldwide, and the Americans will not necessarily suffer, environmentally speaking, from having more pollution rights.

If we return to the theoretical discussion above, we see that this is a case of monopoly. Still, the world simply must reach an agreement in order to prevent extreme climatic change. Peaceful intervention (assuming this could take place) that would prevent the USA from using its power in this way would indeed harm the USA's national autonomy, but would be justified in moral terms both because it prevents ecological disaster and because it fights exploitative monopolies. National self-determination cannot be a strong enough reason to restrict such intervention, especially if this nationality is exploitative and disregards others' rights.

Nationalism is anthropocentric

Any environmental attitude should at least tolerate and be sympathetic to some form of anti-speciesism, that is, to an approach which regards non-human animals and other species as morally speaking equals to humans, at least to some extent. I put this in a minor form, since one could be an environmentalist and defend one's positions by applying *enlightened* anthropocentric arguments; however, while one does not have to accept the theory of intrinsic value in nature and of biocentrism or ecocentrism, one is open to a more egalitarian approach to nature even if one moves from anthropocentrism to *enlightened* anthropocentric theory (Hayward 1998; Brennan 1988).

It is difficult to generalise and assert unequivocally that nationalism is a friend or a foe of non-human species. Nationalists rarely have anything to say about animal welfare, animal rights or the moral status of non-humans. Arguably, nationalism might often stand in contrast with the welfare of the non-human world in the name of the 'national food' (often meat) or 'national industries', which include the abuse of animals, such as in the 'Great American Food Machine' (meat, eggs, dairy industries).[4]

With respect to 'who counts' as a moral agent and a moral client, nationalism is in no way different from anthropocentrism in its worst form. Nationalism treats any non-human species as irrelevant unless it contributes somehow to the nation's ethos, e.g. by being a symbol, and even then it is a rather instrumental attitude. Consider, for example, fox hunting: it is presented as part of a proud national tradition and a noble sport, and any attempt to legislate against it faces the criticism that it threatens a national way of life.

Conclusion

It is not easy to determine whether nationalism and ecology are friends or foes. Arguably, there are some ideas in nationalism that cater for the environment and that may enhance pro-environmental attitudes. At the same time, some features and ideas of nationalism make it difficult to see how it can support the environment: on the contrary, it seems that nationalism often threatens the environment and treats it instrumentally. Altogether, it seems that the tension between nationalism and protecting the environment is too great to be easily resolved. This makes nationality an obstacle to the ecological challenge and to our urgent need to protect Earth.

What does this imply? Does it mean that we must find ways of subduing nationalism? That it is no longer a valid ideology because it contradicts our obligations to the environment? This is a tricky question. Elsewhere I have argued that those who are sceptical about the demand for national self-determination may have a decent moral argument to support this attitude, but it is often not very fair of those who already enjoy self-determination to be critical of nationality. Nationalism seems to be one of these phases through which a people should go in order to acknowledge that perhaps there are much more important and valid political ideals. For some reason, about which I have no room to elaborate here, nations that have not enjoyed self-determination are eager to experience it. Nations whose self-determination is not threatened have developed a sceptical attitude towards it, in my opinion rightly so. Still, it seems wrong to disallow other nations from experiencing it as well.

---

[4] See the novel by Ozeki (1998) as well as Robbins 1987.

At the same time, as I hope to have shown, there are strong environmental reasons why nationalism should be restricted. Perhaps the right solution, then, is to allow those nations that have not experienced it to enjoy self-determination, and to demand that other nations, such as those of North America and Western Europe, switch to a more environment-friendly attitude.

All this is normative, of course. Whether nations will, for example, limit their own self-determining authority in order to protect the environment remains to be seen. No doubt this depends on whether international organisations such as the UN can enforce a collective change of heart.

References

Barry, Brian (1983). 'Self Government Revisited', in David Miller and Larry Siedentrop (eds.), *The Nature of Political Theory*. Oxford: Clarendon Press, 121–54.

Batty, H., and Gray, T. (1996). 'Environmental Rights and National Sovereignty', in S. Caney, D. George and P. Jones (eds.), *National Rights, International Obligations*. Boulder, Colo.: Westview, 149–65.

Beran, Harry (1984). 'The Liberal Theory of Secession', *Political Studies* **32**: 21–31.

Brennan, Andrew (1988). *Thinking About Nature*. Athens, Ga.: University of Georgia Press.

Cuomo Chris (1998). *Feminism and Ecological Communities*. London: Routledge.

De-Shalit (1996a). 'National Self-determination: Political, Not Cultural', *Political Studies* **44**: 906–21.

—— (1996b). 'Ruralism or Environmentalism?', *Environmental Values* **5**: 47–58.

Dobson, Andrew (1998). *Justice and the Environment*. Oxford: Oxford University Press.

Eckersley, Robyn (1992). *Environmentalism and Political Theory*. New York: SUNY Press.

Gopal-Jayal, Niraja (2003). 'Ethics, Politics, Biodiversity: A View from the South', in Andrew Light and Avner de-Shalit (eds.), *Moral and Political Reasoning in Environmental Reasoning*. Cambridge, Mass.: MIT Press, 295–316.

Hayward, Tim (1998). *Political Theory and Ecological Values*. Cambridge: Polity Press.

Johnson, Huey (1997). *Green Plans: Greenprint for Sustainability*. Lincoln: University of Nebraska Press.

Kemball-Cook, David, Baker, Mallen, and Mattingley, Chris (eds.) (1991). *The Green Budget*. London: Green Print.

Krasner, I. S. D. (1993). 'Sovereignty, Regimes and Human Rights', in V. Rittberger and P. Meyer (eds.), *Regime Theory and International Relations*. Oxford: Oxford University Press, 139–67.

Lamb, Robert (1996). *Promising the Earth*. London: Routledge.

Light, Andrew (2002). 'Restoring Ecological Citizenship', in Ben Minteer and Bob Pepperman Taylor (eds.), *Democracy and the Claim of Nature*. New York: Rowman and Littlefield, 153–72.

McCright, Acram, and Dunlap, Riley (2003). 'Debating Kyoto', *Social Problems* 50: 348–73.

McLean, Ian (1996). *Oxford Dictionary of Politics*. Oxford: Oxford University Press.

Miller, David (1995). *On Nationality*. Oxford: Oxford University Press.

— (2000). *Citizenship and National Identity*. Cambridge: Polity Press.

Naess, Arne (1989). *Ecology, Community and Lifestyle*. Cambridge: Cambridge University Press.

O'Neill, John (1993). *Ecology, Policy and Politics*. London: Routledge.

Partridge, E. (1981). 'Why Care about the Future?', in E. Partridge (ed.), *Responsibilities to Future Generations*. Athens, Ga.: Prometheus Books, 203–20.

Ozeki, Ruth (1998). *My Year of Meats*. London: Viking Penguin.

Robbins, John (1987). *Diet for a New America*. Walpole, N.H.: Stillpoint Publishing.

Searle, Denise (ed.) (1997). *Gathering Force: Radical Action for Those Tired of Waiting*. London: The Big Issue Writers.

Tamir, Yael (1993). *Liberal Nationalism*. Princeton: Princeton University Press.

Wissenburg, Marcel (1998). *Green Liberalism*. London: UCL Press.

Young, Stephen (1993). *The Politics of the Environment*. London: Baseline Books.

6   Communitarianism

Robyn Eckersley

Introduction

Can communitarianism meet the ecological challenge? In keeping with the purposes of this volume, I interpret this challenge to mean, 'Does communitarianism provide the appropriate insights, conceptual resources and norms to guide political communities along ecologically sustainable paths?'[1]

This question admits of no straightforward answer because communitarians are an unruly bunch who defy simple political classification. Communitarians can be more easily identified in terms of what they are *against* rather than what they are *for*. We all know that communitarians are critical of cosmopolitanism (see Linklater, chapter 7 in this volume) and the Enlightenment idea of Universal Reason, but it is not always easy to find a common thread in their positive political prescriptions. Some are conservative or traditional while others are civic republicans. Some draw on Aristotle, others on Hegel. Some communitarians have a theoretical affinity with postmodernism while others find common cause with realism. There are also some interesting hybrids, such as liberal communitarians, liberal nationalists and Third Way 'new communitarians', who are keen on rebuilding social capital so we no longer go 'bowling alone'.

Despite this political diversity, it is possible to single out one preoccupation that does unite communitarians, and that is a special preoccupation with questions of identity and the significance of social bonds. It is this preoccupation that partly explains their critique of cosmopolitanism, on the one hand, and the diversity of their political prescriptions, on the other (after all, there are many different ties that bind people together). Communitarians are concerned with the nature of recognition or misrecognition, with how we are situated in the world,

---

[1] Note also that I use the plural 'communities' and 'paths' to acknowledge that there is not only one kind of community nor one true path. There are many types of community and many paths to sustainability.

and how this shapes and constrains the boundaries of our particular moral universes. Understanding 'who are we/who am I?' is logically prior to asking 'what ought we/I to do?' These questions can only be answered by locating people in particular communities, a move that fixes their place in the world and assigns meaning, roles and relationships (Taylor 1992). These questions are also considered basic to understanding how we ought to set our moral horizons and fashion our political institutions. In this respect, we might say that communitarians like to put the ontological horse before the ethical cart.

Now this preliminary account of communitarianism hardly amounts to a clarion call for the green society, especially if it is accepted that most environmentalists tend to be cosmopolitans. Indeed, communitarianism offers some mixed messages for those who are keen to see the flourishing of ecologically sustainable communities across the globe, rather than in isolated, intentional green communities. Nonetheless, in this essay I show that communitarians offer a range of salutary insights about the nature of social bonds and human loyalties that greens ignore at their peril. These insights are important when it comes to understanding the basis of successful citizenship and democracy, along with the more general question of human motivation for environmental reform. The sobering lesson for greens is that there is no point developing political prescriptions or fashioning political institutions that have no grasp on the nature of human identity and motivation. However, there is also a more positive side to this story: focusing on the way human identities are constructed can provide clues as to how greener identities might be created. More generally, I shall seek to show that it is not too difficult to develop an ecologically informed communitarianism by adapting the structure of communitarian arguments to green ends.

The boundedness of human identity and community

Communitarians have been particularly critical of the liberal understanding of the relationship between the individual and the community or society. This critique is waged at both the ontological and the normative levels. That is, the traditional liberal ontology of the self as asocial, detached and radically autonomous is seen as *incoherent*. Moreover, many of the normative prescriptions that flow from this framing of the self are seen as *undesirable* insofar as they neglect or undermine the importance of community belonging and communal responsibilities by emphasising 'arms-length', impersonal contractual obligations over familial and communal ones (e.g. Sandel 1982). Communitarians are typically critical of market relations because they are believed to have a corrosive effect on community life. (Greens need only add here that this applies to both social *and* ecological communities. Since this point is admirably dealt with by Mellor in chapter 3 of this volume, I shall not explore it here.)

In contrast, cosmopolitans typically begin from a normative rather than an ontological starting point: the idea of the equal dignity of each and every human being. Their concern is to develop moral principles and political and legal institutions that might see to the practical realisation of this basic moral precept. However, they are prone to skip over questions of identity or ontology or else assume that human identity can be easily reshaped by new cosmopolitan moral principles and institutions based on Universal Reason rather than loyalty or sentiment. Their concern is to develop universal moral and, in some cases, legal obligations based on our common humanity, which transcend the limitations of particularistic identities and communities. Like communitarians, not all cosmopolitans share the same political analysis or prescription (we need only compare, for example, Marx and Kant!). In this respect, we may describe communitarianism and cosmopolitanism as 'meta-ideologies' or 'meta-theories', since the tensions and debates between these positions cut across many modern political divides. These meta-theoretical differences revolve around disagreement about the proper starting point of political enquiry, the relationship between the self and others, and degree of malleability of human identity.

From a communitarian perspective, human identity is always *bounded* in space and time. This boundedness shapes and constrains the field of ethical and political possibilities; our ethics are correlative with the various particularistic, bounded communities to which we belong. Communitarians disagree among themselves or else are agnostic about the source and scope of this boundedness, that is, whether it is derived from cultural, linguistic and/or place-based ties, and how far it might be enlarged beyond existing horizons. Moreover, the different answers that communitarians give to these questions also provide clues to the kinds of political order they may support (whether traditional or modern, hierarchical or democratic). However, they all agree that there is something about the way humans are socialised that creates primary loyalties and makes it impossible for us to become fully fledged citizens of the world. While communitarians may welcome a cosmopolitan education, they maintain that, however far we manage to extend our circle of compassion for others, our most fundamental allegiances will always be particularistic (i.e. the family, the clan, the nation) rather than universalistic, and especially so when the going gets tough. As Walzer (1994) puts it, we are fundamentally 'tribal'.

Now it necessarily follows that if all humans belong to tribes (loosely understood to include linguistic, national, ethnic and religious communities), then attempts to develop a supra-tribal morality, such as new norms of global environmental justice, will always be fraught. Traditionalists, such as Alastair MacIntyre (1981), maintain that there is no universal morality, only particular moralities that derive from particular traditions. The Enlightenment thinkers had sought to break free from all-embracing traditions, claiming that reason would replace authority and tradition (notably the Church) as the arbiter of what was just or unjust. However, the Enlightenment standards of rational enquiry could not be met; people disagreed as to what principles all rational people might accept. So while we in the West may have broken from an all-embracing tradition, we are left with the problem of choosing among a range of competing and incommensurable traditions. In this context, liberal cosmopolitanism (along with other expressions of cosmopolitanism) must be understood as simply one more tradition. These insights challenge liberal claims of universality, anti-perfectionism and neutrality towards competing ideas of the good. The only place to look for moral guidance is the shared views of the good life, embodied in the social, cultural and religious practices of particular communities.

Those communitarians who have tackled the task of developing a supra-tribal morality have proceeded with great caution, offering only 'thin' rather than 'thick' prescriptions for the global order. For Michael Walzer, if we are to develop a minimal, normative code that is external rather than internal to particular cultures, then it needs to be based on the principle of 'respect for particularity'. As Walzer puts it, such moral minimalism *'leaves room* for the tribes' and for their particularistic versions of justice and criticism (Walzer 1994: 64). Indeed, the principle of self-determination is, according to Walzer, an expression of moral minimalism in international politics. While self-determination is typically thought of in democratic terms, it need not be. It merely means that the members of a tribe *ought to be allowed to govern themselves*, in accordance with their own traditions.

Insights such as these provide the basis of the claim that while thicker principles and prescriptions for global environmental justice may well be *desirable*, they typically won't work because of cultural incommensurability. This is not to say that human identity, particularistic communities and their associated moralities must be understood as fixed and immutable. Quite the contrary, communitarians are constructivists by inclination. Nor does it mean that communitarianism must always be conservative and uncritical. I, for one, consider that communitarianism ought to be both constructivist and critical. However, attempts to expand human moral horizons must be sensitive to local cultures and therefore draw creatively on local resources rather than 'foreign imports' in any refashioning of ideas and practices – environmental or otherwise. This follows from the communitarian insight that ideas of justice (including environmental justice) are embodied within particular traditions; they do not stand outside or above tradition, as the Enlightenment thinkers believed, and as modern liberal cosmopolitans believe. Traditions, along with conceptions of justice, contain their own (revisable) standards of rationality, which have emerged out of a history of engagement (Walzer 1987). Here, communitarians join with postmodernists in seeking to get rid of the rhetoric of Universal Reason. For Richard Rorty, this 'would permit the West to approach the non-West in the role of someone with an instructive story to tell, rather than in the role of someone purporting to be making better use of a universal human capacity' (Rorty 1998: 57). Appeals to Universal Reason are not especially helpful to the process of consensus building in a multicultural world. Efforts to persuade others to interact with their environment on a more sustainable basis must speak across, and appeal to, a wide variety of human cultures (and languages). Wilderness advocates in New World regions have discovered this in their dealings with indigenous peoples. And those cosmopolitan environmental NGOs who have sought to negotiate 'debt-for-nature swaps' or local environmental initiatives in developing countries have likewise been sobered by accusations of 'green imperialism'. Clearly, we must learn to think of sustainability in multicultural terms, in ways that are sensitive to cultural difference.

Communitarianism in a positive green light

So far, I have merely offered a few sobering insights for environmentalists. However, communitarianism also provides scope for a more positive commitment to environmentalism; that is, it is possible to work with the *structure* of communitarian arguments to develop insights that might ground ecological selves, and ecologically sustainable societies. As we have seen, the starting point of communitarian enquiry is the nature of human identity and selfhood. Communitarian ethics and politics flow from a relational rather than atomistic ontology whereby selfhood can only be understood in the context of the network of linguistic and social relationships in which individuals are always embedded. Community is thus a structural precondition of human agency, including moral agency, and the ideal of self-determination is necessarily a collective one, based on the idea of mutual enablement or mutual self-realisation of selves in particular communities. It seems to me a short step to include ecological embeddedness in this ontological understanding of selfhood (e.g. Matthews 1991), to include ecosystem integrity as a structural precondition of human agency and to include non-human species as part of the community to be realised. To be sure, not all communitarians (and certainly not all communities!) have taken this step. However, those who have – many local environmental activists, bioregionalists, ecoanarchists and ecofeminists, to name some of the more prominent examples from within the ecocentric canon – have found it relatively easy to add the 'eco' to communitarianism.

Understanding human *motivation* in terms of bounded and particular loyalties is arguably communitarianism's trump card.[2] So allow me to play this card for what it is worth before exploring how communitarianism's apparent inability to deal with transboundary and global social and ecological problems might be addressed. Let me single out three bounded communities where this kind of ecocommunitarianism has, or might, be played out: the local community, the bioregional community and the national community.

The local community

Local environmental battles, such as campaigns to protest against freeway extensions, high-rise developments, toxic waste dumps and the like, have played a prominent role in the history of modern environmentalism. One of the driving forces of such local activism is a strong 'sense of place' – a deep psychological attachment to a particular place or locale, which encompasses all that dwells within it. It is the deep and intimate knowledge of, and attachment to, particular places (rather than abstract knowledge of abstract spaces) that provides one of the strongest motivations to act to defend threatened historical buildings, neighbourhoods, parks, waterways and other local 'heritage' buildings or ecosystems. Threats to transform the locality are tantamount to an invasion of self and community. At the other extreme, a lack of attachment to particular places can provide the basis for alienation and vandalism or corporate profiteering.

For all the limitations of particularism (and there are many), cosmopolitans have never been able to answer communitarians on this front of the debate with a viable account of why humans might rally in defence of all humans, or all ecosystems, with the same degree of fervour as they would rally in defence of particular communities and

---

[2] Green (post-)cosmopolitans, such as Andy Dobson (2004), have noticed this motivational vacuum within cosmopolitanism.

ecosystems. The flip side of this fervour is, of course, the problem of NIMBY ('not in my backyard') environmentalism, which is also enacted on a grander scale by so many nation states. Yet we should not be so quick to disparage NIMBY environmentalism. Place-based activism enables the ongoing social and ecological learning that is required for communities to reorient their practices on a more sustainable basis. It also provides a fertile opportunity for active political engagement and deeper questioning. NIMBY environmentalism, according to Paul Kingsnorth (2004: 24),

is becoming the struggle of the rooted against the rootless; a battle between those who believe that places matter, and those on the left as well as the right – who see local and national geography as an embarrassing obstacle to a truly global future. This is the struggle of the Mexican Zapatistas and the Welsh road protesters, the Landless Peoples' Movement in Latin America and the family farmers of England, the Narmada Bachao Andolan and the No Airport at Cliffe campaign. Each time, the rallying cry is simple, ancient and deeply democratic: Place matters. This is ours. We decide.

The bioregional community

Psychological attachment to people and places need not be confined to the local. It may be regional or national. Bioregionalism provides perhaps the fullest ecological expression of ecocommunitarian. A bioregion is literally a 'life place' and bioregionalists seek to 'reinhabit' life places in ways that avoid ecological damage and allow local nature to flourish (e.g. Dodge 1981). In this sense, bioregionalists take to heart the ecological insight that human animals – like all animals – are unavoidably biologically embodied and ecologically embedded beings. This acknowledgement demands the development of an intimate knowledge of the species and ecological relationships in one's own bioregion. Such an intimate knowledge provides the basis for both empathy and prudence towards the local life place, treading lightly, restoring damaged ecosystems and, as far as practicable, living sustainably within the particular bioregion. Bioregionalists believe that strong attachments to, and local reinhabitation within, the bioregion grow out of knowledge of, and dependence on, the bioregion. Whereas privileged social classes and nations have managed to remain relatively remote (spatially, temporarily, epistemologically and technologically) from many of the ecological consequences of their lifestyles, bioregionalists remain on much more intimate terms with the ecological consequences of their actions. One of the reasons bioregionalists have had so little to say about co-ordination between bioregions is that, in the ideal bioregional world, all communities would look after their own bioregion, there would be no 'spillover effects' and therefore no pressing need for co-ordination.

One of the many problems facing bioregionalists, however, is that most human communities are tied together by social rather than ecological bonds, and these social bonds have no necessary relationship to the soft and overlapping contours of ecosystems (although many indigenous tribes in Australia tended to live and move within watershed boundaries). Moreover, we now live in a rapidly globalising world where the scale and rate of movement across borders (goods, money, diseases, people, pollution, weapons, seeds, television, music) has intensified. Cosmopolitans would ask: if trade and other 'metabolic' exchanges between bioregions are to be limited, what of the hapless inhabitants of poorly endowed regions? How to address inequalities of wealth and income? Of course, these same arguments can also be directed to defenders of the nation state. I shall return to these questions shortly.

The national community

Attachment to the national community can provide another potential source of mobilisation for sustainability, although there have been few explicit defences of ecological nation building or econationalism. Yet, as Benedict Anderson (1991) has reminded us, capitalist print media have enabled the development of nations as 'imagined communities'; and they are often imagined as 'belonging' to a particular territory or homeland. This is certainly the case for many indigenous peoples. Indeed, Anderson explains that all communities beyond small, face-to-face local villages or tribes are imagined in the sense that each of us does not personally know all the members of the community. Although national communities may be imagined in a variety of different ways, they are always imaged as limited and sovereign. As Anderson puts it, 'No nation imagines itself coterminous with mankind' (Anderson 1991: 5–7).

The environment is often imagined as part of the national community, and protecting (or exploiting) the environment can be part of nation building. Think, for example, of 'national parks', which serve as a source of national pride, or of native fauna or flora that are taken to symbolise the nation (the American eagle, or the kangaroo and emu on the Australian coat of arms). Both enable different kinds of 'environmental patriotism'. Think also of the idea of permanent sovereignty over natural resources, which emerged as developing countries sought to throw off the yoke of colonialism and wrest control of their own 'national' resources and assets, such as oil, timber and minerals.

The Nazi legacy is probably the primary reason why there have been very few explicit defences of econationalism as a source of ecological renewal and restoration. Indeed, it is more common to find analyses of the racist implications of ecological nationalism (e.g. Hage 1998). Historically, nation states have more typically exploited rather than protected the environment for nation-building purposes. Yet this is now becoming more difficult as environmental awareness grows. Environmentalists regularly exploit the idea of the 'national environment' to exhort or persuade. Just as national parks or native species provide a source of national pride (on a par with national galleries), the degradation of such parks or the loss of native species can be described as a 'national disgrace'. To the extent that these parts of nature fall within national jurisdiction, then we ('the nation') have the responsibility to look after these parts as our own, as a national public good. As de-Shalit (chapter 5 in this volume) has pointed out, thinking of the environment in terms of a 'national asset' does at least help to head off individualistic and purely instrumental orientations towards non-human nature. Many developing countries have exploited this idea of the environment as a 'national asset' as something that should be protected against genetic pollution or the rich world's hazardous waste.

Now at this point, the sceptical reader might say: nice try, but surely cosmopolitanism is the 'natural' meta-political theory of environmentalism in our contemporary globalising world? David Held, not Hegel, should be the movement's guiding political philosopher. Cosmopolitanism, like many forms of environmentalism, challenges the way boundaries are drawn around particular communities – including nation states. They all seek to transcend the norms of particularistic communities and encourage the application of more general, abstract principles of justice that apply to all people, irrespective of where or how they are situated. Indeed, bioregionalism and ecoanarchism have attracted concerted critiques from within and beyond green political theory for being out of touch with the forces of globalisation. More generally, developing effective political communication and co-ordination between different polities is crucial to resolving transboundary ecological problems (as it is in so many other issue areas). This challenge emerges most obviously among nation states, but it also applies to relationships between any bounded communities or 'tribes'. Walzer's thin, supra-tribal principle of 'respect for particular communities' (read: 'self-determination of the tribes') does not seem an obvious candidate for ensuring global environmental justice, even if we interpret this principle in democratic terms.

However, before we explore the case for destabilising or transcending political boundaries and moving beyond conventional accounts of citizenship and democracy (via, for example, ecological citizenship and cosmopolitan democracy), I want to take one step back. While I will be making a case for cultivating wider social and ecological loyalties, I still want to defend the loyalties of particular communities, because this is where social learning typically takes place. So rather than begin with the best or worst cases of ecocommunitarianism (reflected in the character of the ideal bioregional citizen or the econationalist xenophobe, respectively), I want to begin somewhere in the middle of these extremes. Exploring the character and motivations of a reasonably well adjusted but not particularly worldly or active citizen might help us explore what it might take to move to a *relatively* more worldly kind of ecological citizen (since a communitarian would not accept that citizens can ever be *completely worldly*).

A children's tale

The character of the Water Rat ('Ratty') in Kenneth Graham's children's tale *The Wind in the Willows* provides a useful entry point into an interrogation of the ecological potential and limitations of communitarianism.[3] Ratty is deeply attached to his riverbank. He knows its moods and currents, and its inhabitants, in all their particularity. Doubtless he would fight the good fight if it were threatened in any way. Ratty *belongs* to the riverbank, and he has little taste for travel or things foreign, as the following conversation with his friend the Mole attests:

'Beyond the Wild Wood comes the Wide World', said the Rat. 'And that's something that doesn't matter, either to you or me. I've never been there, and I'm never going, nor you either, if you've got any sense at all. Don't ever refer to it again, please. Now then! Here's our backwater at last, where we're going to have lunch.' (Graham 1930: 10)

Yet Ratty is not a xenophobe, and he means no harm to strangers. He is a decent friend and a kindly soul – indeed, he is extraordinarily patient with the impudent Toad. He has a strong sense of place and a strong loyalty to those he knows. But his narrow horizons and wilful ignorance of distant lands and their troubles beyond the Wild Woods are unsettling. I suspect that no amount of tutoring in the principles of cosmopolitan democracy or the long-term fate of planetary ecosystems is likely to change his primary loyalties, which lie with his friends and his riverbank.

[3] The inspiration for using Ratty comes from David Miller (2000).

Ratty represents one of the more benign faces of communitarianism. He is clearly not a neo-Nazi. However, a cosmopolitan would say that Ratty is not the type of citizen we need to meet the ecological challenge, particularly if we take that to mean successfully tackling the global ecological crisis. Ratty may care about his own riverbank, but he is too insular to grasp or care about abstract notions such as complex interdependence, global environmental change, the ecological footprint and the increasingly skewed distribution of wealth, environmental amenities and ecological risks. The multifaceted dimensions of globalisation suggest that any environmentalists worth the name must necessarily be cosmopolitan. Ratty appears as the complete antithesis of the well travelled, well read, computer literate, politically aware and actively engaged cosmopolitan citizen of the world. Those who campaign against tropical deforestation, global warming or the transboundary movement of hazardous wastes or GM products are typically engaged and interact in political communities at multiple levels of abstraction – spatially, politically, economically and ideationally. In this respect, such environmental activists conform quite closely to the archetype of the cosmopolitan citizen of the world. Their compassion and concern extends not only to all of humanity, but also the rest of nature – non-human species and ecological communities included. (I must add here that I am acquainted with some of these selfless, frequent-flyer activists, who follow the environmental multilateral negotiations on climate change or hazardous wastes, and are therefore obliged to live out of a suitcase and in a permanent fog of jetlag. They have travelled everywhere, but come to *belong* nowhere, a sad irony to which I shall return).

Both archetypes clearly have their limitations, but Ratty is the foil for this essay not simply because he embodies so many of the strengths and limitations of communitarianism but also because I must confess to feeling some affection for him. Although Ratty, at first blush, may appear too insular and old-fashioned to serve as the exemplar of the modern environmental citizen, I think we have a lot to learn from him nonetheless. Although he is ignorant of so much, his life is grounded and he has a strong sense of place. More importantly for the argument I wish to wage, it would not take much to open Ratty's eyes to the world *since he already has a well-developed capacity for empathy* – something he has learned from his local community and environment. I would wager that his lack of interest in things beyond the Wild Wood stems from local contentment, not complacency or xenophobia, which makes him both lucky and rare. However, Ratty – like most people – could never become a fully fledged citizen of the world.

A cosmopolitan reply

Now it is at this point that green cosmopolitans might wish to pull out their trump card: surely local action is insufficient to arrest the growing gap between those who generate ecological risks and those who suffer the consequences. The complex forces of globalisation have enabled the spread of ecological risks in space and time, and new cosmopolitan norms and political institutions are therefore required to ensure that the generators of these risks are held accountable to the victims. This is the essence of David Held's defence of cosmopolitan democracy, and he draws heavily on environmental examples to make his case. The uneven distribution of ecological risks has created a serious democratic deficit that can only be addressed by the development of an overarching global cosmopolitan law, or 'democratic public law' (Held 1999: 106). In a similar vein, Andrew Dobson has argued that we need to acknowledge new obligations owed by those who have accrued an 'ecological space debt' to those individuals who have been denied their putative share of ecological space (see Dobson, chapter 13 in this volume). Dobson has enlisted the idea of the ecological footprint as the basis for developing norms of global environmental justice that represent 'thick cosmopolitanism', and he has argued that the obligations we in the West owe to others for our oversized footprint is a matter of justice, not charity (Dobson 2004). Linklater (chapter 7 in this volume) has likewise argued that we are most likely to develop cosmopolitan emotions when we realise our actions are causally responsible for harming others and their physical environment.

However, a communitarian would say that whether or not individuals and communities take responsibility for causing harm is context dependent. Just to take two examples: an obligation not to cause harm to combatants is absent during war and it was mostly absent during the colonial period – in both cases because genuine empathy and respect for the other are missing. The fact that soldiers or colonialists might know they are causing harm is not enough to engender any sense of responsibility towards those who are harmed. However, the situation can change dramatically when the 'other' belongs to a community with which one identifies. Harm is important, but it is not enough when respect for the other is absent.

However, even where respect for others is present, it is still unclear whether those who can be shown to *indirectly* cause harm at a distance will *feel compelled* to take steps to change their own behaviour to prevent future harm, and/or to compensate for past harm. The huge difficulties in tracking chains of causation and apportioning blame and responsibility are likely to mean that the situation is typically muddy rather than clear, and that people will not take responsibility in the absence of a clear line of causation that can be tracked back to their own behaviour. In short, the collective action problem here will inevitably to lead to buck-passing of a kind that undermines the crucial motivation issue.

So the *primary* ecocommunitarian response to transboundary ecological problems would still be to work creatively with the moral resources within particularistic communities towards sustainability. Bioregionalists and other ecocommunitarians would say that buck-passing within such communities is much more difficult, and therefore much less likely, the more intimate the social relationships, the thicker the social bonds. In such communities, the basis for taking action to protect or help others in such contexts is a sense of belonging and affinity, not causation per se. It is precisely because social bonds are weak or missing at the global level that cosmopolitans reach for the harm principle or notions of affectedness, rather than the idea of our common humanity or our common planet, as a basis for moral obligations. However, Richard Rorty has argued that we cannot resolve this problem simply by calling it a conflict between reason and sentiment, or justice and personal loyalties, in the hope that the appeal to justice will exert some special pull. From a non-Kantian perspective, these moral dilemmas can only be seen as a 'conflict between alternative selves, alternative self-descriptions, alternative ways of giving meaning to one's life' (Rorty 1998: 48).

We humans belong to many different kinds of community, and the ethical obligations that we owe to others derive from the different relationships that constitute those communities. How far our communities and associated loyalties might extend in time and space will always be a moot point. However, the reason why human loyalties are typically more intense at the more embodied, face-to-face level is because this is how humans *learn* to become social beings.

Martha Nussbaum has described compassion as forming 'a psychological link between our own self interest and the reality of another person's good or ill' (1996: xi). It is something that develops in childhood out of intense attachments to people (and places) with whom (or which) we are in immediate or close relation. Cosmopolitans like Nussbaum, of course, are concerned that human compassion embrace all of humanity (while many cosmopolitan environmentalists wish to extend this to 'all beings'). Patriotism – love of one's territory and community – too often invokes an 'us' against 'them' that can easily degenerate into the neglect or humiliation of the 'them' in times of crisis.

Yet, wherever the circle of human compassion *ends*, it always *begins* with the local. The fact that cosmopolitan arguments must always work by *analogy* with local, embodied relations (such as the family, which is extended to the 'homeland', 'motherland', 'fatherland' or the 'human family') is itself telling. The home, the family, the neighbourhood, the school – this is where we learn the meaning and value of self, society and nature, of citizenship and solidarity with others (sometimes including non-human others). As we have seen, capitalist print media enabled our 'imagined communities' to extend to nations, and further developments in modern communication technologies have enabled the development of a complex and overlapping set of 'virtual communities' that transcend traditional borders. But all of these imagined and virtual communities are still situated somewhere in time and space – they are not boundless.

Translating this discussion back to Ratty, without some knowledge and attachment to our *own* riverbank – to this riverbank, not any old riverbank – I find it hard to understand how one might be motivated to defend *other* riverbanks. The same can be said for concepts such as humanity in general or species or ecosystems in general. Without some knowledge of, or familiarity with, particular persons or particular animals or plants, it is hard to understand how one might be moved to defend the interests of people in general or species in general (since these are abstract categories that cannot be *personally* experienced all at once). And it is these formative, local, social and ecological attachments that provide the basis for sympathetic solidarity with others; the reason for caring in general and not just in particular.

We might say of our cosmopolitan environmental activists that they have selflessly forsaken their own personal embeddedness and sense of place in an effort to turn around the increasing dis-embeddedness brought about by the complex and uneven processes of economic globalisation. Ironically, then, the cosmopolitan activists are campaigning to make it possible for the Ratties of this world to remain content on their own riverbank (or else to discover contentment if they never had it before). They are acting globally *so that others may live locally*.

Now it might be said that the community of humankind is itself a bounded community that is situated in space and time. So is the planet as a whole. Just as newspapers and books have enabled our 'imagined communities' to extend to nations, photographs of the Earth taken from outer space by NASA have enabled many of us to imagine ourselves belonging to a planet that is finite, fragile and floating in a sea of infinite black space. Environmental documentaries invite us to think of the Amazon as 'the lungs of the world'. Wildlife documentaries bring exotic creatures into our living rooms, and teach us their habits and hardships. New media create new, imagined communities and new identities.

From an ecocommunitarian perspective, here lies the possibility of extending our sense of community, our sense of belonging and our sense of affinity with others. This extension must be both affective and cognitive, since the core of the communitarian case is that extending our sense of *belonging* provides a far more potent basis for political motivation to protect non-human species and victims of environmental injustice than does the more abstract idea of *affectedness*. The success of ecological citizenship based on the idea of the ecological footprint (Dobson) or cosmopolitan democracy (Held) presuppose, for their success, a sufficient affinity or social bond between perpetrators and victims for the former to take responsibility for affected others in distant lands. This is an uphill battle, and we therefore need to do a good deal of cultural work before the political work, the new institution building, can succeed (as George Bush Jr. has discovered in the case of Iraq). This cultural work requires ongoing intercultural dialogues of a kind that familiarise the members of different communities with the way of life of the other, in their uniqueness and particularity. This familiarisation process can never reach the levels of intimacy of our local attachments, but it can dispel myths and misunderstandings, and provide a basis for discovering common ground and working on shared problems, including ecological ones. Once the culture of relating becomes sufficiently familiar and respectful, institution building can begin. But this new institutional building cannot and ought not obliterate pre-existing communities.

A final word on democracy

The discussion has finally brought us, in a roundabout way, to democracy. It should hardly be surprising that the communitarian understanding of democracy is based around the idea of community and belonging. The argument here is that democratic politics presupposes a degree of mutual trust and reciprocal recognition based on a common language and cultural identity (e.g. Miller 1995). Self-determination is a *collective* goal of a political community that presupposes a shared political culture and a sufficient degree of social solidarity to enable the pursuit of common goals in ways that transcend individualistic and sectional interests. The principle of self-determination *presupposes a pre-existing self*, understood in collective rather than individualistic terms. Where communitarians divide is over whether this collective 'self' is the national community, the tribe or the linguistic community. I think Kymlicka is perhaps the most convincing here in arguing that democratic politics works best 'in the vernacular', that is, among those who share a common language and mass media (Kymlicka 2001: 121–2).[4]

Perhaps the strongest argument in favour of the communitarian democratic ordering principle of 'belonging' is that the unavoidable and continuing character of linguistic social bonds enables the development of *societal learning*. Sustainability is an uncertain quest that requires social collectivities continually to adapt to new circumstances and challenges. Of course, social learning and mutual understanding can also develop within transnational communities. Take, for example, the community of scientists, state delegates and environmental NGOs that periodically congregate around environmental treaty negotiations. However, it might be said that political communities that merely coalesce around particular, transnational or international debates or problems are occasional and transient political communities where the prospects for collective social learning and hence mutual understanding can never be as deep or lasting as in territorially based communities.

However, for the more heroic cosmopolitans, such as David Held, national, linguistic or cultural ties should have neither moral nor legal significance, since the core question in any democracy should revolve around who is affected by decisions. Held believes that all citizens of the global polity should share 'a common structure of political action' understood as 'a cluster of rights and obligations which cut across all key domains of power, where power shapes and affects people's life-chances with determinate effect on and implications for their political agency' (Held 1999: 105). Only then can power be held accountable wherever it is located – whether in the state, the economy or the cultural sphere. These reforms follow from Held's analysis of the way the processes of globalisation have enabled sites of political, economic and cultural power – including states – to become increasingly *disconnected* from the consequences of exercises of such power. In Held's global polity, individuals would be able to enjoy multiple forms of citizenship at the local, national, regional and global levels. The world would be made up of diverse and overlapping political communities, and each layer of

---

[4] Such vernacular communities are seen as providing the primary forum not only for democratic participation in the world today, but also for the legitimation of other levels of government (federal, international). This is why politics that transcends the vernacular (such as that which takes place in Brussels in the EU or internationally) is invariably elite-dominated, and why mass opinion on the issue of enlargement of the European Union is usually opposed to elite opinion (Kymlicka 2001: 122). For all the talk about the development of a postnational constellation in Europe, the vast majority of environmental organisations are located at the local or national level, not the regional level.

political community would have limited jurisdiction according to a set of filter tests which are largely based on the 'affectedness' principle (Held 1995: 235–6).

However, the great danger of the affectedness principle is that it could be enlisted as a basis for *restricting* participation only to those directly affected by proposed decisions or policies. In this sense, the principle dispenses with the whole idea of community, replacing it with a set of abstract individuals who enforce their rights under a global law. Self-rule is achieved by individuals in possession of abstract rights bestowed by global law, not by participation in the collective life of particular communities. Abstract, legally mediated social integration replaces concrete social interaction in the demos. Understood in these terms, the principle of affectedness – applied without qualification – carries the potential to serve as a basis for exclusion rather than inclusion in political deliberations, preventing those who are merely concerned (as distinct from affected) from engaging in democratic politics. As Saward points out, the application of such a principle would undermine the very concept of citizenship as an inclusive, enduring achievement (Saward 2000: 37–8). This is not to say that 'affectedness' cannot supplement 'belongingness', but it ought not and cannot obliterate it.

Conclusion

Nowadays, it seems both communitarians and cosmopolitans reject both a particularism that excludes the rest of the world and a cosmopolitanism that is blind to local attachments. Yet they reach this apparent consensus from very different starting points – starting points that have different ethical and political consequences. Ecocommunitarians would take particularistic communities as the primary point of focus for building sustainable societies, working with local knowledge and local 'resources' (both 'natural' and moral). This is not enough, to be sure, but it provides the basis for developing ecological selves and wider ecological affinities. Moreover, the task of cultivating wider social and ecological loyalties must happen in the only way that communitarians know how: building additional layers of *community* that loosen (as distinct from dislodge) the hold of local, national and regional affinities so that they may be adjusted to encompass a wider network of still particularistic relationships. In times past, travel was the best cosmopolitan education. In contemporary times, new communication technologies provide a powerful means of building new communities. In this way, our Ratty can learn about other riverbanks and their inhabitants beyond the Wild Wood.

References

Anderson, B. (1991). *Imagined Communities: Reflections on the Origin and Spread of Nationalism*, rev. ed. London: Verso.

Dobson, A. (2003). *Citizenship and the Environment*. Oxford: Oxford University Press.

———(2004). 'Why Be a Cosmopolitan?' Unpublished paper.

Dodge, J. (1981). 'Living by Life: Some Bioregional Theory and Practice', *CoEvolution Quarterly* **32** (Winter): 6–12.

Graham, K. (1930). *The Wind in the Willows*. London: Methuen.

Hage, G. (1998). *White Nation: Fantasies of White Supremacy in a Multicultural Society*. Sydney: Pluto Press, 165–78.

Held, D. (1995). *Democracy and the Global Order*. Cambridge: Polity Press.

———(1999). 'The Transformation of Political Community: Rethinking Democracy in the Context of Globalization', in Ian Shapiro and Casiana Hacker-Cordon (eds.), *Democracy's Edges*. Cambridge: Cambridge University Press, 84–111.

Kingsnorth, Paul (2004). 'Nimbys Are the True Democratic Heroes', *New Statesman* **17**. 805 (3 May): 22–4.

Kymlicka, W. (2001). *Politics in the Vernacular: Nationalism, Multiculturalism, and Citizenship*. Oxford: Oxford University Press.

MacIntyre, A. (1981). *After Virtue*. London: Duckworth.

Matthews, F. (1991). *The Ecological Self*. London: Routledge.

Miller, D. (1993) 'In Defence of Nationality', *Journal of Applied Philosophy* **19**.1: 3–16.

———(1995). *On Nationality*. Oxford: Oxford University Press.

Nussbaum, M. C. (1996). *For Love of Country?* Boston: Beacon Press.

Rorty, R. (1998). 'Justice as a Larger Loyalty', in Pheng Cheah and Bruce Robbins (eds.), *Cosmopolis: Thinking and Feeling Beyond the Nation*. Minneapolis: University of Minneapolis Press, 45–58.

Sandel, M. (1982). *Liberalism and the Limits of Justice*. Cambridge: Cambridge University Press.

Saward, M. (2000). 'A Critique of Held', in Barry Holden (ed.), *Global Democracy: Key Debates*. London: Routledge, 37–8.

Taylor, C. (1992). *Multiculturalism and the Politics of Recognition*. Princeton: Princeton University Press.

Walzer, M. (1987). *Interpretation and Social Criticism*. Cambridge, Mass.: Harvard University Press.

———(1994). *Thick and Thin: Moral Argument at Home and Abroad*. Notre Dame, Ind.: University of Notre Dame Press.

7   Cosmopolitanism

Andrew Linklater

The long-term moral consequences of a series of revolutions in technology and communications which have brought all human societies into a single global political and economic system remain unclear; Kant's question of whether the 'oceans make a community of nations impossible' is relevant two centuries on (Kant 1965: 126). The global media have increased public awareness of suffering in other places, but distance continues to block the extension of solidarity and sympathy beyond the nation state. Global environmental problems have deepened awareness of the interdependence of the species, but it is not certain they will overcome the age-old effects of the 'tyranny of distance' on political loyalty. Will powerful cosmopolitan commitments develop because of global environment problems? What cosmopolitan ethic is most appropriate for a world facing serious environmental threats and challenges?

Kant's answer to his question about the effects of distance on moral and political community frames the present discussion. He pointed to the ambiguities of globalisation in his era. Advances in oceanic navigation created new possibilities 'for doing evil and violence to some place on our globe' (1965: 126). Observers in our time make a similar point when they argue that globalisation allows the most technologically advanced societies to damage the natural environment without great cost to themselves. Kant also stressed that globalisation had positive effects which were evident in growing moral outrage against the violation of human rights everywhere. The modern equivalent is that global environmental problems have reinforced this tendency by promoting a greater sense of responsibility for the biosphere and deeper respect for answerability to other communities for environmental harm.

Current debates about whether the oceans make a world community impossible reflect Kant's perception of the ambiguities of globalisation, but it is important to go beyond Kant's framework in at least one

I am grateful to Toni Erskine, Michael Mason, Matthew Paterson and the editors for their advice on an earlier draft of this chapter.

respect. His examination of the effects of globalisation on human loyalties stressed that Europe's intelligentsia displayed cosmopolitan ethical commitments in their vigorous defence of human rights. We must broaden this analysis to ask if environmental problems such as climate change are creating *popular* as opposed to *elite* cosmopolitanism. Second, Kant believed that the appearance of more cosmopolitan orientations would not weaken the state's position as the dominant form of political community. Indeed, he maintained the republican state was the only assured way of realising the cosmopolitan political project. Turning to the present, many global environmental thinkers lack Kant's faith in the reformist potential of sovereign states and proceed to defend a vision of a post-sovereign world, while others question such pessimism about the prospects for 'ecologically responsible statehood' (Eckersley 2004). For some, Kant's faith in the sovereign state was seriously misplaced, but for others, his focus on the cosmopolitan foundations of responsible statehood provides the right starting point for environmental political theory and practice in the modern age.

The growth of the human rights culture and the development of international criminal law have partly vindicated Kant's prediction of a more cosmopolitan future; however, the legacy of geographical barriers to the development of a human community survives in persistent indifference to distant suffering (Cohen 2001; Smith 2000). Where do human responses to environmental harm belong on this spectrum? On the one hand, it might be argued, global environmental problems have encouraged public recognition of communities of fate or risk which are more inclusive than any national political order; they have promoted the globalisation of shared sentiments in that many non-governmental organisations and ordinary citizens display what Hegel called 'anxiety for the wellbeing of humanity as a whole' and concern for the future of the planet; and they have encouraged many to assume new ethical responsibilities for the welfare of the global commons. These are among the most radical changes of political orientation of the last three or four decades.

But clearly this is not the whole story, since many barriers to the development of a 'community of nations' exist. The sociopsychological consequences of the age-old 'tyranny of distance' endure, in that large numbers of human beings regard the nation state as the only political association that can satisfy basic goals such as the need for physical security. Affluent societies are generally unwilling to make sacrifices which are commensurate with the part they have played in causing environmental degradation – especially if the costs will fall most heavily on co-nationals. Critics of cosmopolitanism have argued that the widening of moral horizons and the development of globalist projects amongst select groups do not alter such fundamental realities of political life. They are almost certainly right that any cosmopolitan vision which envisages the transformation of political loyalties so that obligations to the human species, to non-human species and to the environment come to be placed above duties to the nation or the state is bound to fail in the immediate future, whatever its merits as an ethical ideal. The following argument supports more modest goals in which sovereign communities and their inhabitants become more sensitive to the ways in which their organising principles and practices, public policies and everyday actions harm other peoples and the global commons. The core assumption here is that efforts to create international institutions which address global environmental harm are unlikely to succeed without profound changes in the emotional lives of the members of separate political communities. The question is whether greater awareness of causal responsibility for distant harm can shift the balance between national loyalties and 'cosmopolitan emotions' (Nussbaum et al. 2002).

There are six parts to the remainder of this paper. Part one makes some brief comments about communitarian and cosmopolitan arguments about the relationship between obligations to co-nationals and obligations to humanity.[1] It argues that their respective strengths can be brought together in the idea of 'the connected self' (Staub 2003) which is deeply reflective about the ways in which its actions (and the social practices in which it is involved) harm others. Part two argues that cosmopolitan emotions are most likely to develop when actors believe they are causally responsible for harming others and the physical environment, and when the emotions of shame, guilt, sorrow or compassion arise in consequence. Part three turns to the ethical claim that the duty to avoid causing unnecessary harm is a fundamental human obligation; it also defends this thesis from the criticism that it disregards positive obligations to rescue 'distant strangers'. Part four identifies different types of environmental harm, and part five asks if they seem likely to engender 'common experiences' which weaken the effects of distance on moral and political communities. Part six argues that concerns about global injustice and the absence of accountability to victims of harm may yet spark the development of deep-seated cosmopolitan emotions.

---

[1] The stress below is not on tensions between communitarian and cosmopolitan traditions and perspectives, but on differences between cosmopolitan and communitarian arguments which are often combined in the same perspective.

Community and cosmopolis

Some cosmopolitan arguments start with the moral duties that each person has to all other members of the human race and then turn to the special ethical obligations which the members of particular social groups can reasonably superimpose on supposedly prior universal duties (Goodin 1985). Many green political thinkers and activists extend the argument by asking what co-nationals or fellow citizens can properly agree among themselves, given duties to other species, unborn generations and the natural environment. Communitarian arguments reject the idea that moral and political theory can begin with the duties that each human being has to all others and to the global environment. Their position is that moral agents acquire their most compelling obligations as embedded selves whose personal identities are shaped by family ties, participation in voluntary associations and citizenship of nation states. They criticise liberal-cosmopolitan thinkers for abstracting individuals from the social arrangements in which they acquire moral personalities; they stress, then, the loyalties which bind individuals to particular societies and thwart the emergence of strong moral attachments to the whole human race.

Some cosmopolitan thinkers protest that many communitarians display a conservative faith in the nation state. The former recognise that communitarians believe that all bounded communities should honour their international obligations, but they accuse them of failing to take global responsibilities for environmental and other world problems with due seriousness (Dower 2000). These are important differences. Cosmopolitan and communitarian orientations disagree about how far global commitments can and should erode national loyalties; however, they often concur that the ties that bind individuals to their nation state leave ample scope for universal obligations such as the negative duty not to injure other communities and the positive obligation to assist desperate strangers where possible. The principle that every separate political community faces the challenge of ensuring that its conduct does not needlessly harm other societies, future generations, non-human species and the natural environment forms part of their common ground.

To adopt this standpoint is to stress the need for awareness of embeddedness in particular social arrangements *and* connectedness with distant strangers in complex chains of global interdependence. A brief comment on feminist approaches to ethics is useful at this point, since they have been at the forefront of efforts to reflect on the importance of connectedness as opposed to what they regard as the dominant Western normative standpoints which have privileged the autonomous moral subject in recent centuries. Many feminist approaches have argued that the emphasis on ethical autonomy privileges the experience of Western males and devalues 'the ethic of care and responsibility' which is most apparent in traditional female roles within the family (Gilligan 1982). The accent on connectedness is a direct challenge to the notion of *homo clausus* – the conception of the self as separate from society, and as possessing rights independently of it – which has enjoyed unusual pre-eminence in the modern West (see Elias 1987; Lupton 1998: 72ff.). Emphasising connectedness is designed to reverse the long-term trend of separating individuals from each other which divides Western modernity from the Middle Ages. The ecological defence of duties to the environment aims to consolidate this counter-movement by urging human beings to turn their minds to repairing ruptured connections with nature.

The idea of the connected self which is sensitive to how personal conduct and institutional behaviour can harm others is immensely important for cosmopolitan and environmental ethics. It contains a telling response to a powerful criticism of some cosmopolitan positions which is that human beings rarely warm to moral principles which are divorced from immediate social ties and everyday experience. The evidence is that cosmopolitan ethical ideals lack practical influence when they rely on the notion of 'bloodless' individuals separated from the social contexts in which they acquire their primary identities and loyalties. Ultimately, the success of these ideals depends on the extent to which they engage such powerful influences on human conduct as the emotions of shame, guilt and compassion (Tangney and Dearing 2002; Schopenhauer 1995). Arguably, these ideals are most likely to connect with the emotional lives of individuals when they are persuaded that they are directly or indirectly responsible for the suffering of others.

Cosmopolitan emotions

No society – not even the most cruel and violent – can survive unless most members have internalised the principle that they should not cause unnecessary harm to family members, friends and associates and unless they have acquired requisite moral emotions including the capacity for shame and guilt when fundamental norms are violated (Scheff 1988). The members of every society must internalise norms that prohibit some forms of violent harm while condoning others such as the use of force against external groups. As a broad generalisation, most human beings are averse to harming members of the in-group and can be swayed by peer pressure not to harm them or be complicit in their suffering – at least, most recognise it is wrong to cause needless harm to immediate others. Of course, sharp distinctions between 'in-groups' and 'out-groups' have confined the circle of human sympathy throughout human history. As far as the modern world is concerned, basic moral emotions have been wedded to the 'imagined community' of the nation for the last two centuries. Individuals have felt shame when they have transgressed norms that prohibit forms of harm to other members of the nation; they have experienced guilt when their actions have fallen short of social expectations about the need to assist co-nationals. The important question which arises for cosmopolitans is whether *universal* emotions such as shame or guilt can become the grounds on which a stronger sense of moral obligation to the human race, future generations, non-human species and the natural habitat can be established.

This approach to cosmopolitanism starts, then, with emotional dispositions not to harm at least a limited circle of others which first develop in family relations and are then extended to other members of society and possibly to all members of the human race. Quite how this process takes place is a matter for developmental psychologists. Suffice it to note that the capacity to recognise pain and suffering in others, and to develop the propensity for sympathy, is one dimension of a learning process which occurs within and between societies. Some philosophers have argued that cosmopolitanism is best promoted by convincing human beings that their shared vulnerability to pain and humiliation is more important than cultural, racial and other differences (Rorty 1989). They contend that human beings are more likely to overcome invidious distinctions between 'insiders' and 'outsiders', and more certain to extend their moral community to include all human beings and all sentient creatures, if they are implored to enlarge the sphere of emotional identification in this way. From this standpoint, philosophical claims about universal obligations which are inherent in human reason are unlikely to be as effective as the quest to promote human solidarity through a 'sentimental education'.

This line of argument raises complex questions about the relationship between reason and the emotions which fall outside the present discussion. What is clear is that social and political change rarely takes place through appeals to reason which disregard the emotions. Those who spearheaded struggles against the cruelties of colonial domination, slavery and the slave trade, and apartheid appealed to human sympathies as well as to the capacity for ratiocination (Crawford 2002). Developments in the humanitarian law of war have occurred because efforts to extend the boundaries of human sympathy have had similar success. This is true of the laws of war which prohibit 'unnecessary suffering' and 'superfluous injury' to civilians and to military personnel, and of human rights law that prohibits 'serious bodily and mental harm' to national, racial and other minorities. In each case, political change took place because of the importance of appeals to identify with the suffering.

Of course, the absence of a 'global conscience' mattered less prior to the age of total war (which has compelled all societies to reflect on the rights and wrongs of industrialised warfare) and before the unprecedented violence of the twentieth century (which has made universal moral principles which start with individual human rights more central than ever before). Promoting a global conscience which keeps pace with the economic and technological unification of the human race is one of the great moral and political challenges of the contemporary age. Its retarded development emerged as a matter of growing public concern when the possible social and political effects of global environmental degradation became more widely understood. The question is whether various forms of environmental harm will consolidate the progress that has been made in forming cosmopolitan personality structures so that independent political communities and other actors will face greater public pressure to arrest and reverse damage to the environment.

In part, the answer depends on whether human beings acquire feelings of compassion and sympathy for the suffering in the manner that Rorty suggests. It also depends on how far they come to feel directly or indirectly responsible for harm elsewhere, with the result that emotions such as guilt and shame support projects of global as opposed to national reform. The development of the universal human rights culture and the humanitarian law of war owes much to the human capacity for 'expanding the circle' of sympathy. International legal conventions have drawn on, and sought to encourage, feelings of shame which can attend the breach of global legal or moral prohibitions on harm; and they have sought to promote guilt when, for example, the international community has failed to use available resources to help the victims of genocide. Whether global environmental problems have a similar capacity to foster cosmopolitan emotions such as shame when human beings harm other humans and non-humans, and guilt when little or nothing is done to alleviate distant suffering, is the interesting question, and one that leads inevitably to a discussion of the significance of the 'no harm' principle for cosmopolitan ethics.

The 'no harm' principle

Is the 'no harm' principle the keystone of a cosmopolitan response to global environmental problems? Those who believe it is reasonable that human societies privilege the interests of their own members may answer in the affirmative. From their vantage point, persuading states not to harm one another is the central ethical problem in world politics; trying to convince them to stretch their benevolence to encompass all members of the human race is not the main issue. The counter-argument is that the negative obligation to avoid harm fails desperate strangers; they require assistance from those who are in a position to help them rather than their faithful adherence to the principle, 'do no harm'. It is essential to explore the tension between these approaches before turning to different forms of environmental harm and considering whether they are capable of engendering common experiences which answer Kant's question about the political significance of the oceans.

Ross (1930) provides one of the more robust defences of the 'no harm' principle. He argues that moral agents have many prima facie obligations to each other including the duty of beneficence, but they cannot be expected to be heroic if this will cause their downfall. However, the duty not to harm others should always weigh heavily on them (although it can be overridden when faced with threats to survival). Ross's stance echoes Mill's claim that the 'moral rules which forbid mankind to hurt one another ... are more vital to human wellbeing than any other maxims ... a person may possibly not need the benefits of others; but he always needs that they should not do him hurt' (see Mackie 1977: 135). In short, compliance with the 'no harm' principle is more important than munificence for the survival of civil society. Ross further observed that support for the 'no harm' principle might be a first step in the evolution of close forms of social co-operation. His supposition was that individuals who trust one another to respect this principle can more easily proceed to weave positive obligations of assistance into their social interaction.

The unspoken assumption here is that *self-regarding* individuals must first learn how to build the 'no harm' principle into their relations. As noted earlier, starting with the implicit assumption of *homo clausus* – and asking how separate individuals can most easily create a way of life together – may simply reflect the masculinist properties of the modern West. Nevertheless, Ross's approach is relevant to international politics, which is dominated by what other philosophers have called 'limited sympathies' and 'confined generosity' in human affairs (Mackie 1977; Warnock 1971). These concepts indicate the existence of definite limits to what individuals and associations such as nation states are pre-pared to do – or can reasonably be expected to do – for the benefit of 'strangers'. They suggest that moral agents cannot always be blamed for failing to rescue 'outsiders', given obligations to family members and others, but such duties do not justify needless harm to other groups and communities. Warnock (1971) has argued that this obligation can reasonably be regarded as one of the most basic universal ethical principles precisely because it is integral to every form of life – though often respected only in relations between members of the same in-group. This contention resonates with an earlier claim that most human beings are vulnerable to similar forms of pain and suffering; most can sympathise with those who experience pain (or suffer in some other way); and most can feel remorse when they cause or contribute to suffering elsewhere.

An important objection to this line of argument is that the victims of humanitarian emergencies do not benefit from the other's respect for the 'no harm' principle; what they need is the commitment to rescue (Geras 1998).[2] The argument is not that all potential rescuers are obliged to risk their lives to assist others – only that privileging the 'no harm' principle can lead to an impoverished morality which abandons the desperate to their fate. It is not clear, however, that this argument overturns Mill's and Ross's conviction that the duty not to cause harm is the most basic of all ethical obligations. Some moral thinkers argue that respect for the 'no harm' principle requires acts of Good Samaritanism; they contend that the failure to rescue can be harmful in its own right. Their central point is that lasting psychological harm and profound damage to self-esteem can occur when the desperate are left to conclude that their lives are so unimportant that bystanders have no obligation to help them (see Feinberg 1984; Wiesel 1977; Goldhagen 2002: 171ff.).

There are good reasons for thinking that moral responsibility can exist independently of causal responsibility for the suffering of others – alternatively, that those who have caused harm are not the only ones with obligations to do something about it. Be that as it may, belief in a moral responsibility to assist others is often stronger when evidence of causal responsibility for suffering exists. The sense of moral responsibility often depends on whether agents believe they have harmed others or benefit from political arrangements which cause harm (whether or not they played any part in their creation). Shame can be a potent emotion when individuals and groups decide they have violated public norms which prohibit harming others; guilt can be a significant influence on conduct when actors believe they have done less than they could to assist the desperate, or benefit unfairly from social arrangements. To return to an earlier point, these emotional dispositions exist in all societies, although the extent to which they influence human behaviour

---

[2] It is assumed for the purpose of this argument that potential rescuers are not responsible for the humanitarian emergency.

depends, for example, on how far they recognise others as members of their community or think outsiders have rights against them. This leads to the question of whether global environmental harm has an unusual capacity to generate cosmopolitan identities which transcend the parochialism of the nation state.

Varieties of environmental harm

Environmental problems come in many forms with different consequences for moral and political life. It is important to distinguish between three types of global environmental harm and then to ask how far they seem capable of engendering common experiences. They are:

- deliberate environmental harm designed to disadvantage others
- negligent behaviour or lack of 'due diligence' where harm is caused by exposing others to unnecessary risk
- unintended environmental harm which results from unplanned global social and economic processes.

Iraq's destruction of Kuwaiti oil fields during the 1990 Gulf war is an example of deliberate harm where particular agents set out to disadvantage specific others. This form of harm has led to discussions about extending international criminal law to cover deliberate damage to the environment. International environmental law has already established the obligation not to harm the environment of other states or the global commons (see below), and criminalising serious environmental harm is an obvious way of extending this commitment. There have been no serious diplomatic discussions about establishing an international environmental court with parallel functions to the International Criminal Court (ICC), and there can be little doubt that claims for immunity from prosecution which have run through recent US policy towards the ICC would surface if such discussions seemed likely to bear fruit. However, expectations that states and other actors should be punished for causing serious environmental harm may well grow, and bystanders may come under more frequent criticism for not taking steps to create global legal institutions which punish wrongdoers. For reasons given earlier, progress in this direction may ultimately depend on the growth of cosmopolitan shame and guilt.

The gas explosion in the pesticide plant in Bhopal in 1984 is the most notorious example of harm caused through the lack of due care, but the literature on exporting hazards including hazardous waste has addressed a central issue raised by the Bhopal incident – how far a double standard of morality exists in world politics so that peoples in the poorer parts of the world do not have the level of environmental protection which the populations of more industrialising societies have come to expect (Shue 1981). The idea of 'environmental apartheid' embodies the crucial point (Shiva 2000). Those who make such arguments do not accuse the powerful of intending to harm others, but of indifference to the risks they face. Ways of addressing this problem include the establishment of principles of corporate responsibility and appropriate means of ensuring compliance, but transnational business enterprises often frustrate such measures by clouding the issue of legal liability. Underlying their strategy is a belief in the sanctity of property rights – and in primary duties to shareholders – which places the burden of seeking compensation on the victims, a standpoint whose failings have been extensively documented with respect to the Bhopal incident (Eckersley 2004: 105, 219; Shrivastava 1992). Evasiveness does not encourage confidence in the prospects for a global conscience, although the cosmopolitan must hope that world norms will emerge that facilitate the shaming of organisations which are indifferent to the risks associated with the employment of hazardous technologies. Whether those norms develop will depend in part on how far efforts to draw attention to double standards in world politics increase the level of popular guilt.

A third form of harm is dispersed across frontiers by global industrial processes and by the cumulative effect over many decades of individual or group actions, each apparently trivial in itself. Climate change is the result of decades of industrial production and patterns of consumption whose consequences have only recently begun to be understood. The dominant kind of global environmental harm has not been deliberate, but has arisen from the unintended consequences of industrial systems of production and modern forms of consumption. Recognition of its existence has led to the development of international environmental law which proclaims that states do not have a sovereign right to be indifferent to harm to neighbouring societies and the global commons (compare the Harmon Doctrine of 1895 with the Trail Smelter Arbitration of 1941 and the more recent Principle 21 of the Stockholm Agreement of 1972).[3] Global environmental law insists the exercise of

---

[3] The Harmon Doctrine is named after the US Attorney General, Hudson Harmon, who in 1895 dismissed Mexican claims that US use of the Rio Grande caused environmental damage in Mexico. The Harmon Doctrine stated that the fundamental principle of international law is 'the absolute sovereignty of every nation, as against all others, within its own territory' (see Dobson 2003). The Trail Smelter Arbitration involving the US and Canada held that no state has 'the right to use or permit the use of its territory in such a manner as to cause injury ... to the territory of another or the properties and persons therein'. Principle 21 of the Stockholm Agreement claims that states have a duty not to cause harm to the environment of neighbouring states or to the global commons.

sovereignty must conform with the principle, *sic utere tuo ut alienum non leadas* – 'one must use one's property so as not to injure others'. The aim is to alter social behaviour in the light of scientific evidence that unchecked industrialisation processes and consumption patterns are having disastrous effects. The upshot is that indifference to environmental harm should be deemed morally reprehensible.

Responses to unintended environmental harm include a new vocabulary of politics which includes the tenet, 'polluter pays'. The precautionary principle is designed to reduce the chances of accumulative harm caused by industrial policies and social practices. The focus on 'ecological footprints' attempts to uncover the hidden environmental consequences of different forms of commodity production (see Dobson, chapter 13 in this volume). A striking feature of the vocabulary of environmental politics is its attempt to secure fundamental changes in the organisation of industrial societies *and* to make new forms of cosmopolitan awareness and responsibility central to the everyday experience of individuals – especially in affluent societies that are most inculpated in global environmental degradation. This is an unprecedented development. Earlier generations were not required to reflect on how individual and group behaviour contribute to climate change, create health risks which may haunt future generations and cause the unparalleled loss of biological diversity.

The point can be rephrased to stress that earlier generations did not live with a standing summons to ponder their 'complex' (or 'reflexive') as well as their 'simple' responsibilities (Davis 2001: 6). Simple responsibility exists when actors are primarily concerned with whether they have breached established social conventions. Complex or reflexive responsibility exists when actors take the initiative in asking whether their actions – and the social practices in which they are involved – have unintended but not proscribed harmful consequences for other peoples as well as for non-human species and the natural environment. Complex responsibility arises when persons heed the call of conscience rather than act from a more rudimentary desire to comply with established social norms.

Environmental movements have called for higher levels of complex responsibility on the part of individuals, business enterprises and nation states. The idea of global environmental citizenship has been invoked to encourage cosmopolitan identities which are aware of connectedness with distant others and with the physical environment. It has been used to argue for a global conscience which replaces the myopia of *homo clausus* (Davis 2001: 7–8). Many individuals have replied to such appeals by choosing lifestyles which minimise harm to the environment and which reduce complicity in ecological damage, but it is impossible to tell whether efforts to change individual psychologies and alter everyday conduct will yield cosmopolitan emotions which have no historical precedent.[4] What is clear is that green political thought and environmental activists have created a new vocabulary of politics which makes movement in this direction entirely possible.

Common experiences?

As Kant observed over two centuries ago, the globalisation of social and economic life may not lead inexorably to a global conscience; as Halliday (1988) has argued, there is no historical guarantee that internationalisation will spawn internationalism. One reason is that untrammelled social and economic processes do not affect all human beings in identical ways; societies do not have equal incentives to seize control of unplanned forces or reverse environmental harm. Inequalities of political power mean that indifference to environmental harm can persist without fear of public sanction; and as Hume argued, self-interest shows no sign of losing its ability to block the advance of human sympathy.

If sea levels rise over the next few decades, coastal dwellers in societies such as Bangladesh will suffer disproportionately. Distant observers may feel pity for them, but this may not lead to political action. Aristotle's definition of this emotion is worth considering in this context. According to his usage, pity arises when an observer witnesses 'destructive or painful harm *in one not deserving to encounter it*' (italics in original), when the pain is something 'which one might expect oneself, or one of one's own, to suffer', and importantly, 'when it is near' (quoted in Konstan 2001: 34).

Two points are worth noting about this definition: first, that pity only arises when the pain involved is something one can imagine happening to oneself or to a close associate and, second, when it is 'near'. What it means to be 'near' is a crucial question raised by Aristotle's conception of pity. As noted earlier, green theorists and activists have argued that nearness is not about physical proximity but about social and economic connectedness. The question, 'who is near?', is answered by thinking imaginatively about whether one's actions have harmful effects on those who live further along the line of global networks of interdependence.

---

[4] The stress here is on how emotions affect 'character' and 'self-control', and how they predispose agents to act in certain ways, as opposed to simply responding to external constraints. For a discussion, see Harré and Parrott (1996: 3, 18) and Barbalet (1998: 27).

Calculations of this kind do not alter the fact that it is hard to imagine some forms of harm befalling oneself or one's closest associates. With respect to floods in Bangladesh, for example, affluent populations may sympathise with the victims, but the scale of their suffering is often unimaginable and it is hard to identify closely with them. The stress on pity does not solve the problem Adam Smith (1982: 136–7) identified – namely, that a man who cannot sleep because he will 'lose his little finger to-morrow ... will snore with the most profound security over the ruin of a hundred million of his brethren', provided he never sees them. Hume (1962: 229) raised the same point when stating that not only is sympathy with 'persons remote from us ... much fainter than with persons near and contiguous'; it is invariably 'much fainter than our concern for ourselves'. Two other obstacles to converting pity into effective political action must be added – that actors are not always sure who is best placed to assist the suffering, and that the repetition of media images of remote suffering can do more to dull the moral senses than to spark humanitarian involvement (Moeller 1999).

Global environmental problems may not generate cosmopolitan solidarities for those reasons. Those who do not suffer environmental harm may gaze sympathetically on distant sufferers but fail to help them – especially when they have no (perceived) causal responsibility for their plight. The discussion turns inevitably to the 'bystander phenomenon', and specifically to what it is 'in societies that makes for a pervasive tendency to help and what makes for widespread non-involvement in the problems of others' (Barry 1980: 460). In response, Barry argues that 'the more things are arranged so that people really do share a common fate, the better the chance that people will respond to the plight of others', while 'whatever insulates people from sharing common experiences, and facing common problems ... makes it more likely that they will fail to recognise the common humanity of a stranger' (1980: 460). Modern populations know that climate change does not respect national borders, but they are perhaps more deeply aware of differential exposure to environmental harm. Global environmental obligations are unlikely to develop far through appeals to 'common experiences' and a 'common fate'.

Global justice and accountability

Where are the countervailing moral forces to be found when agents with few or no common experiences think about appropriate responses to environmental harm? Dobson (2005: 270) argues that 'the obligation to compensate for harm, or to take action to avoid it, is not an obligation of charity to be met through the exercise of compassion but of justice'. His position is that justice requires that the affluent members of humanity should do most to solve environmental problems because they are largely to blame for them. This crucial point can be extended to argue that the affluent benefit unfairly from global social and political arrangements which cause environmental problems. It can be developed still further by arguing that the sense of injustice, which Aristotle (1955: 155) defined as 'an excess of the harmful and a deficiency of the beneficial', might produce forms of guilt or shame which stand in for common experiences and common fate as sources of global political action.

Dobson is critical of cosmopolitan approaches which begin with the duty to engage all others in unconstrained dialogue (Linklater 1998). He argues that faced with rising sea levels, the Alliance of Small Island States does not require further dialogue but serious efforts on the part of 'net contributors to global warming to reduce their impact on the global environment' (Dobson 2005: 268). In short, its members require justice rather than dialogue. This leads Dobson to argue that the move from harm to dialogue is less helpful than the move from harm to 'redistributive or restorative justice'. His central claim is that 'if harm is being done, then surely more *justice* rather than more talking is the first requirement' (Dobson 2005: 269).

One might query this line of argument by asking whether the claims of societies which are most vulnerable to the consequences of rising sea levels have been taken seriously in the relevant diplomatic fora and whether societies which have less to fear from rising sea levels are guilty of a profound failure to think from the standpoint of others. It might also be suggested that efforts to decide appropriate levels of compensation in line with commitments to restorative justice should proceed through forms of dialogue in which all affected parties enjoy the right to have their claims taken seriously. Justice, in short, requires equal access to forms of dialogue in which actors strive to be accountable and answerable to one another. The fact that the interests of the Alliance of Small States have been neglected can be regarded as evidence of the need for more discourse of this kind rather than for promoting justice set apart from the cosmopolitan project of promoting the dialogic ideal.

Green political theorists and activists have argued that those who cause environmental harm (whether intentionally or otherwise) must be morally and politically answerable to those who suffer the consequences. The argument leads to a central theme in discourse approaches to morality, which is that all people have the right to be consulted about actions and decisions which affect them (Eckersley 2004). Customary international law already invokes this moral principle by requiring states to exercise their sovereignty in such a way as to avoid unintended harm to other societies and to the global commons; it creates 'the obligation of prior notification of and consultation with states likely to be affected by a potentially harmful activity'; and it establishes the specific duty to co-operate to prevent the transfer to other states of 'any activities and substances that cause severe environmental degradation or are found to be harmful to human health' (Kummer 1999: 13–24). These are essential principles of 'ecologically responsible statehood' and crucial ways of promoting the Kantian goal of defining state sovereignty in the light of cosmopolitan ideals. Such principles find their strongest defence in the vision of a world order in which peoples enjoy the right of equal access to transnational public spheres where they can protest against all forms of actual or potential harm including the three forms of environmental harm mentioned earlier (O'Neill 1991; Mason 2001; Eckersley 2004).

Cosmopolitan accountability is crucial for realising justice in the Aristotelian sense of fairly distributed costs and benefits. In this context, Douglas's claim that a culture is 'a system of persons holding one another mutually accountable' warrants attention (Douglas 1992: 31). She adds that in general each member of a culture 'tries to live at some level of being held accountable which is bearable and which matches the level at which that person wants to hold other persons accountable'. However, the search for 'mutual accountability' is often 'fraught' with difficulty precisely because social actors often disagree about what counts as a fair distribution of rights and responsibilities (1992: 31).

Douglas's comments are a reminder that the international political system has not reached the stage where different societies agree about cosmopolitan forms of mutual accountability, but global environmental harm has almost certainly increased support for the cosmopolitan principle that all human beings have the right to be consulted about any decisions or practices which may adversely affect them; and some progress has been made in promoting support for the moral principle that distinctions between citizens and non-citizens are morally irrelevant when harm spills over national frontiers. Global environmental problems may have an unusual ability to foster the sense of connectedness with 'distant strangers' and to make concern about harm to others a central feature of everyday life. Emphasising causal responsibility for harm and the practice of benefiting unfairly from long-distance networks of economic interdependence may be the best way of bridging internationalisation and internationalism. This orientation can substitute for 'common experiences' and a 'common fate' in producing cosmopolitan emotions without which a more just global order is unlikely to develop, but the omens do not suggest that these sentiments are about to become determining influences on world politics.

Conclusion

It is impossible to predict whether the gap between cosmopolitan ideals and current political practice will close, although international non-governmental organisations and other political actors will doubtless continue to work for the development of a global conscience. Environmental harm does not produce the 'common experiences' which have been central to national political communities, but it may promote changes in the emotional order which make the extension of moral and political community possible. These include the idea of the 'connected self' which responds with shame and guilt to harm that crosses national borders, and they include related concerns about global injustice and the lack of cosmopolitan accountability. How far cosmopolitan expressions of such universal emotions as guilt, shame, sorrow and compassion can develop is the central question. This will decide how long it will be meaningful to ask Kant's question about whether the oceans make 'a community of nations impossible'.

References

Aristotle (1955). *Ethics*. Harmondsworth: Penguin.

Barbalet, J. (1998). *Emotion, Social Theory and Social Structure: A Macrosociological Approach*. Cambridge: Cambridge University Press.

Barry, B. (1980). Review of L. S. Scheleff, *The Bystander: Behavior, Law, Ethics, Ethics* **90**.4: 457–62.

Beck, U. (1992). *Risk Society: Towards A New Modernity*. London: Sage.

Bendelow, G., and Williams, S. (1998). *Emotions in Social Life: Critical Themes and Contemporary Issues*. London: Routledge.

Boltanski, L. (1999). *Distant Suffering: Morality, Media and Politics*. Cambridge: Cambridge University Press.

Cohen, S. (2001). *States of Denial: Knowing about Atrocities and Suffering*. Cambridge: Polity Press.

Crawford, N. C. (2002). *Argument and Change in World Politics: Ethics, Decolonization and Humanitarian Intervention*. Cambridge: Cambridge University Press.

Davis, W. (ed.) (2001). *Taking Responsibility: Comparative Perspectives*. London: University Press of Virginia.

Dobson, A. (2003). 'States, Citizens and the Environment', in Q. Skinner and B. Strath (eds.), *States and Citizens*. Cambridge: Cambridge University Press, ch. 12.

(2005). 'Globalisation, Cosmopolitanism and the Environment', *International Relations* **19**.3: 259–73.

Douglas, M. (1992). *Risk and Blame: Essays in Cultural Theory*. London: Routledge.

Dower, N. (2000). 'The Idea of Global Citizenship', *Global Society* **14**.4: 553–67.

Eckersley, R. (2004). *The Green State: Rethinking Democracy and Sovereignty*. Cambridge, Mass.: MIT Press.

Elias, N. (1987). *Involvement and Detachment*. Oxford: Blackwell.

Feinberg, J. (1984). *Harm to Others: The Moral Limits of the Criminal Law*. Oxford: Oxford University Press.

Geras, N. (1998). *The Contract of Mutual Indifference: Political Philosophy after the Holocaust*. London: Verso.

Gilligan, C. (1982). *In a Different Voice: Psychological Theory and Women's Development*. Cambridge, Mass.: Harvard University Press.

Goldhagen, D. J. (2002). *A Moral Reckoning: The Role of the Catholic Church in the Holocaust and its Unfulfilled Duty of Repair*. New York: Alfred A. Knopf.

Goodin, R. (1985). *Protecting the Vulnerable: A Reanalysis of our Social Responsibilities*. Chicago: University of Chicago Press.

Halliday, F. (1988). 'Three Concepts of Internationalism', *International Affairs* **64**.2: 187–98.

Harré, R., and Parrott, W. G. (eds.) (1996). *Emotions: Social, Cultural and Biological Dimensions*. London: Sage.

Hume, D. (1962). *An Enquiry Concerning Human Understanding*. New York: Collier Books.

Kant, I. (1965). *The Metaphysical Principles of Virtue*. New York: Bobbs-Merrill.

Konstan, D. (2001). *Pity Transformed*. London: Duckworth.

Kummer, K. (1999). *International Management of Hazardous Waste*. Oxford: Oxford University Press.

Linklater, A. (1998). *The Transformation of Political Community: Ethical Foundations of a Post-Westphalian Era*. Cambridge: Polity Press.

Lupton, D. (1998). *The Emotional Self*. London: Sage.

Mackie, J. L. (1977). *Ethics: Inventing Right and Wrong*. Harmondsworth: Penguin.

Mason, M. (2001). 'Transnational Environmental Obligations: Locating New Spaces of Accountability in a Post-Westphalian Order', *Transactions of the Institute of British Geographers* **26**.4: 407–29.

Moeller, S. D. (1999). *Compassion Fatigue: How the Media Sell Disease, Famine, War and Death*. London: Routledge.

Nussbaum, M. et al. (2002). *For Love of Country*. Boston: Beacon Press.

O'Neill, O. (1991). 'Transnational Justice', in D. Held (ed.), *Political Theory Today*. Cambridge: Polity Press, 276–304.

Rorty, R. (1989). *Contingency, Irony and Solidarity*. Cambridge: Cambridge University Press.

Ross, W. D. (1930). *The Right and the Good*, Oxford: Clarendon Press.

Scheff, T. (1988). 'Shame and Conformity: The Deference-Emotion System', *American Sociological Review* **53**.3: 395–406.

Schopenhauer A. (1995). *On the Basis of Morality*. Oxford: Berghahn Books.

Shiva, V. (2000). 'Ecological Balance in an Era of Globalization', in P. Wapner and L. Ruiz (eds.), *Principled World Politics: The Challenge of Normative International Relations*. Lanham, Md.: Rowman and Littlefield.

Shrivastava, P. (1992). *Bhopal: Anatomy of a Crisis*. London: Paul Chapman Publishing.

Shue, H. (1981). 'Exporting Hazards', in P. G. Brown and H. Shue (eds.), *Boundaries: National Autonomy and Its Limits*. Totowa, N.J.: Rowman and Littlefield.

Smith, A. (1982). *The Theory of Moral Sentiments*. Indianopolis: Liberty Press.

Smith, D. M. (2000). *Moral Geographies: Ethics in a World of Difference*. Edinburgh: Edinburgh University Press.

Staub, E. (2003). *The Psychology of Good and Evil: Why Children, Adults and Groups Help and Harm Others*. Cambridge: Cambridge University Press.

Tangney, J. P., and Dearing, R. L. (2002). *Shame and Guilt*. London: Guilford Press.

Walzer, M. (2002). 'Spheres of Affection', in M. Nussbaum et al., *For Love of Country*. Boston: Beacon Press, 125–7.

Warnock, G. (1971). *The Object of Morality*. London: Methuen.

Weisel, E. (1977). *Dimensions of the Holocaust*. Evanston, Ill.: Nortwestern University Press.

Part 2

Political concepts and the ecological
challenge

8   Democracy

Terence Ball

Several years ago I participated in a round table discussion on 'Our Responsibilities Toward Future Generations' at a small liberal arts college in the American midwest. One of my fellow discussants was a theologian, the other a state legislator. Despite our differences, we all agreed that we do not pay sufficient heed to the health and wellbeing of our distant descendants and that this represents a kind of moral myopia that calls for correction. Sometime during the discussion I turned to the state legislator – a thoughtful and sensitive man of enlightened outlook – and asked him point-blank why our elected representatives don't pay much (if any) attention to the fate of future people, and still less to that of non-human creatures. 'Because they don't vote', was his prompt reply. (He might have added that future people and animals don't contribute money to political campaigns either.)

That, in a nutshell, sums up one of the chief shortcomings of democracy, at least from an environmental or green perspective. I should perhaps qualify this by saying that I am talking about democracy *as presently understood*. My contention throughout will be that 'democracy' has been, and doubtless will continue to be, a contested concept whose meaning(s) can be challenged and perchance changed. My argument proceeds in the following way. I shall begin on a cautionary note by briefly suggesting that there is no logically or conceptually necessary connection between democracy and environmentalism; indeed the latter can take, and in several significant instances has taken, authoritarian and anti-democratic forms. And, too, democratic majorities can and frequently do favour decisions and policies that degrade or destroy the natural environment. Even so, I believe that there is a better 'fit' between environmentalism and democracy than between environmentalism

For helpfully criticising an earlier version of this chapter, I thank Richard Dagger, Andrew Dobson, Robyn Eckersley, Matthew Festenstein, Mathew Humphrey, Cary Nederman and Lauret Savoy. Further useful criticisms came from audiences at the universities of Sheffield, Oxford, and Exeter and from my hosts there – Michael Kenny, Michael Freeden and Iain Hampsher-Monk.

and anti-democratic authoritarianism. I then briefly consider the 'essential contestability' of moral and political concepts in general, of 'democracy' in particular. The history of 'democracy' shows it to be, if not essentially contested, then at least 'contingently contested' in light of new problems and developments. Democracy as heretofore understood is under increasing pressure from arguments advanced by theorists allied with the environmental or green movement, and for several rather compelling reasons. I conclude with several conjectures about what green democracy – or perhaps one should say 'ecodemocracy' or even 'biocracy'[1] – would look like, and the practical and institutional innovations that would be required to sustain it.

Anti-democratic environmentalism

I begin by sounding a cautionary note. There is no logically or conceptually *necessary* connection between a commitment to the natural environment and a commitment to democracy. One can be 'green' and yet be opposed to democracy on either philosophical or strategic grounds. Conversely, one can of course be a democrat without having much, if any, sympathy for the natural environment and nature's myriad creatures.

Consider first those greens who oppose democracy on philosophical or ideological grounds. Lest we forget: one of the most murderous regimes of the twentieth century extolled environmental values. Hitler and the German Nazi party were strongly supportive of environmental protection and condemned cruelty to animals.[2] Hitler and several of his high-ranking henchmen, including Heinrich Himmler (head of the SS), were strict vegetarians. One of the first acts of the Nazi regime was the passage in 1933 of the *Tierschutzgesetz*, the wide-ranging law protecting both domestic and wild animals from cruel treatment. This was followed a year later by the *Reichsjagdgesetz*, the law limiting hunting, and then in 1935 by the sweeping *Reichsnaturschutzgesetz*, the law protecting nature itself from human plunder and predation (Ferry 1995: 91). Admirable as these acts might have been, they were promulgated by a regime that was anti-democratic and totalitarian to its core. Murderous as it was to humans, this regime went out of its way to protect animals and wild nature. Indeed, it extolled and sometimes practised a kind of 'nature worship' (Pois 1986).

Sometimes greens are antipathetic towards democracy for strategic and tactical reasons. They believe that the interest-group politics of

---

[1] I owe the neologism 'biocracy' to my friend and colleague Richard Dagger.
[2] Bramwell 1985; Pois 1986; Ferry 1995: ch. 5; see further Wenz 1997 and, with particular reference to the American green movement, Zimmerman 1997.

Western-style liberal democracies are unable to achieve significant environmental ends, and hold that if greens organise themselves into political parties and pressure groups, nominate candidates for election to public office and lobby on behalf of their green agenda, they will be 'co-opted' and their movement corrupted. They will be forced to compromise in hopes of gaining piecemeal political victories. Insofar as the give-and-take politics of liberal democracy requires compromise, the green programme will be enacted (if at all) in dribs and drabs and pieces. And this will not do, inasmuch as the green programme is of a piece and must be taken whole (Goodin 1992). Thus democratic politics is both ineffective and corrupting to those who engage in its endless give-and-take. The motto of one radical or 'dark green' group, Earth First!, is 'No compromise in defence of Mother Earth.' And since compromise is central to democratic politics, many radical environmentalists are deeply suspicious of, if not hostile to, conventional democratic politics. They therefore maintain that the greens should remain a radical and politically pure movement, aloof from partisan wrangling and pressure-group politics, and immune from temptations to tailor their message to appeal to a broad band of the electorate.[3] After all, nature is not merely one 'interest group' among many; its interests are not on a par with those of (say) corporate polluters and should not be viewed as negotiable.

Other greens are antipathetic toward democracy for still other reasons. Some hold that the environmental crisis may prove so severe and protracted as to give rise to authoritarian rule, whilst others predict that the complexity of environmental problems may require rule by expert elites (Ophuls 1977; Catton 1980; Heilbroner 1991). They do not, to be sure, necessarily *advocate* authoritarian solutions to environmental problems; they merely fear that democratic politics may not be up to the sheer scale, complexity and difficulty of the task at hand.

Most greens, however, profess to be grass-roots democrats who favour widespread political participation and decision-making by majorities at the local level. 'Think globally and act locally' is their motto and recurring admonition. As Andrew Dobson notes, 'Greens argue for a radically participatory form of society in which discussion takes place and explicit consent is asked for and given across the widest possible range of political and social issues. All this implies the kind of decentralist politics associated with the Green movement' (1990: 25–6). Whilst this tenet is central to green democratic theory, it can and often

---

[3] Tensions of this sort split *die Grünen*, the German Green party, in the 1980s. Self-described realists or 'realos' wanted the Greens to be a political *party*, while purists or 'fundis' wanted the Greens to remain a political *movement* that brooked no compromise on environmental values.

does, in practice, result in distinctly anti-green outcomes. Consider, by way of example, the current controversy over whether to drill for oil in Alaska's ecologically fragile and pristine Arctic National Wildlife Refuge. American environmentalists are ardently opposed to drilling. Yet survey after survey shows that if the decision were made locally and democratically by Alaskans themselves, roads, oil rigs and pipelines would quickly cover Alaska's North Slope, the very real threat of oil spills would be ever present, and little or no heed would be given to the destruction of wildlife habitat or of the starkly beautiful scenery of that remote place. An overwhelming majority of Alaskans are more interested in jobs and in boosting the state and local economy than in protecting the natural environment. And they blame the (as they see it) anti-democratic 'environmental elitists' from the 'lower 48' for opposing the drilling that would raise their incomes and standard of living.

In light of such considerations, some greens have suggested that decentralised grass-roots democracy is not necessarily friendly to the environment, and that local control can result in environmental degradation that can extend far beyond local boundaries (Foreman 1991). In practice, then, democracy need not result in green outcomes. As Robert Goodin observes,

To advocate democracy is to advocate procedures, to advocate environmentalism is to advocate substantive outcomes: what guarantees can we have that the former procedures will yield the latter sorts of outcomes? (Goodin 1992: 168)

Apparently the answer is: none. For, as Michael Saward notes, 'If governments, to be democratic, must respond to the felt wishes of a majority of citizens, then greens have little comeback if a majority does not want green outcomes' (1996: 93). In short, environmentalists have good grounds for fearing at least some democratically decided outcomes.

Might there be some way to allay those fears while, at the same time, avoiding anti-democratic tendencies or temptations? Might there be an alternative and distinctly green conception of democracy that retains the virtues and yet avoids the vices and shortcomings of democracy as heretofore theorised and practiced? The answer to both questions, I believe, is yes.

Towards biocracy

It is by now a truism that 'democracy' is a contested concept – if not 'essentially contested' (Gallie 1955–6), then at least historically and contingently contested (Ball 1988: 13–14). Contests over the meaning of the concept have come from various quarters: from the 'protectionist' theory of Jeremy Bentham and James Mill, the 'educative' theory of John Stuart Mill, the 'elite' theory proposed by Joseph Schumpeter (and picked up by Anthony Downs and others: Ball 1988: ch. 6), and the more recent attempts by Iris Young (1990) and others to recast democracy in a 'multicultural' mould. But perhaps the greatest challenge yet comes from the environmental or green movement which has of late been tugging 'democracy' in a distinctly green direction. We now need to ask how 'ecodemocracy' or perhaps 'biocracy' might differ from earlier variants of democratic theory and practice – all of which are, as Dryzek notes, anthropocentric to their core: 'democracy, however contested a concept, and in however many varieties it has appeared in the last two and a half thousand years, is, if nothing else, anthropocentric' (Dryzek 2000: 147). And, as Freya Matthews observes, liberal democracy – the dominant variant in the modern West – owes much, as the adjective 'liberal' implies, to 'liberalism [which] as it stands is of course anthropocentric: it takes human interest as the measure of all value' (quoted in Dryzek 2000: 147). But she casts her critical net too narrowly, for all the major ideologies – and the variants of democracy to which they give rise – are anthropocentric; all assume without argument that human interests are paramount.[4]

This is exactly what green democracy or biocracy does *not* do. While biocracy certainly does not exclude human interests, neither does it – like liberal democracy, social democracy and people's democracy – place them at the apex of a hierarchical pyramid of moral considerability; rather, biocracy counts human interests as one set within a web of complexly interdependent interests.[5]

How then might we move from democracy to biocracy? The relatively new field of 'conceptual history', with its attendant theory of 'conceptual change', suggests an answer: concepts lose old meanings and acquire new ones through a process of external challenge and immanent

---

[4] Western liberal democracies have had, on the whole, better environmental records than communist governments. For a particularly depressing account of the ways in which one communist regime deliberately despoiled the natural environment, see Shapiro 2001.

[5] Some green theorists (e.g. Goodin 1992: 30–41) hold that 'natural objects' such as animals and ecosystems have value in and of themselves and quite apart from any value that humans might place upon them. I believe that this is a misleading way to talk, and therefore to think, about ecological value. After all, greens emphasise the *interdependence* of natural entities; but to speak of their having 'intrinsic value' is to speak of their having value independently of one another. I believe it better to say that natural objects have interdependent value within natural systems. For example, wolves have value insofar as they cull weak, lame or otherwise defective members of the deer population, thereby aiding that species. And since deer eat and sometimes extinguish certain plants within fragile ecosystems, keeping their numbers down aids those ecosystems. See, further, Johnson 1991: chs. 3–6; Ball 2003: 539–43.

critique, in which internal tensions and contradictions within belief systems are detected and exposed and supporting arguments criticised and countered (Ball 1983, 1988: ch. 1; Farr 1989). I believe that 'democracy' as presently conceived is now being subjected to the 'ecological challenge' and is open to such an immanent critique and transformation.

If there is a single – and singular – feature that distinguishes green democracy from other variants, it is surely this: the immense widening of the moral and political community to encompass what Aldo Leopold called the entire 'biotic community'. The idea of such an inclusive community is predicated on a 'land ethic [which] enlarges the boundaries of the community to include soils, waters, plants and animals, or collectively, the land' (Leopold 1949: 240). This ethic also takes into account the interests of future generations of humans, non-humans and the ecosystems and habitats that sustain them. 'In short', Leopold writes, 'a land ethic changes the role of *Homo sapiens* from conqueror of the land-community to plain member and citizen of it. It implies respect for his fellow-members, and also respect for the community as such' (Leopold 1949: 240). Leopold was a forest ecologist, not a political theorist; but his conception of the biotic community and the land ethic have been adopted and adapted by green political theorists. As Mike Mills notes, 'If we consider what greens argue is distinctive about their ideology, their political theory and their practical concerns, it is invariably the case that these can be reduced to a concern to expand the moral community' (Mills 1996: 102). By this he means 'the increase in the number of individuals, species or systems which become morally considerable' (Mills 1996: 113 n. 2). Since the issue of the expansion of the moral community 'is logically prior to all others' (1996: 97), we need to attend to arguments against and in favour of its expansion.

There are several reasons for expanding the moral community by widening the circle of moral considerability. Perhaps surprisingly, some of these reasons are less radical or novel than one might suspect. Indeed, two are very old and quite traditional. The first is the Golden Rule: treat others as you would wish to be treated. It does *not* say that these others must or can only be presently living human beings. It seems no great stretch to say that the 'others' include members of past and future, as well as present, generations. I would not (for example) wish to have my health and wellbeing threatened by toxic wastes generated and carelessly disposed of by long-dead ancestors; and I am quite certain that my distant descendants will feel the same way about my actions. A second reason for expanding the moral community draws upon the venerable principle *quod omnes similiter tangit ab omnibus comprobetur* – 'what touches all should be decided by all'[6] – which, if taken seriously, suggests that some way must be found to take account of the interests of future people and of creatures who have interests that they are unable to articulate and defend. Not surprisingly, the political and institutional implications of this ancient principle are far-reaching. A more inclusive land ethic or ecocentric outlook will require innovations in democratic theory and institutional design and practice. The result would then be, not a democracy comprised exclusively of presently existing humans, but rather, as Robyn Eckersley puts it, 'a democracy of the affected' or, perhaps more precisely, 'a democracy *for* the affected' (2000: 119). And those whose interests are or will be affected by democratically made decisions would include future generations of human beings and animals, and the ecosystems and habitats that sustain them. Politically and democratically speaking, the changes required to recognise and respect these interests would amount to nothing less than 'enfranchising the earth' (Goodin 1996).

In what follows I shall use the term 'interest' to mean simply this: x is in A's interest if x is necessary for and/or conducive to A's functioning and/or flourishing. A need not be consciously aware of or able to articulate the claim that x is in A's interest. For example, I did not know (until quite recently) that I, like all humans, need to ingest very small or 'trace' amounts of zinc in order to bolster my immune system and thereby ward off illness or infection. Whether I know it or not, it is in my interest to ingest trace amounts of this otherwise toxic metal. My ignorance did not preclude my having an interest. Indeed it would be absurd to say that I didn't have an interest in ingesting small doses of zinc until I knew I did, and was able to articulate and communicate that fact. The upshot is that interests can be 'objective' and unknown to and unarticulated by the bearers of those interests. Moreover, A need not be alive and present in order for us to ascribe interests to A.

Had I space to do so, I would argue that animals and future generations of humans have interests that are morally considerable and are, if not full members of our moral community, then at least adjunct members. But since I have elsewhere attempted to advance arguments in favour of (and refute arguments against) expanding the circle of moral considerability to include future generations of humans and non-human animals (Ball 2005), I shall not repeat myself here. Here I shall simply assert without argument that we treat future generations fairly and justly

---

[6] Justinian, *Codex*, 5.59.5.2. Although this passage has become a mainstay of the 'protectionist' theory of democracy, it referred originally to the duties of tutors. I thank Quentin Skinner for correcting my Latin and for supplying the reference to the original source.

by not avoidably harming or disadvantaging them. We may not have a positive or 'thick' duty to help them; but at the very least we have a negative or 'thin' duty to refrain from harming them. This is Mill's harm principle extended into the indefinite future.[7] We should also leave our distant descendants with their autonomy intact and with more choices instead of fewer (Ball 2001: 103). To cite two admittedly anthropocentric examples of the latter: if whales become extinct, future people will not have the option of watching whales migrate and give birth to their young in the Gulf of California. If we dam the Grand Canyon to create a large and very deep lake, future people will not have options that we now enjoy, including rafting down the ofttimes frightening and dangerous Colorado River as it wends its way through the canyon. Surely we have a minimal moral duty to bequeath to posterity a world as rich and varied and beautiful – and, yes, as frightening and dangerous – as the one we now inhabit. We have, in short, a duty to treat future people as members of our moral community, with all the rights and privileges that go with adjunct if not full membership. They are, as it were, members-in-waiting, with interests that are as morally considerable as our own.

The reasons standardly given for denying that animals have interests and for excluding them from membership in the moral community turn out, upon close critical examination, to be much less sound than one might believe.[8] We, along with animals and future people (and the natural systems that sustain us all), belong to the same community – the biotic community – and our interests are not only morally but *politically* considerable. And that is because laws and policies are the means by which interests are recognised, respected and protected by law. But why should the politics of environmental protection be *democratic* politics? Can't the interests of animals, future people and ecosystems be (better?) protected by a non- or even anti-democratic authoritarian regime? Or, to put it another way, how and why make the move from *moral* to *political* considerability to *democratic-political* considerability? I shall suggest one answer here, and another closely related one in my conclusion. Consider the following argument from analogy. Suppose that black former slaves in the American South had been told after the Civil War, 'We white, privileged, propertied males now recognise you as members of our moral

---

[7] To discuss whether liberalism (or any other ideology) has the conceptual resources required to recognise, respect and protect future generations of people (and perhaps animals as well), while relevant to the present discussion of democracy, is not part of my purpose here; but see Ball 2001: 100–8. For a different view, see Plumwood 1995.

[8] See Singer 1988; Johnson 1991; and James Sterba's critique of anthropocentrism in the present volume.

community; we acknowledge that you have morally considerable interests which we will take into account; but we will not extend political recognition or representation, or enfranchise you, now or ever. All you need do is trust us to recognise, respect and promote your interests.' Suppose also that female suffragists had been told the same thing. Would either group have been satisfied with receiving moral but not political – and more especially democratic-political – recognition and representation of their interests? Obviously not, and for very good reason. For to extend moral recognition but not democratic-political representation does not offer adequate (or indeed any) protection of their interests; it is to leave those interests in the uncertain care of those who may well have conflicting interests. In a democracy, unlike an authoritarian or totalitarian system, there are checks and restraints upon those who claim to represent and protect the interests of their constituents but do not in fact do so.[9] A free press, freedom of speech and discussion, and other features of modern liberal democracy make for a degree of openness and accountability that is absent in authoritarian systems. Any democratically elected representative who claims to represent the interests of nature but instead favours the interests of its destroyers can, in principle if not always in practice, be criticised, exposed and called to account.

This points us in the direction of a greatly expanded democracy or biocracy in which we living and legally enfranchised humans view ourselves, and act, as plain members and citizens of the broader biotic community who represent its interests as well as our own. This is of course easy to say; but it might prove damnably difficult to do as a matter of political practice.

Biocracy in practice: institutional implications

One of the chief challenges posed by ecodemocracy or biocracy is how – by what institutional means – might constituencies without voices be represented? That is, how might the interests of animals, ecosystems and future generations be recognised and represented? The typical and traditional route – extending the franchise to include them (as with

---

[9] The *locus classicus* of this 'protectionist' argument for democratic representation is James Mill (1992 [1820]). Mill was also a paternalist who held that the interests of women and children are encapsulated or 'included in' the interests of husbands and fathers. In representing the interests of future generations and of nature, however, such paternalism may well be defensible and, indeed, unavoidable. For a defence of 'encapsulated interests' see Goodin 1996: 841–4. For a variation on the protectionist defence of democracy, see Dobson 1996b. And for a critique of this approach, see Plumwood, this volume.

blacks and women) – is obviously a non-starter. We cannot, except in a metaphorical sense, enfranchise the earth (Goodin 1996). Democratic politics have heretofore been predicated on an anthropocentric perspective and a relatively short time horizon. But technological innovations – and perhaps particularly nuclear power and the accompanying production of very long-lived radioactive wastes – have given the present generation of human beings the capacity to affect people, animals and ecosystems tens of thousands of years into the future. Indeed, for the first time *ever*, geological time scales must now figure in our moral calculations of the costs and consequences of our actions (Ball 2001: 101–2). This is especially true of the decisions we make (or fail to make) collectively, as democratic citizens. And this will in turn require a reconfiguring or reconceptualisation of democracy in the direction of biocracy. This chapter will conclude by briefly exploring a number of possible and perhaps desirable conceptual, theoretical and institutional innovations.

One of the cornerstones of green political thought is that green democracy will ideally and perhaps even necessarily be decentralised direct democracy – that is, a system in which citizens participate locally and directly in making decisions that affect all. I believe this to be a wholly inadequate view that requires radical rethinking. My view is that green democracy or biocracy cannot, in practice or in principle, be both direct and participatory in the sense that all those affected can come together at particular times and places to discuss, debate and decide matters of common concern; it must instead be indirect and representative, at least for those who are not literally present and participating. And that is simply because the range of creatures and entities who have interests – but are without voice and agency – is much more extensive than most democratic theorists have heretofore recognised (or rather, perhaps, theorised in any adequate way). The interests of such creatures and entities must, in the nature of the case, be *represented* by humans who do have voice and agency.[10] Let me attempt to unpack and clarify these claims.

First, in a biocracy or 'democracy of the affected', do those affected need to be present to communicate and defend their interests before we

---

[10] Andrew Dobson, in criticising an earlier draft of this chapter, objected that the interests of any creature can be 'represented without that representation taking a democratic form. A lawyer, for example, might represent my interests, but not do so democratically.' On the contrary, I 'elect' my lawyer; and if he does not, in my judgement, represent my interests adequately, I can remove him from the 'office' to which I 'elected' him.

can take those interests into account? The answer is no, and is contained in the very meaning of the term 'representation'. As Hanna Pitkin notes,

representation means ... *re-presentation*, a making present again ... [T]aken generally, [representation] means the making present *in some sense* of something which is nevertheless not present literally or in fact ... [I]n representation something *not* literally present is considered as present in a nonliteral sense. (Pitkin 1967: 8–9)

And what is being represented in a legislative assembly is not people (or even animals or ecosystems) per se, but their *interests*. To say that my elected representative 'represents me' is not to say that she speaks or acts as I would if I were present in some legislative assembly (a frightening thought, that!); it is, rather, a shorthand way of saying that she represents my interests and/or the interests of those who resemble me in some relevant respect(s).[11]

Secondly, as I noted earlier, biocracy will be vastly more inclusive than democracy as presently understood, i.e. a democracy of those human beings now living and legally enfranchised. The moral and political community will be coextensive with the biotic community. Among the *political* objections to such a widening of the moral community, the most commonly voiced are the following. For starters, even if we acknowledge that future generations, non-human animals and ecosystems have interests, these entities – unlike us – are unable to speak or give voice to their interests, tastes and preferences; and it is impossible to represent or otherwise take account of that which is unsaid and perhaps unsayable. After all, theorists from Aristotle to Habermas have agreed that politics is about discussion and debate which is made possible by speech – a point nicely captured by Bertrand de Jouvenel's observation that 'the elementary political process is the action of mind upon mind through speech' (Jouvenel 1957: 304). No speech, no communication; no communication, no politics – democratic or otherwise. Without speech (or at least a signalling system of some kind), political preferences cannot be communicated and policy proposals debated and decided upon.

This seemingly weighty objection can be countered in a number of ways. The first is that we are concerned not with the 'tastes' or 'preferences' of future generations of humans or of animals and ecosystems but (as noted earlier) with their *interests*. It makes little or no sense to speak of ecosystems (for example) having preferences; but it makes perfect sense to speak of their having interests (as defined earlier).

---

[11] For further discussion, see Michael Saward on 'representation', chapter 11, below.

Moreover, they need not know about or be able to articulate these interests in order for us to recognise, respect and protect them. Democracy does indeed require speech and deliberation and listening (Bickford 1996); but listening need not be coextensive with hearing human speech. An inclusive democracy or biocracy requires not only or literally listening to those who can speak – i.e. human beings – but to entities that are dumb but not mute.

Here it might help, I think, to draw a distinction between two kinds of listening: listening *to* and listening *for*. When I was a young father I would listen for (and not merely to) my infant son's cries, especially cries of distress. He did not say (because he could not yet speak) 'My nappy needs changing' or 'I'm hungry; feed me' or 'I want attention; hold me.' But these were on various occasions what he meant, and communicated to me. Nor is this communicative capacity confined to human beings. My dog and two cats likewise communicate with me. When Rosie, my aged black lab, scratches at the back door, or picks up a tennis ball and drops it at my feet, or wakes me by nuzzling my face with a cold wet nose at 6 a.m. – none of which are 'tricks' she was taught – I know exactly what she wants to do, and wants me to do. The same is true of my two middle-aged cats, Sid Vicious and Tabby, who are markedly more direct and less polite in communicating with me. 'Listening *for*' is a way of paying attention to communications that do not necessarily come via human speech. Listening for is closely akin to what Robert Lane (1962) calls 'listening with the third ear', i.e. picking up on things that are not spoken literally and articulately, but are accessible through sympathetic listening (where 'listening' is understood in its most extended sense), attentiveness to 'body language' and to other non-verbal cues.

In a biocracy, however, 'communication' can and must be construed more broadly still, to encompass communications coming from such non-sentient entities as ecosystems, habitats and soils. John Dryzek argues suggestively that we can 'listen' to (or, as I would prefer to say, listen for) nature's cries of distress. He contends – quite rightly, I think – that nature can and does 'communicate' with us. Not verbally, to be sure, but in myriad other ways:

> while ecosystems cannot literally 'speak' to human subjects, they can communicate in other ways ... If the topsoil on which my crops depend is shrinking, then clearly nature is 'telling' me something. (Dryzek 1987: 207; see further Dryzek 2000: ch. 6)

This will of course require attentiveness of the sort that makes us attuned not merely to human communication but to the unspoken suffering of others – where 'the other' extends well beyond human beings to include not only other sentient beings but the ecosystems and habitats that it is in their interest to conserve, preserve and protect. One cannot, after all, claim to recognise and respect – and still less represent – the interests of animals and future people while, at the same time, degrading or destroying the habitats and ecosystems upon which they (will) depend. To paraphrase Kant, whoever wills the end likewise wills the means to that end. To endorse green ends without supporting the means necessary to achieve them is incoherent or, worse, hypocritical. We must, as Goodin (1992) contends, subscribe both to a green theory of value that specifies the ends and, simultaneously, a green theory of agency that specifies the means required to achieve those ends. This sort of stereoscopic sensibility must be a foundational feature of green thought and action generally, and of green *political* theory and practice in particular. And, not least, this perspective must take into account the interests of not-yet-living and non-human others. Such a sensibility requires a mode or manner of 'enlarged thinking' (Eckersley 2000: 128) that is, at present, relatively rare.

How then to make such enlarged thinking less rare and more common? One obvious way is through the kind of civic education that includes, as a central constitutive feature, environmental education. Such education would, to borrow a distinction from Wendell Berry (1981), require not only 'learning about' environmental problems and their possible solutions but 'learning from' nature itself by listening to and for what nature communicates to us. An education of this sort will enable living human citizens of a biocracy to think of themselves – and to act – as plain members and citizens of an inclusive biotic community. Thus there is ineluctably an educative dimension to biocracy. And what this education imparts is not merely the acquistion of 'information' or 'data'; it is the formation of individual and civic character of a distinctively biocentric sort. To sketch that civic character type in bold but admittedly crude outline: the character of the biocratic citizen is not acquisitive but contributive to the larger and more inclusive biotic community. Biocratic citizens will have an ecocentric outlook, viewing themselves and their species as a small but important part of a much larger and more inclusive biotic community; they will be motivated by a love of and respect for the natural world and its myriad creatures; their satisfactions and pleasures will not, in the main, be materialistic; their wants will be few and satisfiable in sustainable ways; they will whenever possible act non-violently; their time horizon will extend into the further future; and their moral and political community will consist of creatures and entities which are not human, not necessarily sentient and not (yet) present. Only agents and citizens with such characters can represent the interests of nature.

Conclusion

It has been *de rigueur* in recent democratic theorising to denigrate the 'protectionist' theory of democracy, according to which the point and purpose of democratic politics is to protect the interests of various constituencies, and to laud the uplifting and educative effects of deliberative democracy. Without wishing to deny the latter, I believe that biocracy offers a bracing combination of both theories. As I've just emphasised, there is a strongly educative element in biocracy inasmuch as one learns not only from other sentient and articulate contemporaries but from nature itself. Yet, as I suggested earlier, biocracy also necessarily relies on some version of the protectionist theory. The interests of non-deliberating entities – future people, animals, ecosystems – require protection. How these interests are to be given voice and protected and by whom is a matter for debate, deliberation and reflection by those who are capable of doing so. Protecting and accommodating those interests along with our own is best accomplished by the kind of trans-generational and trans-species representative democracy that I call biocracy. The idea of representing the interests of those who cannot speak or vote is really not so radical, after all. For we already do this in the case of minors, severely retarded adults and others. (They don't elect trustees to represent their interests; but the terms and conditions of trusteeship are set by democratically enacted laws.) Such a practice is therefore not a radical departure from, but merely an extension of, present practices. We, the living and articulate, are trustees and stewards.

How is such stewardship to be exercised, and by whom? Ideally, by all of us, both in our capacities as individuals and as citizens. But, short of that, we might elect or have our elected representatives appoint spokespersons or ombudsmen to reflect on and articulate nature's interests before larger legislative bodies (Dobson 1996b: 164–5). Or perhaps the members of various environmental organisations can, as they already do, articulate and lobby for those interests (Goodin 1996). Or we might establish an 'Environmental Defenders Office, staffed by a multidisciplinary team and charged with responsibility for environmental monitoring, political advocacy and legal representation' of nature's interests (Eckersley 2000: 130).[12] In any case, some sentient and

---

[12] In the United States, alas, supposedly independent regulatory agencies (such as the Environmental Protection Agency) have lagely been taken over by the very interests and

articulate human being(s), acting in some civic or political capacity, must listen for, articulate, and protect the interests of nature.

I began by noting that there is no logically necessary connection between green values and democratic politics. Even so, there are a number of affinities between them, including the following. The first can be posed negatively, as a question: why can't an authoritarian system represent and take into account the interests of (say) animals and eco-systems (as indeed Hitler's Nazi regime purported to do) as well as, if not better than, a democracy? One answer, as J. S. Mill noted, is that authoritarian governments discourage or forbid deliberation and the educative character-formation that results from participation, discussion and debate; they encourage or even require that their subjects have 'passive characters' (Mill 1951 [1861]: 283). Authoritarian regimes replace education with indoctrination, and rational persuasion with propaganda and coercion. A second answer is that authoritarian regimes also lack the degree and kind of political and legal accountability that characterises democracy. By contrast, a democracy – or, better, a biocracy – requires a civically (and environmentally) educated and engaged citizenry whose members have what Mill called 'active char-acters'. Such active and attentive citizens demand accountability from their government and their representatives. Finally, though not least, democracy is by its very nature committed to diversity: authoritarian rule is, politically speaking, a monoculture, whilst democracy is a mul-ticulture consisting of diverse and sometimes cacophonous voices, interests and agendas. Democracy, reconceptualised and retheorised as biocracy, widens the circle of those whose interests are included and whose 'voices' are heard and heeded.

References

Ball, Terence (1983). 'Contradiction and Critique in Political Theory', in John S. Nelson (ed.), *What Should Political Theory Be Now?* Albany: State University of New York Press, 127–68.

(1988). *Transforming Political Discourse: Political Theory and Critical Conceptual History*. Oxford: Blackwell.

(2001). 'New Ethics for Old? Or, How (Not) to Think About Future Generations', *Environmental Politics* **10**.1: 89–110.

(2003). 'Green Political Theory', in Terence Ball and Richard Bellamy (eds.), *The Cambridge History of Twentieth-Century Political Thought*. Cambridge: Cambridge University Press, 534–50.

industries that they are supposed to regulate. In light of the so-called 'capture' theory of regulatory agencies, the prospects for Eckersley's Environmental Defenders Office are not particularly promising, at least in the USA.

Ball, Terence (2005). 'Duties Beyond Borders: The Expanding Ethical Universe', in Peter French and Jason A. Short (eds.), *War and Border Crossings: Ethics When Cultures Clash*. Totowa, N.J.: Rowman and Littlefield, 165–76.

Berry, Wendell (1981). *The Gift of Good Land*. San Francisco: North Point Press.

Bickford, Susan (1996). *The Dissonance of Democracy: Listening, Conflict and Citizenship*. Ithaca, N.Y.: Cornell University Press.

Bramwell, Anna (1985). *Blood and Soil: Richard Walther Darré and Hitler's 'Green Party'*. Bourne End, Buckhinghamshire: Kensal.

Catton, William R. (1980). *Overshoot: The Ecological Basis of Revolutionary Change*. Urbana: University of Illinois Press.

Dobson, Andrew (1990). *Green Political Thought*. London: Routledge.

    (1996a). 'Democratising Green Theory: Preconditions and Principles', in Brian Doherty and Marius de Geus (eds.), *Democracy and Green Political Thought*. London: Routledge, pp. 132–48.

    (1996b) 'Representative Democracy and the Environment', in William Lafferty and James Meadowcroft (eds.), *Democracy and the Environment: Problems and Prospects*, Cheltenham: Elgar, 124–39.

Doherty, Brian, and de Geus, Marius (eds.) (1996). *Democracy and Green Political Thought*, London: Routledge.

Dryzek, John S. (1987). *Rational Ecology: Environment and Political Economy*. Oxford: Blackwell.

    (2000). *Deliberative Democracy and Beyond: Liberals, Critics, Contestations*. Oxford: Oxford University Press.

Eckersley, Robyn (1999). 'The Discourse Ethic and the Problem of Representing Nature', *Environmental Politics* **8**.2: 24–49.

    (2000). 'Deliberative Democracy, Ecological Representation and Risk: Towards a Democracy of the Affected', in Michael Saward (ed.), *Democratic Innovation: Deliberation, Representation and Association*. London and New York: Routledge, pp. 117–32.

Farr, James (1989). 'Understanding Conceptual Change Politically', in Terence Ball, James Farr and Russell L. Hanson (eds.), *Political Innovation and Conceptual Change*. Cambridge: Cambridge University Press, pp. 24–49.

Ferry, Luc (1995). *The New Ecological Order*, trans. Carol Volk. Chicago: University of Chicago Press.

Foreman, Dave (1991). *Confessions of an Eco-Warrior*. New York: Crown.

Gallie, W. B. (1955–6). 'Essentially Contested Concepts', *Proceedings of the Aristotelian Society* **56**: 167–98.

Goodin, Robert E. (1992). *Green Political Theory*. Cambridge: Polity.

    (1996). 'Enfranchising the Earth, and Its Alternatives', *Political Studies* **44**: pp. 835–49.

Gottlieb, Roger S. (ed.) (1997). *The Ecological Community: Environmental Challenges for Philosophy, Politics, and Morality*. New York: Routledge.

Heilbroner, Robert (1991). *An Enquiry Into the Human Prospect*, 3rd ed. New York: Norton.

Johnson, Lawrence E. (1991). *A Morally Deep World: An Essay on Moral Significance and Environmental Ethics*. Cambridge: Cambridge University Press.

Jouvenel, Bertrand de (1957). *Sovereignty: An Enquiry into the Public Good*, trans. J. F. Huntington. Chicago: University of Chicago Press.

Lane, Robert E. (1962). *Political Ideology: Why the American Common Man Believes What He Does*. New York: Free Press.

Leopold, Aldo (1949). *A Sand County Almanac*. New York: Oxford University Press.

Mill, James (1992 [1820]). 'Government', in *James Mill: Political Writings*, ed. Terence Ball. Cambridge: Cambridge University Press, pp. 1–42.

Mill, John Stuart (1951 [1861]). *Considerations on Representative Government*, in *Utilitarianism, Liberty, and Representative Government*, ed. A. D. Lindsay. New York: Dutton.

Mills, Mike (1996). '*Green Democracy: The Search for an Ethical Solution*', in Brian Doherty and Marius de Geus (eds.), *Democracy and Green Political Thought*. London: Routledge, pp. 97–114.

Ophuls, William (1977). *Ecology and the Politics of Scarcity*. San Francisco: W. H. Freeman.

Pitkin, Hannah F. (1967). *The Concept of Representation*. Berkeley: University of California Press.

Plumwood, Val (1995). 'Has Democracy Failed Ecology? An Ecofeminist Perspective', *Environmental Politics* **4**: 134–68.

Pois, Robert A. (1986). *National Socialism and the Religion of Nature*. London: Croom Helm.

Sagoff, Mark (1988). *The Economy of the Earth*. Cambridge: Cambridge University Press.

Saward, Michael (1996). 'Must Democrats be Environmentalists?', in Brian Doherty and Marius de Geus (eds.), *Democracy and Green Political Thought*. London: Routledge, pp. 79–96.

Shapiro, Judith (2001). *Mao's War Against Nature*. Cambridge: Cambridge University Press.

Singer, Peter (1988). *Animal Liberation*, 2nd ed. New York: New York Review Books.

Wenz, Peter S. (1997). 'Environmentalism and Human Oppression', in Roger S. Gottlieb (ed.), *The Ecological Community: Environmental Challenges for Philosophy, Politics and Morality*. New York: Routledge, pp. 3–21.

Young, Iris Marion (1990). *Justice and the Politics of Difference*. Princeton: Princeton University Press.

Zimmerman, Michael E. (1997). 'Ecofascism: A Threat to American Environmentalism?', in Roger S. Gottlieb (ed.), *The Ecological Community: Environmental Challenges for Philosophy, Politics and Morality*. New York: Routledge, pp. 229–54.

9 Justice

James P. Sterba

Justice requires giving what is deserved. That in turn requires figuring out both what is deserved and who it is that deserves it. Here priority should be given to *who* it is that is deserving rather than *what* it is that is deserved. This is because the more there are who are deserving, other things being equal, the fewer good things each of them can deserve. Political philosophers have long recognised this priority when they are trying to determine what the human members of a particular society or state deserve; they have acknowledged that this question cannot be conclusively resolved without taking into account distant peoples and future generations as also deserving. Unfortunately, most political philosophers tend to stop there. Even environmentalists who argue for environmental justice and oppose the imposition of undeserved risks to health and wellbeing on people of colour usually start from an anthropocentric perspective; they do not take the next logical step of asking whether non-human living beings are also deserving. In this chapter, in a quest for a truly non-arbitary, non-question-begging conception of justice, I will ask that question and answer it in the affirmative. Having established that all individual living beings, as well as ecosystems, are deserving, I will go on to begin to establish what it is that they deserve.

The moral deservingness of all living beings

Most political philosophers, as I have indicated, are committed to anthropocentrism; they just assume without argument that all or only human beings are deserving or have moral status. In order to show that a particular version of non-anthropocentrism is morally preferable to anthropocentrism, then, I will need a really good argument that non-human living beings are deserving. A really good argument, by definition, must be a non-question-begging argument. So what we need is a non-question-begging argument that non-human living beings are deserving, which is to say that they should count morally. Is there such an argument?

Consider. We clearly have the capacity of entertaining and acting upon both anthropocentric reasons that take only the interests of humans into account and non-anthropocentric reasons that also take the interests of non-human living beings into account. Given that capacity, the question we are seeking to answer is what sort of reasons it would be rational for us to accept.

Now right off, we might think that we have non-question-begging grounds for only taking the interests of humans into account, namely, the possession by human beings of the distinctive traits of rationality and moral agency. But while human beings clearly do have such distinctive traits, the members of non-human species also have distinctive traits that humans lack, like the homing ability of pigeons, the speed of the cheetah, and the ruminative ability of sheep and cattle. Nor will it do to claim that the distinctive traits that humans possess are more valuable than the distinctive traits that members of other species possess, because there is no non-question-begging standpoint from which to justify that claim. From a human standpoint, rationality and moral agency are more valuable than any of the distinctive traits found in non-human species, since, as humans, we would not be better off if we were to trade in those traits for the distinctive traits found in non-human species. Yet the same holds true of non-human species. Generally, pigeons, cheetahs, sheep and cattle would not be better off if they were to trade in their distinctive traits for the distinctive traits of other species. So there would appear to be no non-question-begging perspective from which to judge that distinctively human traits are more valuable than the distinctive traits possessed by other species, and so no non-question-begging justification for only taking anthropocentric reasons into account. Judged from a non-question-begging perspective, we would seemingly have to grant the prima facie relevance of both anthropocentric and non-anthropocentric reasons to rational choice and then try to determine which reasons we would be rationally required to act upon, all things considered.

In this regard, there are two kinds of cases that must be considered. First, there are cases in which there is a conflict between the relevant anthropocentric and non-anthropocentric reasons. Second, there are cases in which there is no such conflict.

It seems obvious that where there is no conflict and both reasons are conclusive reasons of their kind, both reasons should be acted upon. In such contexts, we should do what is favoured both by anthropocentrism and by non-anthropocentrism.

Now, when we turn to rationally assess the relevant reasons in conflict cases, three solutions are possible. First, we could say that anthropocentric reasons always have priority over conflicting non-anthropocentric reasons. Second, we could say, just the opposite, that non-anthropocentric reasons always have priority over conflicting anthropocentric reasons. Third, we could say that some kind of compromise is rationally required. In this compromise, sometimes anthropocentric reasons would have priority over non-anthropocentric reasons, and sometimes non-anthropocentric reasons would have priority over anthropocentric reasons.

Once the conflict is described in this manner, the third solution can be seen to be the one that is rationally required. This is because the first and second solutions give exclusive priority to one class of relevant reasons over the other, and only a question-begging justification can be given for such an exclusive priority. Only by employing the third solution, and sometimes giving priority to anthropocentric reasons, and sometimes giving priority to nonanthropocentric reasons, can we avoid a question-begging resolution. What we need, therefore, are conflict resolution principles that specify these priorities.

Conflict resolution principles

But how are these priorities to be specified? Now surely, even if we hold that all living beings should count morally, we can justify a preference for humans on grounds of preservation. Accordingly, we have

A Principle of Human Preservation: Actions that are necessary for meeting one's basic needs or the basic needs of other human beings are permissible even when they require aggressing against the basic needs of individual animals and plants, or even of whole species or ecosystems.[1]

Now needs, in general, if not satisfied, lead to lacks or deficiencies with respect to various standards. The basic needs of humans, if not satisfied, lead to lacks or deficiencies with respect to a standard of a decent life. The basic needs of animals and plants, if not satisfied, lead to lacks or deficiencies with respect to a standard of a healthy life. The basic needs of species and ecosystems, if not satisfied, lead to lacks or deficiencies with respect to a standard of a healthy living system. The means necessary for meeting the basic needs of humans can vary widely from society to society. By contrast, the means necessary for meeting the basic needs of particular species of animals and plants tend to be much less variable. Of course, while only some needs can be clearly classified

---

[1] For the purposes of this paper, I will follow the convention of excluding humans from the denotation of 'animals'.

as basic, and others clearly classified as non-basic, there still are other needs that are more or less difficult to classify. Yet the fact that not every need can be clearly classified as either basic or non-basic, as similarly holds for a whole range of dichotomous concepts like moral / immoral, legal / illegal, living / non-living, human / non-human, should not immobilise us from acting at least with respect to clear cases.

In human ethics, there is no principle that is strictly analogous to this Principle of Human Preservation. There is a principle that permits actions that are necessary for meeting one's own basic needs or the basic needs of other people, even if this requires *failing to meet* (through an act of omission) the basic needs of still other people. For example, we can use our resources to feed ourselves and our families, even if this necessitates failing to meet the basic needs of people in underdeveloped countries. But, in general, we don't have a principle that allows us to *aggress against* (through an act of commission) the basic needs of some people in order to meet our own basic needs or the basic needs of other people to whom we are committed or whom we happen to care about. One place where we do permit aggressing against the basic needs of other people in order to meet our own basic needs or the basic needs of people to whom we are committed or whom we happen to care about is our acceptance of the outcome of life and death struggles in lifeboat cases, where no one has an antecedent right to the available resources. For example, if you had to fight off others in order to secure the last place in a lifeboat for yourself or for a member of your family, we might say that you justifiably aggressed against the basic needs of those whom you fought to meet your own basic needs or the basic needs of the members of your family.

Now the Principle of Human Preservation does not permit aggressing against the basic needs of humans even if it is the only way to meet our own basic needs or the basic needs of other human beings. Rather, this principle is directed at a different range of cases with respect to which we can meet our own basic needs and the basic needs of other humans simply by aggressing against the basic needs of non-human living beings. With respect to those cases, the Principle of Human Preservation permits actions that are necessary for meeting one's own basic needs or the basic needs of other human beings, even when they require aggressing against the basic needs of individual animals and plants, or even of whole species or ecosystems.

Moreover, beyond the prudential value of such implicit non-aggression pacts against fellow humans, there appears to be no morally defensible way to exclude some humans from their protection. This is because any exclusion would fail to satisfy that most basic principle of morality, the 'ought' implies 'can' principle, given that it would impose a sacrifice on at least some humans that would be unreasonable to ask and/or require them to accept.

But what about the interests of non-human living beings? Doesn't the Principle of Human Preservation impose a sacrifice on non-humans that it would be unreasonable to ask and/or require any would-be human guardian of their interests to accept? Surely, we would expect the animals and plants to fight us however they can to prevent being used in this fashion. Why, then, would it not be reasonable for would-be human guardians of the interests of non-human living beings to also try to prevent their being used in this fashion? But this would mean that it would be morally permissible for would-be human guardians of the interest of non-humans to prevent other humans from meeting their own basic needs, or the basic needs of other humans, when this requires aggressing against the basic needs of non-humans. Understood as 'strong permissibility', it would imply that other humans would be *prohibited* from interfering with such preventive actions, even if it meant that their own basic needs would not be met as a result. But surely, this would be an unreasonable requirement for humans to impose on other humans – one that would not accord with the 'ought' implies 'can' principle.

But suppose we understood the permissibility involved to be that of weak permissibility, according to which virtually everything is permissible and virtually nothing is morally required or prohibited. Then the Principle of Human Preservation would imply that it was permissible, in this weak sense, for humans to aggress against the basic needs of non-humans when this was necessary for meeting their own basic needs, and at the same time imply that it was permissible, in this same weak sense, for would-be human guardians of the interests of non-humans to prevent humans from meeting their basic needs by aggressing against the basic needs of non-humans. Since under this interpretation of moral permissibility, virtually nothing is morally required or prohibited, what gets done will tend to depend on the relative power of the contending parties. The purpose of morality, however, is to provide resolutions in just such severe conflict-of-interest situations. Assuming, then, that a moral resolution must satisfy the 'ought' implies 'can' principle, it cannot impose moral requirements on humans that it would be unreasonable for them to accept.[2] This would seem to suggest that the permissibility in the Principle of Human Preservation must be that of strong permissibility, which means that would-be human guardians of the interests of non-humans would be prohibited from interfering with humans who are

---

[2] Nevertheless, as I shall argue, this assumption does not always hold. Moral resolutions can also permit actions that they cannot require, as, for example, in lifeboat cases.

taking the necessary action to meet their basic needs, even when this requires them to aggress against the basic needs of non-humans.

But are there no exceptions to the Principle of Human Preservation? Consider, for example, the following real-life case (Rolston 2001). Thousands of Nepalese have cleared forests, cultivated crops and raised cattle and buffalo on land surrounding the Royal Chitwan National Park in Nepal, but they have also made incursions into the park to meet their own basic needs. In so doing, they have threatened the rhino, the Bengal tiger and other endangered species in the park. Assume that the basic needs of no other humans are at stake.[3] For this case, then, would would-be human guardians of these non-human endangered species be justified in preventing the Nepalese from meeting their basic needs in order to preserve these endangered species? It seems to me that before the basic needs of disadvantaged Nepalese could be sacrificed, the would-be human guardians of these endangered species first would be required to use whatever surplus was available to them and to other humans to meet the basic needs of the Nepalese whom they propose to restrict. Yet clearly it would be very difficult to have first used up all the surplus available to the whole human population for meeting basic human needs. Under present conditions, this requirement has certainly not been met. Moreover, insofar as rich people are unwilling to make the necessary transfers of resources so that poor people would not be led to prey on endangered species in order to survive, the appropriate means of preserving endangered species should be to use force against such rich people rather than against poor people, like the Nepalese near Royal Chitwan National Park.[4] So for all present purposes, the moral permissibility in the Principle of Human Preservation remains that of strong permissibility, which means that other humans are prohibited from interfering with the aggression against non-humans that is permitted by the principle.

Nevertheless, preference for humans can still go beyond bounds, and the bounds that are required are captured by the following:

A Principle of Disproportionality: Actions that meet non-basic or luxury needs of humans are prohibited when they aggress against the basic needs of individual animals and plants, or even of whole species or ecosystems.

---

[3] This did not hold in the real-life case that Rolston actually presented. See my response in Sterba 2001: 451–2.

[4] In a non-ideal world, the Nepalese and their human allies should press against rich people to acquire the available surplus to meet the basic needs of the Nepalese until their own lives are threatened, and then, regrettably, the Nepalese would be justified in preying on endangered species as the only way for them to survive.

This principle is strictly analogous to the principle in human ethics that similarly prohibits meeting some people's non-basic or luxury needs by aggressing against the basic needs of other people. Without a doubt, the adoption of such a principle with respect to non-humans would significantly change the way we live our lives. Such a principle is required, however, if there is to be any substance to the claim that the members of all species count morally. We can no more consistently claim that the members of all species count morally, and yet aggress against the basic needs of some animals or plants whenever this serves our own non-basic or luxury needs, than we can consistently claim that all humans count morally, and then aggress against the basic needs of other human beings whenever this serves our non-basic or luxury needs. Consequently, if saying that species count morally is to mean anything, it must be the case that the basic needs of the members of non-human species are protected against aggressive actions that only serve to meet the non-basic needs of humans, as required by the Principle of Disproportionality. Another way to put the central claim here is to hold that counting morally rules out domination, where domination means aggressing against the basic needs of some for the sake of satisfying the non-basic needs of others.

To see why these limits on preference for the members of the human species are what is required for recognising that species and their members count morally, we need to understand the non-domination of species by analogy with the non-domination of humans. We need to see that just as we claim that humans should not be dominated but treat them differently, so too we can claim that species should not be dominated but also treat them differently. In human ethics, there are various interpretations given to human non-domination that allow for different treatment of humans. In ethical egoism, everyone is *equally at liberty* to pursue his or her own interests, but this allows us to always prefer ourselves to others, who are understood to be like opponents in a competitive game. In libertarianism, everyone has an *equal right to liberty*, but although this imposes some limits on the pursuit of self-interest, it is said to allow us to refrain from helping others in severe need. In welfare liberalism, everyone has an *equal right to welfare and opportunity*, but this need not commit us to providing everyone with exactly the same resources. In socialism, everyone has an *equal right to self-development*, and although this may commit us to providing everyone with the same resources, it still sanctions some degree of self-preference. So just as there are these various ways to interpret the non-domination of humans that still allow us to treat humans differently, there are various ways that we can interpret the non-domination of species that allow us to treat species differently.

Now, one might interpret the non-domination of species in a very strong sense, analogous to the interpretation of non-domination found in socialism. But the kind of non-domination of species that I have defended here is more akin to the non-domination found in welfare liberalism or in libertarianism than it is to the non-domination found in socialism. In brief, this form of non-domination requires that we not aggress against the basic needs of the members of other species for the sake of the non-basic needs of the members of our own species (the Principle of Disproportionality), but it permits us to aggress against the basic needs of the members of other species for the sake of the basic needs of the members of our own species (the Principle of Human Preservation). In this way, I have argued that we can endorse the non-domination of species, while avoiding imposing an unreasonable sacrifice on the members of our own species.

Nevertheless, in order to avoid imposing an unacceptable sacrifice on the members of our own species, we can also justify a preference for humans on grounds of defence. Thus, we have

A Principle of Human Defence: Actions that defend oneself and other human beings against harmful aggression are permissible even when they necessitate killing or harming individual animals or plants, or even destroying whole species or ecosystems.

This Principle of Human Defence allows us to defend ourselves and other human beings from harmful aggression, first against our persons and the persons of other humans beings that we are committed to or happen to care about, and second against our justifiably held property and the justifiably held property of other humans beings that we are committed to or happen to care about.

Here there are two sorts of cases. First, there are cases where humans are defending their own basic needs against harmful aggression from non-humans. In cases of this sort, not only would the human defenders be perfectly justified in defending themselves against aggression, but also no would-be human guardians of non-human interests would be justified on grounds of what we could reasonably require of humans in opposing that defence.

Second, there are cases where humans are defending their non-basic needs against harmful aggression from non-humans which, let's assume, are trying to meet their basic needs. In cases of this sort, would it be justified for would-be human guardians of the interests of non-human living beings to assist them in their aggression against humans? In analogous cases in human ethics, we can see how just this type of aggression can be justified when the poor, who have exhausted all the other means that are legitimately available to them, take from the surplus possessions of the rich just what they require to meet their basic needs. Expressed in terms of an ideal of negative liberty endorsed by libertarians, the justification for this aggression is the priority of the liberty of the poor not to be interfered with when taking from the surplus possessions of the rich what they require to meet their basic needs, over the liberty of the rich not to be interfered with when using their surplus for luxury purposes (Sterba 1998: ch. 3) Expressed in terms of an ideal of fairness endorsed by welfare liberals, the justification for this aggression is the right to welfare that the needy have against those with a surplus. And expressed in terms of an ideal of equality endorsed by socialists, the justification for this aggression is the right that everyone has to equal self-development. Under each of these justifications, would-be guardians of the poor (e.g. real or idealised Robin Hoods) would certainly be justified in assisting the poor in their aggression against the rich. Would then would-be human guardians of non-human living beings (e.g. real or idealised Earth Firsters) be similarly justified in assisting plants and animals in their aggression against the non-basic needs of humans to meet the basic needs of non-humans?

There are two reasons why this is unlikely to be the case. First, as the above justifications from human ethics suggest, achieving either libertarian, welfare liberal or socialist justice for humans will require a considerable redistribution of resources in order to meet the basic needs of humans in both existing and future generations (Sterba 1998: ch.3) So if justice is done in this regard, it will significantly constrain the availability of resources for legitimately meeting non-basic human needs, and thereby limit the possibilities where humans could be justifiably defending their non-basic needs against aggression from non-humans.

Second, the Principle of Disproportionality further constrains those possibilities where humans could be justifiably defending their non-basic needs against aggression from non-humans. This is because the principle prohibits humans from aggressing against the basic needs of non-humans in order to meet their own non-basic needs, and thereby significantly constrains the ways that humans could legitimately acquire resources that are used simply for meeting non-basic human needs. For these two reasons, therefore, the possibilities for legitimately exercising the Principle of Human Defence for the sake of non-basic needs would be drastically limited, thus providing few occasions where would-be human guardians of the interests of non-humans could have any role with regard to its exercise. Of course, some non-basic human needs can still legitimately be met indirectly through meeting basic human needs.

But any attempt by would-be human guardians of the interests of non-humans to help non-humans aggress against the non-basic needs of other humans in such contexts would most likely result in aggressing against the basic needs of those humans as well, and thus would not be justified. Of course, in the non-ideal societies in which we live, many humans still have access to a surplus for meeting non-basic needs. But in these circumstances, other humans would surely have a claim to significant part of that surplus, and much of what remains would have been illegitimately acquired in violation of the Principle of Disproportionality. In any case, the Principle of Human Defence would rarely apply because it presupposes for its application that the means for meeting the non-basic needs of humans have been legitimately acquired.

Lastly, we need one more principle to deal with violations of the above three principles. Accordingly, we have

A Principle of Rectification: Compensation and reparation are required when the other principles have been violated.

Obviously, this principle is somewhat vague, but for those who are willing to abide by the other three principles, it should be possible to remedy that vagueness in practice. Here, too, would-be human guardians of the interests of non-humans could have a useful role figuring out what is appropriate compensation or reparation for violations of the Principle of Disproportionality, and, even more importantly, designing ways to get that compensation or reparation enacted.

Taken altogether, these four principles, I claim, constitute a defensible set of principles for resolving conflicts between human and non-human living beings.

Individualism and holism

It might be objected, however, that I have not yet taken into account the conflict between holists and individualists. According to holists, the good of a species, or the good of an ecosystem, or the good of the whole biotic community can trump the good of individual living things.[5] According to individualists, the good of each individual living thing must be respected.

---

[5] Aldo Leopold's view is usually interpreted as holistic in this sense. Leopold wrote: 'A thing is right when it tends to preserve the integrity, stability and beauty of the biotic community. It is wrong when it tends otherwise.' See Leopold 1949.

Now, one might think that holists would require that we abandon my Principle of Human Preservation. Yet consider. Assuming that people's basic needs are at stake, how could it be morally objectionable for them to try to meet those needs, even if this were to harm non-human individuals, or species, or whole ecosystems, or even, to some degree, the whole biotic community? Of course, we can *ask* people in such conflict cases not to meet their basic needs in order to prevent harm to non-human individuals or species, ecosystems or the whole biotic community. But if people's basic needs are at stake, it will be a very unusual case where we can reasonably *demand* that they make such a sacrifice.

We could demand, of course, that people do all that they reasonably can to keep such conflicts from arising in the first place, for, just as in human ethics, many severe conflicts of interest can be avoided simply by doing what is morally required early on. Nevertheless, when lives or basic needs are at stake, the individualist perspective seems generally incontrovertible. We cannot normally require people to be saints.

At the same time, when people's basic needs are not at stake, we would be justified in acting on holistic grounds to prevent serious harm to non-human individuals, or species, or ecosystems, or the whole biotic community. Obviously, it will be difficult to know when our interventions will have this effect, but when we can be reasonably sure that they will, such interventions (e.g. culling elk herds in wolf-free ranges or preserving the habitat of endangered species) would be morally permissible, and would even be morally required when the Principle of Rectification applies. This shows that it is possible to agree with individualists when the basic needs of human beings are at stake, and to agree with holists when they are not.

Yet this combination of individualism and holism appears to conflict with recognising that all species count morally, by imposing greater sacrifices on the members of non-human species than it imposes on the members of the human species. Fortunately, appearances are deceiving here. Although the proposed resolution only justifies imposing holism when people's basic needs are not at stake, it does not justify imposing individualism at all. Rather, it would simply permit individualism when people's basic needs *are* at stake. Of course, we could impose holism under all conditions. But given that this would, in effect, involve going to war against people who are simply striving to meet their own basic needs in the only way they can, as permitted by the Principle of Human Preservation, intervention is such cases would generally not be justified.[6]

---

[6] See, however, the last section of this chapter.

It would involve taking away the means of survival from people, even when these means are not required for one's own survival.

Nevertheless, this combination of individualism and holism may leave animal liberationists wondering about the further implications of this resolution for the treatment of animals. Obviously, a good deal of work has already been done on this topic. Initially, philosophers thought that humanism could be extended to include animal liberation and eventually environmental concern (Singer 1975). Then Baird Callicott argued that animal liberation and environmental concern were as opposed to each other as they were to humanism (Callicott 1980). The resulting conflict Callicott called 'a triangular affair'. Agreeing with Callicott, Mark Sagoff contended that any attempt to link together animal liberation and environmental concern would lead to 'a bad marriage and a quick divorce' (Sagoff 1984). Yet more recently, such philosophers as Mary Ann Warren have tended to play down the opposition between animal liberation and environmental concern, and even Callicott now thinks he can bring the two back together again (Warren 1983; Callicott 1989: ch. 3). There are good reasons for thinking that such reconciliation is possible.

Right off, it would be good for the environment if people generally, especially people in the developed world, adopted a more vegetarian diet of the sort that animal liberationists are recommending. This is because a good portion of livestock production today consumes grains that could be more effectively used for direct human consumption. For example, 90% of the protein, 99% of the carbohydrate and 100% of the fibre value of grain is wasted by cycling it through livestock, and currently 64% of the US grain crop is fed to livestock. So by adopting a more vegetarian diet, people generally, and especially people in the developed world, could significantly reduce the amount of farmland that has to be keep in production to feed the human population. This, in turn, could have beneficial effects on the whole biotic community by eliminating the amount of soil erosion and environmental pollutants that result from raising livestock. For example, it has been estimated that 85% of US topsoil lost from cropland, pasture, range land and forest land is directly associated with raising livestock. So, in addition to preventing animal suffering, there are these extra reasons to favour a more vegetarian diet.

But even though a more vegetarian diet seems in order, it is not clear that the interests of farm animals would be well served if all of us became complete vegetarians. Sagoff assumes that in a completely vegetarian human world people would continue to feed farm animals as before (Sagoff 1984: 01–5). But it is not clear that we would have any obligation to do so. Moreover, in a completely vegetarian human world, we would probably need about half of the grain we now feed livestock to meet people's nutritional needs, particularly in underdeveloped countries. There simply would not be enough grain to go around. And then there would be the need to conserve cropland for future generations. So in a completely vegetarian human world, it seems likely that the population of farm animals would be decimated, relegating many of the farm animals that remain to zoos. But raising farm animals can be seen to be mutually beneficial for humans and the farm animals involved. Surely, it would benefit farm animals to be brought into existence, maintained under healthy conditions, and hence not in the numbers sustainable only with factory farms, but then killed relatively painlessly and eaten, rather than that they not be brought into existence or maintained at all.[7] So a completely vegetarian human world would not be in the interest of farm animals. Of course, no one would be morally required to bring farm animals into existence and maintain them in this manner. Morally, it would suffice just to maintain representative members of the various subspecies in zoos. Nevertheless, many will find it difficult to pass up an arrangement that is morally permissible and mutually beneficial for both humans and farm animals.

Nor, it seems, would it be in the interest of wild species that no longer have their natural predators not to be at least therapeutically hunted by humans. Of course, where possible, it may be preferable to reintroduce natural predators. But this may not always be possible because of the unavoidable proximity of farm animals and human populations, and then if action is not taken to control the populations of wild species, disaster could result for the species and their environments. For example, ungulates (hooved mammals such as white-tailed and mule deer, elk and bison), as well as elephants, in the absence of predators regularly tend to exceed the carrying capacity of their environments. So it may be in the interest of these wild species and their environments that humans intervene periodically to maintain a balance. Of course, there will be many natural environments where it is in the interest of the environment and the wild animals that inhabit it to be simply left alone. But here, too, animal liberation and environmental concern would not

---

[7] There is an analogous story to tell here about 'domesticated' plants, but hopefully there is no analogous story about 'extra humans' who could be raised for food. Given the knowledge these 'extra humans' would have of their fate, a similar use of humans would not be mutually beneficial and would most likely make their lives not worth living. But even assuming that this were not the case, with the consequence that this particular justification for domestication would be ruled out because of its implications for a similar use of humans, it still would be the case that domestication is justified in a sustainable agriculture to provide fertiliser for crops to meet basic human needs.

be in conflict. For these reasons, animal liberationists might seem to have little reason to object in this regard to the proposed combination of individualism and holism that is captured by these conflict resolution principles.

An objection from a somewhat alien perspective

There remains, however, at least one serious objection to the non-anthropocentrism that I have been defending. It might be argued that from a somewhat alien perspective my view is not non-anthropocentric enough. Consider the following.

Suppose our planet were invaded by an intelligent and very powerful species of aliens who could easily impose their will upon us. Suppose these aliens have studied the life history of our planet and they have come to understand how we have wreaked havoc on our planet, driving many species into extinction, and how we still threaten many other species with extinction. In short, suppose these aliens discover that we are like a cancer on our biosphere.

Suppose further that these aliens are fully aware of the differences between us and the other species on the planet. Suppose they clearly recognise that we more closely resemble them in power and intelligence than any other species on the planet. Even so, suppose the aliens still choose to protect those very species we threaten. They begin by forcing us to use no more resources than we need for a decent life, and this significantly reduces the threat we posed to many endangered species. However, the aliens want to do more. In order to save more endangered species, they decide to exterminate a certain portion of our human population, reducing our numbers to those we had when we were more in balance with the rest of the biosphere.

Now, if this were to happen, would we have moral grounds to object to these actions taken by the aliens? Of course, we could argue that it would be unreasonable for us to do more than restrict ourselves to the resources we need for a decent life, and so we are not morally required to do more. But these aliens need not be denying this. They may recognise that the extermination of a certain portion of the human population is not something the humans could reasonably require of each other. What they are claiming, as champions of endangered species, is just the right to impose a still greater restriction on humans, recognising, at the same time, a comparable right of humans to resist that imposition as best they can. Of course, in the imagined case, any resistance by humans would be futile; the aliens are just too powerful.

In so acting, the aliens have placed themselves outside that morality captured by my conflict resolution principles. The moral permissibility to meet one's basic needs and to defend oneself, guaranteed by the Principles of Human Preservation and Human Defence respectively, was that of strong permissibility. It implied that any would-be guardians of the interests of non-human earthly species were morally prohibited from interfering with humans who are taking the necessary actions to preserve and defend themselves, even when this required that the humans aggress against the basic needs of non-humans. In our imaginary tale, however, the aliens have rejected this moral prohibition, claiming instead that it is morally permissible for them to ally themselves with the interests of some of the endangered species on our planet. They claim that we cannot morally blame them, or morally object to what they are doing. They say that they have a right to try to impose greater restrictions on our species and that we have a right to resist. And they would be right. How could we object to the actions of these non-human-species-loving aliens?

Likewise, we could not object if similar actions were undertaken by radical Earth Firsters who, so to speak, chose to 'go native' and renounced, to some extent, their membership in the human community so as to be able to take stronger steps to protect endangered species. Of course, we might argue that there are other more effective ways for these Earth Firsters to protect endangered species, but if their actions proved to be the most effective at protecting endangered species, what could our objection be? Of course, we could oppose them if they went beyond what is morally required, as we could oppose the aliens on those same grounds, but, as in the case of the aliens, we don't seem to have any moral objection against what they are doing. What this would show is that while morality cannot impose requirements that would be unreasonable to accept (i.e. requirements that violate the 'ought' implies 'can' principle), it can permit (as in this case) actions that it cannot impose, as in lifeboat cases.[8]

Even so, before these radical Earth Firsters could sacrifice the basic needs of fellow humans for the sake of endangered species, they would be first required to use whatever surplus was available to them and to other humans to meet the basic needs of the humans they propose to restrict. Yet clearly it would be very difficult to have first used up all the surplus available to the whole human population for meeting basic human needs. Under present conditions, this requirement has certainly

---

[8] The direct analogy is to a lifeboat case in which you are trying to secure a lifeboat for one person from someone else who has an equal claim to it.

not been met. So unlike our imaginary aliens, whom we assumed were first able to force us to use no more resources that we needed for a decent life, before they started killing us to further reduce the threat we pose to endangered species, the efforts of radical Earth Firsters would probably never get beyond that first step. All of their efforts would be focused on trying to benefit endangered species by forcing humans to use no more resources than they needed for a decent life. Unlike our imaginary aliens, real-life radical Earth Firsters would probably never be able justifiably to get to the second step of taking the lives of fellow humans for the benefit of endangered species.

Accordingly, even though we can envision the perspective of hypothetical aliens and radical Earth Firsters and recognise that it is a morally permissible stance to take, that still doesn't undercut the moral defensibility of the Principles of Human Preservation, Disproportionality, Human Defence and Rectification. These principles still capture the moral requirements we can reasonably require all human beings to accept. In fact, the first step of this somewhat alien perspective requires the enforcement of just those principles. It is only at the second step, hypothetically justified in the case of the aliens, and virtually never justifiably realised in the case of real-life radical Earth Firsters, that we have a departure from the principles. Hence, the mere possibility of this somewhat alien moral perspective does not undercut the real-life moral defensibility of these conflict resolution principles. A non-arbitrary, non-question-begging conception of justice, giving what is deserved to whom it is deserved, therefore, will at least require a commitment to these conflict resolution principles.

References

Callicott, Baird (1980). 'Animal Liberation: A Triangular Affair', *Environmental Ethics* **2**: 311–28.

(1989). *In Defense of the Land Ethic*. Albany: State University of New York Press.

Leopold, Aldo (1949). *A Sand County Almanac*. Oxford: Oxford University Press.

Rolston, W. Holmes III (2001). 'Enforcing Environmental Ethics: Civil Law and Natural Value', in James P. Sterba (ed.), *Social and Political Philosophy: Contemporary Perspectives*. New York: Routledge, 249–369.

Sagoff, Mark (1984). 'Animal Liberation and Environmental Ethics: Bad Marriage, Quick Divorce', *Osgoode Hall Law Journal*. **22**.2: 297–307.

Singer, Peter (1975). *Animal Liberation*. New York: New York Times Publication.

Sterba, James P. (1998). *Justice for Here and Now*. New York: Cambridge University Press.

(2001). 'Toward a Reconciliation on Social and Political Philosophy', in James P. Sterba (ed.), *Social and Political Philosophy: Contemporary Perspectives*. New York: Routledge.

Taylor, Paul (1987). *Respect for Nature*. Princeton: Princeton University Press.

Warren, MaryAnn (1983). 'The Rights of the Nonhuman World,' in Robert Elliot and Arran Gare (eds.), *Environmental Philosophy*. University Park: Penn State University Press, 109–34.

10 The state

Andrew Hurrell

'The view of world order to which we have fallen heir is dominated by the conception of statehood' (MacCormick 1996: 554). The deeply entrenched statism of both political theory and international relations has many sources. For some, it rests simply on the historical rise of the modern state as the dominant form of social and political order and on its continued strength as both a source of authority and an apparatus of power in the face of would-be challengers and potential competitors, be they transnational firms, international organisations or transnational social movements. For others, it rests on the role of the nation state as the primary focus for human loyalty and communal allegiance. But, whatever its foundations, it is impossible to ignore the immense power of the idea and ideology of the state in the Western political imagination and the way in which this ideology became globalised in the course of European imperial expansion and in the process of decolonisation. The emergence of the modern state was complex, the history of state formation contested, and the variety of actually existing states and the inequalities amongst them have always been hard to square with the ideal-typical character of the 'modern state'. But, once established, the state came to dominate the ontological landscape of politics, as well as many of the most powerful traditions of political theory, moral reflection and international legal analysis. It also became, and has remained, extremely difficult to avoid seeing the world except through the eyes of the state. As James Scott has argued, the development of the state and the expansion of its goals involved the creation and institutionalisation of many of the simplified categories through which both the social and natural worlds could be understood, made 'legible', and thereby controlled and manipulated (Scott 1998).

On this basis, then, it has appeared natural to understand political order primarily in terms of the state: the enforcement by the state of its laws, the development of other non-coercive governance mechanisms, and the sense of community that is embodied in the state. Equally, if the state is viewed as the primary locus of social order within its borders, then world or global order involves asking how these islands of localised order can be related to each other; how some broader political framework for their interaction might be created and sustained; and how far such a framework might be capable of meeting three recurring political and moral challenges – capturing common interests, managing unequal power, and mediating difference and value conflict. Historically, this broader political framework has often been understood in terms of a limited 'society of states' or an 'anarchical society' – anarchical in that there was no common power to enforce law or to underwrite co-operation amongst states; but a society in that its members recognised some common interests and shared in the operation of common institutions (Bull 1977/2002).

In order to capture the sheer extent of the ecological challenge, it is important to underscore the minimalism of this classical pluralist conception. On this view, interstate co-operation could never be expected to provide a stable and universal peace but only to mitigate the inevitable conflicts that would arise from the existence of a multiplicity of sovereignties. The relevant question was not: how might human beings create forms of international society that embodied all their aspirations for justice or which universalised some particular conception of the good society? It was rather: how might states and other groups do each other the least possible harm and, in an age of total war and nuclear weapons, survive as a species? So the core goals of international social order were survival and coexistence; the political framework was made up of the core institutions of a pluralist international society – international law, Great Powers, the balance of power, diplomacy and war; and the legal framework was built around the reciprocal recognition of sovereignty, with its corollaries of non-intervention, sovereign equality and state consent. Even as the environment emerged as an international issue from the early years of the twentieth century, the response of states could be well captured within this traditional conception: limited bilateral or small group contractual agreements to deal with specific problems (for example, managing shared rivers or common fishery stocks).

Given the very prevalent suspicion of the state on the part of many ecologists, it is important to note the normative claims made for this kind of pluralism. In the first place, the state as an institution (but not necessarily any particular state) and the apparatus of state sovereignty provide a container for pluralism and a framework for the protection of diversity. The importance of diversity might rest on claims about cultural autonomy (perhaps religious, but most often national) which, in turn, might be seen as having either an intrinsic or an instrumental value. Or it might rest on arguments about collective self-governance, particularly in cases such as republican liberalism where a high value is placed on active and engaged citizens within a small and cohesive polity. Second, this limited interstate order provides a morally significant means of promoting coexistence and limiting conflict in a world in which consensus on more elaborate forms of co-operation does not exist and in which more elaborate international institutions are liable to be captured by the special interests and particular values of the most powerful. We should also note that some variety of this pluralist view continues to be upheld by many of the most influential western political theorists (including, for example, John Rawls and Michael Walzer); and that it continues to express the preferences of many major states (including India, China, Russia, Brazil), as well as capturing powerful currents of thought and practice in the United States. It is wholly wrong therefore to see pluralism as belonging solely to a vanished Westphalian world. Indeed, green arguments that economies should be brought back under firm national control and that 'excessive' immigration should be resisted attest to the continued power of the pluralist impulse.

The ecological challenge is so important and so profound because of the way in which it calls into question both the practical viability and the moral adequacy of this pluralist conception of a state-based global order; and because of the way in which responding to the ecological challenge has pushed states towards new forms of international law and global governance. The chapter is divided into three sections. The first examines the nature and extent of the challenge posed. The second examines some of the principal ways in which the state has evolved and adapted to the ecological challenge. It is certainly the case that very important processes of adaptation to the ecological challenge have occurred within individual states: through the 'greening' of domestic politics; through the increased emphasis on environmental issues within state administrations; through varied processes of ecological moder- nisation; and through the different ways in which the environment has been connected to the problem of state legitimacy (for a recent com- parative study of these changes see Dryzeck et al. 2003). And yet it has always been problematic to look at the state as an isolated, discrete institution. State sovereignty needs to be understood not as a discrete set of claims based solely on state power, but rather as a historically con- stituted 'bundle of competences' whose character depends on the changing constitution of the international legal, political and economic order as a whole (for an excellent discussion of these claims and the problems that arise, see Litfin 1998). Discussions of the ecological challenge are often couched in terms of a move 'beyond sovereignty' – either in terms of the changes that have already occurred or in terms of the changes that need to take place if the ecological challenge is to be met. In order to assess such claims and to understand the ways in which the state has engaged with the environment, we need to trace the ways in which different conceptions of the state and of the system of sovereign states have evolved. For this reason, the second section sets the response of the state to the ecological challenge within the context of the changing constitutional structure of international society – the move towards a solidarist state system on the one hand and the emergence of increasing elements of transnational governance on the other. The concluding section considers the implications of the ecological challenge for political theory.

The nature of the challenge

There are four principal aspects to the ecological challenge. The first derives from increased awareness of the material limits to the kinds of progress and development around which Western political theory has traditionally been constructed, and from the real possibility that our dominant forms of political organisation may be inadequate to manage the relationship between humankind and the natural environment on a lasting and sustainable basis. The international political salience of environmental issues has increased enormously as a result of accelerating rates of environmental degradation, increased scientific knowledge and heightened popular awareness of the seriousness of the ecological challenges facing humanity. Although much of the picture remains contested and obscure, there is increasing evidence that human social and economic activity is placing excessive strains on the physical limits of the ecosphere and that, in a crude but real sense, we are filling up the ecological space available to us.

The second aspect of the challenge concerns the increasingly global character of contemporary environmental issues. There are three senses in which the environment has become a global issue. First, and most obviously, humanity is now faced by a range of environmental problems that are global in the strong sense that they affect everyone and can only be effectively managed on the basis of co-operation between all, or at least a very high percentage, of the states of the world: controlling climate change and the emission of greenhouse gases, the protection of the ozone layer, safeguarding biodiversity, protecting special regions such as Antarctica or the Amazon, the management of the sea bed, and the protection of the high seas are among the principal examples. Second, the increasing scale of many originally regional or local environmental

problems, such as extensive urban degradation, deforestation, desertification, salination, or water or fuel-wood scarcity, now threaten broader
international repercussions: by undermining the economic base and
social fabric of weak and poor states, by generating or exacerbating
intra- or interstate tensions and conflicts and by stimulating increased
flows of refugees. The third, and most important, aspect of increased
globalisation derives from the complex but close relationship between
the generation of environmental problems and the workings of the now
effectively globalised world economy. On the one hand, there is the
range of environmental problems caused by the *affluence* of the industrialised countries; by the extent to which this affluence has been built
upon high and unsustainable levels of energy consumption and natural
resource depletion; and by the 'ecological shadow' cast by these
economies across the economic system. On the other, there is the widely
recognised linkage between *poverty*, population pressure and environmental degradation. Sustainable development is an inherently global
issue both because of the high levels of economic interdependence that
exist within many parts of the world economy and because it raises
fundamental questions concerning the distribution of wealth, power and
resources between rich and poor.

The third aspect of the challenge concerns the character of co-
operation that is required to deal with ecological challenges. The
management of globalisation necessarily involves the creation of deeply
intrusive rules and institutions, and debate on how different societies are
to be organised domestically. This is a structural challenge. Effective
international policies on the environment necessarily involve engagement with a complex array of international and transnational actors, and
interaction not just with central governments but with a much wider
range of domestic players. The fourth aspect of the challenge concerns
the increasing number of individual nation states that are no longer able
to provide localised order and an adequate degree of environmental
management within their own borders. Many of the most serious
obstacles to sustainability have to do with the domestic weaknesses of
particular states and state structures. In some cases these stem from the
limits of economic development: the fragility, inefficiency and corrup-
tion of government bureaucracies; the absence of appropriate human,
financial and technological resources; the prevalence of deep-rooted
economic problems; and the increasing susceptibility to international
and transnational economic forces. But in many cases the problems are
directly political: the opposition of powerful political interests that
benefit from unsustainable forms of development and the difficulties of
the state in regulating both itself and the many areas of economic life in

which it is directly involved. Clearly these problems are most severe in many of the weakest states, such as Haiti, El Salvador or many parts of Africa. But, even in states that have not in any sense 'failed', the capacity of governments to control or manage access to natural resources is often far from clear. The story of the Brazilian Amazon provides a parable of how a quintessentially 'strong' state came to grief: an extensive state-led development programme built around a powerful ideology of national integration and national development; the attempt to achieve direct centralised control, displacing traditional local elites and replacing them with new bureaucratic structures of control; and the gradual erosion of the capacity of the state to control the powerful and contradictory forces that had been unleashed. Moreover, the Brazilian case does not stand alone, as shown by the role of environmental degradation and environmental protest in the collapse of communist regimes in the Soviet Union and Eastern Europe. And there are worrying signs that China's shaky environmental foundations may yet force a dramatic reassessment of the much vaunted 'Chinese miracle' and of the image of China as a strong state (Shapiro 2001).

These challenges would be serious even if we were to see the state as an environmentally neutral form of social organisation. For many ecological theorists, however, the state is anything but neutral. In the first place, ecological thinking is necessarily about relationships, interconnections and community. The state can, at best, form only one part of this broader whole. Second, green political theory has long suspected that the bureaucratic logic of Weberian state machines is deeply antithetical to viewing nature in anything other than the narrowest of instrumental terms. Third, as it has emerged historically, the state has been very closely connected with the development of capitalism and hence with the productivism, expansionism and emphasis on ever-higher levels of material consumption that is such a central target of the ecological critique. And finally, the anarchical character of interstate politics generates a logic of security competition that leads to recurrent conflicts, with their attendant environmentally destructive effects; that presses political leaders to look to their short-term interests and to their power position relative to other states; and that reinforces narrow and exclusivist conceptions of national community.

Whatever view one takes about the state itself, the ecological challenge has undoubtedly served to undermine both the practical viability and the moral acceptability of state-based pluralist international order. It becomes impossible to think about world politics in terms of the distinction drawn by Martin Wight (Wight 1966): on the one hand, we have domestic society as the political arena within which understandings of the 'good life' might be debated, developed and, potentially, realised; on the other, we have international relations which is condemned to remain forever an arena concerned with the imperatives of 'mere survival'. In relation to the safeguarding of the global environment, 'mere survival' depends fundamentally on how societies are organised domestically and on how their various conceptions of what the good life entails can be brought together and reconciled. Given the extent of the ecological challenge, what possible sense can it make to build political theory around the idea of the state as a bounded political community whose basic structure is defined in terms of 'self-sufficient schemes of co-operation *for all the essential purposes of human life*'? (Rawls 1993: 301, emphasis added).

There is a wide spectrum of opinion as to the seriousness of many environmental problems and a great deal of scope for legitimate uncertainty. For the environmental optimists, the ecological challenge is not nearly as severe as suggested above, and both technology and continued economic development will allow human societies both to achieve higher levels of sustainability and to adapt successfully to the environmental changes that will inevitably occur. The environmental pessimist's response is to argue that human capacity to control the natural environment has been greatly and consistently overestimated, in particular because of the lack of attention to complexity, non-linearity and unpredictability. Moreover, a very great deal of the optimism depends on there being a well-functioning set of political institutions capable of achieving historically unprecedented levels of co-operation. Maybe technology will solve many problems; but that technology has to be applied and distributed to where it is needed. Maybe the world is capable of dealing with particular kinds of scarcity in aggregate; but for this to be a meaningful solution, there has to be a global mechanism for distribution and allocation and one that is able to take into account both efficiency and equity. To a much greater extent than they acknowledge, it is the environmental optimists who are most dependent on answers to some of the most intractable political problems facing international relations.

Responses

The seriousness of the ecological challenge and suspicion of the state have led some to look to radical political solutions. At one end of the spectrum, this has involved arguments either for world government or for strong global centralism of a kind that would certainly change the character and role of the state. Yet arguments in favour of world government have always faced very powerful objections, most importantly that any effective concentration of power would pose a severe threat to liberty. After all, if one of the purposes of a well-functioning political system is to reflect and promote some conception of the common good, the other is to limit, or at least minimise, domination. In addition, there are many solid ecological arguments against any form of global centralism, above all the critical importance of diversity – both of forms of interaction with nature but also of ecological ideas, possibilities and ways of thinking.

At the other end of the scale, ecological thinking has long stressed the value of decentralisation. The empowerment of both individuals and communities, combined with a strong emphasis on decentralised forms of political organisation, has become a major theme of environmentalist writing. Decentralisation and empowerment facilitate sustainability in various ways: by bringing consumption and production closer together; by strengthening local democracy and focusing public opposition on the seriousness of existing environmental problems; and by building on the extent to which local groups and communities possess special knowledge of sustainable forms of development and provide the social organisations within which that knowledge can be effectively implemented. And yet, however valuable these arguments may be, the global nature of the ecological challenge necessitates a significant degree of co-ordination, regulation and long-term planning (see Eckersley 1992). Even if decentralised or more regionally or locally based communities were to replace the state, some pattern of external or global political relations and institutions would need to be created or recreated. It is hard to see how these could entirely avoid replicating many of the features of contemporary state-based governance, in terms of both its positive possibilities and its recurring dilemmas.

Given these difficulties, much ecological thinking and almost all environmental practice has tended to follow the two principal dimensions along which the normative structure of international society has evolved. The first continues to view political order in terms of states. Crudely speaking, the solidarist conception of international society is a state system that can be made to work better and which strives to narrow the gap between law and power, on the one hand, and between law and morality, on the other, even if the gap can never be fully eliminated. Four dimensions of change are especially important. The first has to do with the increased range, scope and intrusiveness of international legal and political norms. Here we would note the 500 or so multilateral environmental agreements that form the heart of the structure of global environmental governance – 60 per cent of which have been negotiated since the 1972 Stockholm conference, and 85 per cent of which cover domestic (as opposed to transborder) activities (Haas 1999: 109).

The second dimension concerns the source of norms. In a traditional pluralist conception, the dominant norms are created by states and depend directly on the consent and will of states. In a solidarist conception, the process of norm creation is opened to a wider range of actors, and there is an easing of the degree to which states can only be bound by rules to which they have given their explicit consent. The environment provides a particularly clear example of these trends. Witness the increasingly central role of NGOs at the major environmental conferences and the roles of transnational specialist networks in the functioning of so much environmental governance.

The third dimension has to do with the justification and evaluation of norms. Alongside the old idea that actors create and uphold law because it provides them with functional benefits, the post-1945 period has seen the emergence of a range of internationally agreed core principles which underpin some notion of a world common good and some broader basis for evaluating specific rules. Central to multilateral environmental governance has been the emergence not just of an overarching idea of a shared responsibility to safeguard the global environment, but also a range of more specific norms – for example, legal duties to prevent environmental harm, liability for environmental harm, duties to inform and to consult, duties to undertake environmental impact assessment, the precautionary principle, the principle of intergenerational equity; and ideas of common heritage, of shared resources and of common concern.

The fourth dimension has to do with moves towards the more effective implementation of these norms, and the variety of attempts to move beyond the traditionally very 'soft' compliance mechanisms and to give more effective teeth to the norms of this more ambitious society. This is contested ground. On one side, the power of traditional pluralism is visible in the deep reluctance of states to concede significant power to supranational environmental bodies. But on the other, as environmental regimes have become more complex and more interconnected, the degree of institutional enmeshment has increased. More importantly, a good deal of the move towards harder and more coercive forms of implementation has taken place on the fringes of the legal order, most notably in the growth of an increasingly wide range of conditionalities and environmentally related sanctions applied, for example, by international lending agencies.

These changes have diluted and clouded the idea of international law as a state-privileging system and have unsettled the concept of state sovereignty that lay at the heart of the inherited legal and political order. As the constraints on sovereignty have grown more severe, so the theoretical and practical inconsistencies within the inherited sovereignty-based order have grown more serious. Most important is the ambiguity that begins to open up around the idea of states as the principal agents of world order. Within the pluralist world, states could be understood as 'agents' simply in the sense of those acting or exerting power and of doing so for themselves. But the expanding normative agenda of solidarism has opened up a second and different meaning of agency – the idea of an agent as someone who acts for, or on behalf of, another. Within the solidarist order, states are no longer to act for themselves as sovereigns, but rather, first, as agents for the individuals, groups and national communities that they are supposed to represent; and second, as agents or interpreters of some notion of an international public good and some set of core norms against which state behaviour should be judged and evaluated.

Liberals remain inclined to believe that the reality of ecological interdependence will create problems that can only be solved by new and more far-reaching mechanisms of co-operation. Radical environmental degradation of the planet will involve losses for all, and states are locked into a situation from which they cannot escape and about which they will be forced to co-operate. Moreover, for the liberal, increased scientific understanding of environmental problems will work to redirect state interests and to facilitate international co-operation. On this optimistic view, we are already witnessing the emergence of a complex structure of global environmental governance with new sets of institutions and an array of new legal concepts. 'The norms, rules and strategies for environmental governance are no longer widely contested' (Haas 1999: 103). For the optimist, the effectiveness of many environmental regimes does not derive solely from their individual strengths, but rather from the extent to which they tie states into a continuing and institutionalised process of negotiation: hence the importance of provisions for regular meetings and for the generation and dissemination of information; hence the view of regimes as frameworks around which political pressure on states can be effectively mobilised. What matters about the Kyoto protocol, for example, is not that it will have a great impact on climate change (which it will not); but rather that it creates a political framework within which more effective agreements can be negotiated.

Sceptics, on the other hand, continue to highlight the many obstacles to co-operation: the weakness of most international institutions and the absence of sanctioning power; the pressures on states and state representatives to place a high priority on their immediate short-term interests and on the protection of political autonomy; the mismatch between the time horizons of politicians and political processes, on the one hand, and the extended time frames needed to address and deal with many of the most serious environmental problems, on the other; the fact that there is no easy link between increased scientific knowledge and the growth of international co-operation; and the extent to which the loose rhetoric of 'interdependence' disguises a wide variety of problems whose specific character may sometimes work to promote co-operation (as in the case of ozone) but may also militate against co-operation (as in the case of global climate change). Most serious of all are the enormous difficulties facing states in their efforts to manage the global economy in the interests of ecological rationality. International environmental regulation has traditionally relied on separating issues and negotiating particular agreements to deal with particular problems. Yet attempting to give meaning to sustainability in the context of economic globalisation is necessarily about managing the environmental implications of a diverse and highly politicised set of relationships (for example, between trade and environment, between debt and environment, between military spending and environment). The impasse on trade and environment linkages within the WTO provides a clear example of the difficulties involved.

In order to assess the impact of these changes on the state, it is helpful to unpack the different ways in which the problem of interstate co-operation has been understood. Most of the writing on environmental governance over the past couple of decades has been rationalist in method and technocratic in character. The proliferation of international institutions is commonly associated with globalisation and with increased levels of transnational exchange and communication. Institutions are analysed in terms of how self-interested egoists overcome the collective-action problems arising from increased interdependence and interaction. Norms, rules and institutions are generated because they help states deal with common problems and because they enhance welfare.

Although analytically powerful, this rationalist, technocratic approach has systematically underplayed the severity of the obstacles to effective environmental governance, and hence has tended to exaggerate the degree to which the role of the state has in fact been transformed. In the first place, it has neglected the problem of value diversity and value conflict. All communities and polities have to find ways of dealing with diversity and with value conflict. The environment provides a particularly significant example of the problem. Thus liberal governance approaches to global environmental negotiations overlook the absence of a shared cultural or cognitive script that allows the largely rhetorical consensus value of 'sustainability' to be translated into stable and effective operational rules. Definitions of sustainability are inextricably bound up with the allocation of values and the distribution of costs and benefits both between individuals and groups within this generation and across time. Whilst there is widespread agreement that the benefits of environmental protection and the costs of environmental damage need to be made far more explicit and internalised within both markets and government policymaking, there can be no 'objective' and universal way of determining these costs and benefits. This is especially so when it comes to assessing the intrinsic value to be placed on the natural world and its preservation, the idea that what makes nature valuable to human beings is its very 'naturalness' and irreplaceability. It is not simply that environmental agendas will vary across different parts of the world, in terms of their substantive priorities and their underlying values (Allier 2003). It is also that understandings of a 'nature' and 'humanity' have been constructed very differently according to both culture and context. Finally, the common appeal in ecological thought and practice to moral intuition as a mode of reasoning and debate (rather than abstract rationalism) pushes environmentalism towards engagement with the different and varied moral cultures that exist across the world. Ecological thinking has rightly laid great emphasis on diversity. But to do so is to add a further twist to an already deep-rooted problem in the constitution of the society of states.

The second great challenge concerns power and the way in which conflicting values are intertwined with patterns of unequal power. The classical state system was a system that was both marked by inequality and structured around inequality. The environment is deeply implicated in the patterns of unequal power that continue to dominate world politics – in at least four ways. First, there is the role that the past use of environmental resources has played in the practices of imperialism and the creation of present inequalities. Second, there is the unequal impact of environmental change on different states and communities and the vastly different capacity of states and communities to cope and adapt to environmental change. Third, there is the role of power in setting the agenda of environmental politics, including the deeply contested issue of what counts as a global challenge and the way in which ecological ideas are translated into policy. The case of 'liberal environmentalism' provides a good example (Bernstein 2001) – the way in which the concept of sustainability was picked up by the OECD and the international financial institutions in the post-Brundtland period and transformed into a set of technical understandings that purged it of its radical elements so as to do as little harm as possible to orthodox ideas of economic development. And finally, there is the fundamental question as to the future ecological impact of how the developing world will choose or be able to develop and how the global environment will be politically managed in a system in which the industrialised world comprises only 20 per cent of world population (projected to shrink to 13 per cent by 2050).

Unequal power is also central to our understanding of the changing problem of political legitimacy. It is often argued that the increasing moves towards solidarism have undermined the state as a viable basis for democratic political community, and that the expansion of governance beyond the state has opened up new problems of legitimacy. But the legitimacy problematic has two distinct sources which are often insufficiently disentangled. In the first place, the problem might result from a general tendency of governance to seep beyond the confines of the state and of the political community represented by that state. Such accounts lay great stress on generalised, even systemic, processes of institutional enmeshment and on the thickening of an ever-expanding regulatory layer of governance both above states and across societies. As a result, many have highlighted the democratic deficits of international bodies from the EU to the WTO and the absence of adequate systems of accountability and representation. On the second view, however, the problem of legitimacy does not rest on any such general tendency, but rather on the degree to which the structures of global governance are contaminated by the preferences and special interests of the powerful. It is not the generalised seepage of authority that matters most, but rather the unequal impact of these changes. The dominant trend in the post-Cold War world has not been towards the erosion of sovereignty; it has been the return to a world of unequal and differentiated sovereignties.

If one kind of political, institutional and normative change looks to an improved society of states united by a far higher degree of solidarity, another looks beyond the state, or at least comes to view the state within the context of a broader legal order. This conception of transnational governance builds on many of the trends already visible in the contemporary international legal system: the pluralism of the norm-creating processes; the role of private market actors and civil society groups in articulating values which are then assimilated in interstate institutions; and the increased range of informal, yet norm-governed, governance mechanisms often built around complex networks, both transnational and transgovernmental. Tied closely to processes of social and economic globalisation, this view sees traditional interstate law as increasingly subsumed within a broader process in which old distinctions between public and private international law and between municipal and international law are being steadily eroded. The state loses its place as the privileged sovereign institution and instead becomes one of many actors and one participant in a broader and more complex social and legal process.

Transnational governance has formed an important part of the political response to the ecological challenge. On many issues (such as deforestation, biodiversity, ozone, fisheries, hazardous waste), environmental governance is characterised by a complex and shifting array of actors, including states, NGOs, transnational social movements and civil society organisations (CSOs), and specialist transnational communities. The roles of such groups have increased very significantly: first, in the formal process of norm creation, standard-setting and norm development; second, in the broader social process by which new norms emerge and find their way on to the international agenda; third, in the detailed functioning of many international institutions and in the processes of implementation and compliance; and finally, in direct participation in many governance activities (disbursing an increasing proportion of official aid, leading efforts on the ground to promote sustainable development). In all of these areas the analytical focus has been on transnational networks – for example, knowledge-based networks of economists, lawyers or scientists; or transnational advocacy networks which act as channels for flows of money and material resources but, more critically, of information, ideas and values.

In order to unpack the potential implications of these changes for the state, two streams of thinking can be identified. The first presses in a functional-contractual direction. Under this heading we would place those aspects of environmental governance that involve epistemic communities of technical specialists and the many regulatory networks that are responsible for the development, diffusion and implementation of an increasing range of environmental norms, rules and regulations. On this view, institutions, including state institutions, should not be seen at representative of sovereign power or as embodiments of a particular community, but rather as functional bodies that compete with one another to provide efficient solutions to governance problems. There is no prior normative preference as to what governance functions should be undertaken at what level, by what kinds of actors, or by what social mechanism (state, market, civil society). State functions are substitutable and may be assumed by external agencies, by private actors and, given the nature of the ecological challenge, by a range of transnational actors. On this account, states would still exist; but the status and the protection conferred by the norm of sovereignty would disappear. Sovereignty would become overtly contractual and defeasible. The normative arguments in favour of such moves tend to stress efficiency and effectiveness. Thus environmental regulatory networks are able to penetrate sovereignty without the need for cumbersome political negotiation; they can draw on a selected range of relevant public and private actors; they are informal and flexible; and they help close the space between the creation of new rules and the enforcement of those rules (Slaughter 2004).

A second stream presses in a deliberative-democratic direction. Here international law becomes the law of a cosmopolitan community. It regulates states but does not depend on the will of the state for its existence, content or implementation. The state is at least partially constituted by the will of this transnational civil society. The nature of the ecological challenge pushes towards more open and diverse governance arrangements, with substantially greater power for local communities, increased autonomy for various ethnic and territorial groups, and legal recognition for civil society organisation. Again the state continues to exist, but it loses its place as an autonomous institution and instead become one of many participants in a broader and far more complex social, political and legal process.

Very important claims have been made about the normative potentiality of global civil society as an arena of politics that is able to transcend the inside-outside character of traditional politics; to fashion and provide space for new forms of political community, solidarity and identity; and to provide modes of representing previously marginalised communities – for example, transnational cultural communities (such as indigenous peoples) and those affected stakeholders on whom the impact of environmental change falls most heavily. Sometimes the emphasis is on global civil society as a relatively autonomous, self-organised public sphere in which genuine deliberation among competing positions can take place and through which some notion of international public reason can be developed. In other cases, global civil society and its linked network of 'domestic' civil societies feed positively into state-based order through the provision of legitimacy and consent and into market-based order as the repository of the trust and other forms of social capital without which markets will not function. But on both views, global civil society represents a pluralist and open arena for the negotiation of rules and norms based on genuine and unforced consent. It serves as a regulative ideal, but one whose potential can be gauged from the changing real practices of world politics.

Assessing the normative strengths and weaknesses of these two streams has become a central task for political theory. Assessing the impact that these developments have already had on the role of the state would involve an empirical analysis that is well beyond the scope of this chapter. But the three perennial questions need to be addressed. First, how far have we seen the emergence of new sources of political authority, as opposed to new actors with power, ideas and influence? Second, how autonomous is the world of transnational governance from the state? State action may by shaped by NGOs, by regulatory networks, by specialist communities; but it is often state action and specific state policies that are crucial in fostering the emergence of such forums in the first place and in providing the institutional framework that enables them to flourish. More importantly, state power itself is increasingly determined by the ability of governments to work successfully within civil society and to exploit transnational and transgovernmental coalitions for their own purposes. Hence these changes may well work to undermine the power and autonomy of some states, but hardly of 'the state' as an institution. Finally, we have to ask about links between examples of transnational governance and the power of particular parts of the international system. Here we have to face the argument that NGOs, CSOs and regulatory networks favour the values and interests of Northern states and societies, magnifying still further the power of the already powerful.

Conclusion

Three conclusions can be drawn from the increasingly close engagement between the state and the environment.

In the first place, for political theorists concerned directly with the environments, the central preoccupation is likely to be with the varied ways in which the state has responded to the increasingly complex set of ecological challenges that it has faced, and with the adequacy of those responses. Here the focus is likely to remain on the uneven and highly contested role of the state and on its ambiguous relationship with the environment: on the one hand, as an agent deeply implicated in many of the most serious processes of environmental harm; and, on the other, as the still-dominant form of political organisation that will inevitably have to play a central role in facilitating progressive environmental change. Many enquiries of this kind stress the limits and obstacles that block progress, and connect many of those limits to the state and the constraining logics of both domestic and international politics. The state may not be about to fade away any time soon, but it is clear that the greening of sovereignty is an enormously difficult process. From this perspective, the task for political theory is to imagine and think through innovative ways in which the environmentally destructive potential of the state can be tamed and its emancipatory potential enhanced (Eckersely 2004).

Second, the environment challenge is likely to play an ever more central role in the work of those political theorists concerned with the problem of how we can establish some minimally secure foundations for rational moral debate in a diverse and deeply divided world, and of how some shared notion of a global moral community can be created within which moral ideas and projects can achieve some argumentative and deliberative purchase, and perhaps even persuasion. The limits of an appeal to some universal notion of human reason suggest an increasing need to engage with normative practices that are embedded in particular communities. The central role within environmental thinking and environmental practice of diversity and particularity, on the one hand, and commonality and community, on the other, makes it a particularly rich source for such work.

Third, the adequacy of the state's response to the ecological challenge needs to be seen as analytically separate from the extent to which the character of the state has in fact evolved or changed (although there may be important interconnections). Here political theory will be concerned with the extent to which changes in relation to the environment are reflective of a broader evolution in the character of the state and of broader possibilities for normatively driven change, even transformation. Environmental writing has often been well ahead of the field in suggesting that we are witnessing a reconfiguration of political space in which traditional notions of the state and of state sovereignty are being transformed. Such claims are usually closely related to a broader reading of contemporary world politics.

As this chapter has indicated, the ecological challenge has indeed been one of the most important factors contributing to the changes that have taken place in the changing normative structure of international society. And yet, even in relation to the environment, there is a real danger that transformationist claims overstate the scale of the changes that have actually taken place and, more important, that this exaggeration might lead to a misdiagnosis of the challenges to be faced. This is still more the case if we place the environment in the context of the many other issues with which political theory is inevitably concerned: security, for example, where solidarist ambitions towards the collective management of security remain largely frustrated; or the management of the global economy, where formal institutions are often weak and where market-based modes of transnational governance seem even more reflective of the power and interests of particular states and private economic actors. In relation to the environment (and more generally), the precarious and insecure political foundations of both solidarism and of transnational governance mean that major states, international institutions and many other social groups are constantly forced back to the older pluralist norms of coexistence and to the power-political ordering mechanisms that supported them. We are therefore not dealing with a vanished or vanishing Westphalian world, as much transformationist writing suggests, but rather with a world in which solidarist and cosmopolitan conceptions of governance coexist, usually rather unhappily, with many aspects of the old pluralist order.

References

Allier, J. M. (2003). *The Environmentalism of the Poor: A Study of Ecological Conflicts and Valuation*. London: Edward Elgar.

Bernstein, S. (2001). *The Compromise of Liberal Environmentalism*. New York: Columbia University Press.

Bull, H. (1977/2002). *The Anarchical Society: A Study of Order in World Politics*, 3rd ed. Basingstoke: Palgrave.

Dryzek, J. S., Downes, D., Hunold, C., and Schlosberg, D. (2003). *Green States and Social Movements: Environmentalism in the United States, United Kingdom, Germany and Norway*. Oxford: Oxford University Press.

Eckersely, R. (1992). *Environmentalism and Political Theory: Toward an Ecocentric Approach*. London: UCL Press.

—— (2004). *The Green State: Rethinking Democracy and Sovereignty*. Cambridge, Mass.: MIT Press.

Haas, P. M. (1999). 'Social Constructivism and the Evolution of Multilateral Environmental Governance', in Aseem Prakesh and Jeffrey A. Hart (eds.), *Globalization and Governance*. New York: Routledge.

Litfin, K. T. (ed.) (1998). *The Greening of Sovereignty in World Politics*. Cambridge, Mass.: MIT Press.

MacCormick, N. (1996). 'Liberalism, Nationalism and the Post-Sovereign State', *Political Studies*, **44**, (special issue): 553–67.

Rawls, J. (1993). *Political Liberalism*. New York: Columbia University Press.

Scott, J. C. (1998). *Seeing Like a State: How Certain Schemes to Improve the Human Condition Have Failed*. New Haven: Yale University Press.

Shapiro, Judith (2001). *Mao's War Against Nature: Politics and the Environment in Revolutionary China*. Cambridge: Cambridge University Press.

Slaughter, A.-M. (2004). *A New World Order*. Princeton: Princeton University Press.

Wight, M. (1966). 'Why Is There No International Theory?', in Martin Wight and Herbert Butterfield (eds.), *Diplomatic Investigations*. London: Allen and Unwin, 17–34.

11   Representation

Michael Saward

'Political theory' is a wide and diverse body of work; in this book's title, it comes across as inert, the receptor, the thing that is acted upon. The active ingredient, the 'challenge', is ecological. There is, of course, no given, bounded body of political theory to be acted upon, but rather a shifting set of arguments and assumptions. And the ecological challenge is in fact many challenges – to conventional views of the state, social justice, democracy, progress, individualism and more. Which of a range of possibilities to pick when it comes to 'representation'? How to represent the problem of representation?

Political representation is normally discussed in terms of how accurately elected representatives reflect the interests of voters. In this chapter, I argue that representation happens in many more places than just elected legislatures, and in many more ways than the accurate capturing of human interests. I start from the view that representative claims are made by a great variety of political actors, and that representation involves the active portrayal of constituencies rather than simple reflection of them. From that base, it quickly becomes clear that adding some 'proxy' representatives of nature into conventional legislatures (Dobson 1996), for example, is just one part of the ecological challenge, and probably not the most important part. Broader portrayals or representations of nature matter in politics, and they matter beyond just parliamentary politics.

The concept of political representation we need will move us beyond the influential style of analysis of the (deserved) contemporary classic on political representation, Hannah Pitkin's *The Concept of Representation* (Pitkin 1967). Pitkin sets up the problem of representation in a distinctive way. She describes her basic task as a metaphorical search for 'a rather complicated, convoluted, three-dimensional structure in the

The author would like to thank Karin Bäckstrand, Andrew Dobson, Robyn Eckersley, Phil Sarre and Grahame Thompson for helpful comments on previous versions of this chapter.

middle of a dark enclosure' (1967: 10). Political theorists – Hobbes, Burke, Madison and others – have given us photographs of this structure, she says, taken from various angles. These photographs offer different images or interpretations of representation. 'Yet', says Pitkin, 'there is something there, in the middle in the dark, which all of them are photographing; and the different photographs together can be used to reconstruct it in complete detail' (1967: 10–11). There is, in other words, an essence of representation, a full view of it, three-dimensional and complete.

It is easier to admire Pitkin's work than to share her confidence. I suspect that in fact any way or style of capturing the problem of representation is more like a freeze-frame – one fragmentary, passing moment amongst others – than the definitive three-dimensional photograph. Pitkin is searching for a master metaphor which points to the essence of representation. The problem is that the metaphor – rich and compelling as it may be – remains a metaphor. Metaphors substitute for essences, or so we often like to think, precisely because those essences are so elusive. The trouble is that there are always other metaphors which depict their object in a different light, with different emphasis. We cannot reach a point where we say: 'this is the right metaphor, this captures it, the work is done.'

The elusiveness of the concept of representation itself is repeated for the world of representations in which we live. No one picture or representation of a thing, a person, an animal or whatever can securely be thought to capture its essence. That sounds limiting and negative. But there is another side to the coin. Metaphors or representations do crucial work for us. We use them to find entry points to gaining some understanding of processes, phenomena, people. But they do more even than that. Often our metaphors *create* our entry points; what we cannot imagine, what we cannot evoke with metaphor, we find difficult to see and therefore study. In his writing on representation, Derrida (1982) implies that we have to construct the concepts that bring into focus the objects of our study in order to study them.

Both the necessity and unreliability of such representations are crucial to carry into a discussion of political representation and the ecological challenge.

A new approach to political representation

My approach is informed by a view of political representation which is based on three key background assumptions. First, in the words of Dennis Thompson, 'we must understand representation not as a relationship between constituents and representatives at particular moments, but as a *process* in which the relationship between citizens and representatives continues over time' (1988: 136). Second, we should see that representation as a process centres upon the practice of making *claims to be* representative, and varied efforts to substantiate and to contest those claims; and third, that 'constituents' and 'representatives' need *not* be members of electoral districts and elected parliamentarians or councillors respectively – only by narrow political science conventions do we confine discussion of political representation to parliamentary politics and electoral processes.

Representation is always something in the making rather than something achieved or completed, not least because it is tied up with an economy of *claim-making* rather than fact-establishing. A representative claim is a claim to represent, or to know what represents, the interests of someone or something. The claim could be expressed in a variety of ways. For example, I could claim to represent the interests of a person, or the needs of a country or region, or the needs of non-sentient nature. I could claim to embody the desires of my co-religionists, or that a painting accurately represents a particular landscape (and so on). Any claim can be and normally is subject to dispute, and may be accepted, ignored or rejected by individuals or groups.

Representative claims differ enormously from one to the next, but there are common elements at an abstract level. Claims have a *maker* – the one who asserts them. The maker puts forward a *subject* – perhaps herself, perhaps a symbol, perhaps a social group or party – as standing for or signifying an *object*, such as a human electoral constituency or an endangered species. The object of a representative claim is a concept, an idea of a real thing rather than the thing itself; the latter is more helpfully understood as the *referent*. Finally, claims have an *audience*, which may accept or reject claims. Critics may argue that to put all these elements together is to pack too much into a conception of representation, but it seems to me that all are vital. If we drop the maker or audience, for example, and concentrate on signification (subject as signifier, object as signified), we catch the technical side but miss vital political and cultural aspects of representation.

An example of a conventional representative claim would be: the member of parliament (M) offers herself (S) as the embodiment of constituency interests (O) with respect to a legally defined set of people in a constituency (R) to that constituency (A). Or: the green party (M) offers itself (S) as the protector of the interests of endangered species (O) with respect to the animals in question (R) to governments and the broader media and public (A).

Contained within the notion of the representative claim is an argument that aesthetic and cultural modes of representation are themselves political, and need to be seen as an integral part of what political representation is all about.

There is an indispensable *aesthetic* moment in political representation because the maker has to be an artist, to operate aesthetically, to evoke the represented. If for example an electoral constituency's interests were transparent, then a representative could simply 'read off' those interests and act on them. But the signified, or the object, is not the same as the collection of people who make up the constituency (the referent). It is a picture, a portrait, an image of that electorate. The 'interests' of a constituency have to be 'read in' via a subject or signifier, not 'read off'. This is an active, creative process, not one of passive reception of signals from below. The business of political figures, parties, lobby groups and social movements is aesthetic *because* it is political.

And political representation is necessarily *cultural* in the sense that there are cultural limits to the types of subject – object links that can plausibly be made in a given context. Potential audiences of representative claims have cultural codes which will make them receptive to some claims and unreceptive to others. In Stuart Hall's terms, '[c]odes fix the relationship between concepts and signs [subject and object in my terms]. They stabilise meaning within different languages and cultures' (Hall 1997: 21). These are codes which would-be political representatives can exploit.

A full account would require exploring the representative claim much more. For example, we would need to think about how an audience may or may not hear a message as it was intended, or dispute it by constructing its own alternatives. But my focus here is green political theory representations of 'nature' – constructions of nature as an object, intended for professional or political audiences. Constructions of nature, like those of other phenomena, are aesthetic creations using cultural resources. Green challengers to 'grey' or 'brown' political theory and politics question existing representations of nature and offer new ones. I turn now to specific examples and to raise some questions about them in the light of the preferred approach to political representation.

Green political theory and the challenge to representation

Selected works by Andrew Dobson, John Dryzek, Robyn Eckersley and Robert Goodin examined here are sophisticated green attacks on conventional representative democratic institutions. What I want to do is to deploy elements of the framework outlined above to shed light on some lesser-noticed aspects of what is going on in the ecological challenge's representations of nature especially.

Dobson invokes a 'species' as having interests which might adequately be represented when 'assured of the conditions to provide for its survival and flourishing' (1996: 137). Faced with the question of which animals are to be represented, and to what extent, Dobson invokes the rich metaphor of the 'hierarchy of moral considerability' which his proposed special parliamentary representatives for non-human animals – the proxies – should debate and decide for political purposes. Finally, he offers us a representation of future generations, people who will exist and who will 'want both a viable environment in which to live and the possibility of satisfying their basic needs' (1996: 132). In short, here are 'representations' of another sort, choices about the depiction of potential new 'constituencies' – one might say choices about how to constitute constituencies. The theorist (M) puts forward proxy representatives carrying hierarchies and flourishing conditions assumptions (S) as defining and standing for the needs of animals and of future generations (O) with respect to animals and presumed future people (R) for consumption by a human political audience (A). The assumptions about flourishing and needs look general and reasonable, but in theory they are not the only ones that proxies might come up with. They are the theorists' creations, his preferred representations of the problem. The creations are theoretical, but they are also political in a deep way: they involve particular claims about what interests are, how they need to be construed. And those particular claims play their role in making a new potential political constituency visible, of defining it through representation.

Let me turn to Eckersley's essay, 'Deliberative Democracy, Representation and Risk' (2000). This piece is an account of the limits of conventional representative machinery in the face of pressing ecological problems and demands. Future generations and other species form 'communities of fate' which have the potential to be harmed by political decisions and industrial processes. Therefore they are interests that ought to be represented within our political structures. Future generations and other species cannot represent themselves, so they must be represented in some other way. Eckersley considers positively the potential of a modified version of deliberative democracy to assist in bringing about a more ecologically sensitive democracy.

There are two points here. The first is an interesting tension in Eckersley's account of representation. On the one hand, she places weight on the idea of stretching elected representatives' imaginations, as a way of ensuring that the interests of future generations and other species are taken on board in decision-making. On the other, she tends to regard the interests of these constituencies as real and singular. Admittedly this needs to be read between the lines of her account, but there are plenty of relevant lines to read. For example, she refers to 'the perspectives of differently-situated others', 'the concerns and interests of differently-situated others', of adopting 'the standpoint of differently-situated human and non-human others' (2000: 128–9). The main challenges to representatives being able to imagine these interests, she argues, are epistemological and motivational. The epistemological challenge is how to know, to recognise, those interests. An institutional mechanism that can help us to meet this challenge is 'mandatory state-of-the-environment reporting' (2000: 129). In short, there is an emphasis on the singular knowability of the interests concerned. Here, I want to suggest, is an example of *unidirectionality*. A unidirectional approach to representation proceeds from the assumed given character of the represented to the adequacy of the representatives' perception of that character. In the terms of the model, two things are happening. First, the distinction between object and referent is glossed over – future people (R) have determinate interests (O) just because they will exist. And second, the process of knowing those interests involves *discovery* by appropriate technique (state-of-the-environment reporting). The maker and the subject are set aside, missing therefore the necessarily con-stitutive role played in these elements of representation. My argument will be that representation should instead be seen as bidirectional (or multidirectional), recognising the interpretative and selectively creative role of makers and subjects in representation. Using Eckersley's own terms, I am suggesting that the imagination or 'enlarged thinking' of her subjects, the elected representatives, stretches beyond the role of knowing by discovery what is already there (the interests of future generations, for example), to actively evoking one or more potential versions of what is there to be represented. It might be protested that techniques like state-of-the-environment reporting have a scientific status that overcomes the partiality and selectivity of representations; I shall say more on scientific representations of nature in a moment.

I now turn to some brief comments on discursive and decentralist green challenges as exemplified in works by Goodin and Dryzek.

Goodin, like the other green theorists, wants to find a way to make nature's interests figure in political decision-making. Beyond general comments in favour of decentralist and participatory democracy, he builds a conception of democracy in which the internalisation of the interests of others plays a central part. Interests, whatever their source and whoever or whatever bears them, should be represented; if their bearers cannot represent themselves, then a notion of interests 'encapsulated' by others who can, becomes acceptable, even desirable.

Goodin argues that 'In so far as natural objects have objective values that can properly be construed as interests, those ought be politically represented just as any others' (1996: 837). So, values in nature are *objective* – *there*, given, regardless of human recognition or not. Again, the necessary gap between object and referent is closed off – the concept of what value natural objects may have is collapsed into the material of those objects themselves. These values, according to Goodin, require an 'appreciator' to turn them into interests, to represent them politically. Goodin the theorist is the maker of this representation, and the appreciator is his subject. The appreciator's skills are subjective, of course, and Goodin recognises this fact. But the values, on his account, are objective, to be discerned rather than creatively construed (as I argue they can only be). His model offers us a transmission belt, transferring objective values to the passive receptor that is the appreciator. The very idea of an appreciator implies such one-way traffic – an appreciator has (merely) to see what's already there.

Nature, then, has interests that ought to be represented. These are to be discovered, appreciated. Then they need to be internalised. The one-way traffic continues at this point. To 'internalise' implies that there is a single external reality to be transferred – there is something specific outside that can be brought inside our heads. There is no guarantee, Goodin writes, that 'people will necessarily internalise nature's interests completely or represent them perfectly' (1996: 844). The idea that in principle these interests *could be* represented 'completely' or 'perfectly' reinforces their presumed single and unalterable character. These interests require no active mediation and little interpretation; the appreciator's role remains that of a passive receptor. Interests are to be *read off* nature, not *read into* it (my words, not Goodin's).

My suggestion is that Goodin emphasises too much the objectivity of nature's value and interests, and that this leads to an overly unidirectional view of the transmission of those interests into politics. To be sure, we are dealing with matters of *emphasis* here rather than black-and-white distinctions. Nevertheless, it leaves aside the necessarily creative role of the representative, one that requires the incumbent to construct, reconstruct, choose, depict and portray that which needs to be represented ('nature', in this case). The process is two-way, as I have tried to argue above. The representative / politician must be a maker of representations, an artist, even if a bad or unwitting one. Much less is given, much less is capable merely of being 'read off' than Goodin presumes.

In other words, we have here (I suggest) an example of a problematic *objectivity assumption* along with one of *unidirectionality*.

Let me turn to Dryzek's radical analysis and prescription. As a discursive democrat, for whom unconstrained communication is the ideal political mechanism, Dryzek seeks to deepen and extend radically the meaning and spaces of political communication, seeking 'a more egalitarian interchange at the human / natural boundary' (2000: 145). Nature is not only a source of 'interests', which are 'affected'. In Dryzek's eyes, nature is an agent too; it is not 'passive, inert, and plastic'. Instead, this world is truly alive, and 'pervaded with meanings' (2000: 148). This agency means we must recognise and respect nature in wholly new ways. For Dryzek, the key metaphor here involves 'listening' – 'we should listen to signals emanating from the natural world with the same sort of respect we accord communication emanating from human subjects, and as requiring equally careful interpretation' (2000: 149).

My main point here, echoing others above, is that listening implies a passivity on the part of the listener, mere receptiveness of what is given. Dryzek's listener is blood brother to Goodin's appreciator in this key respect – he or she is the subject within the representative claim being made. 'Effective listening' is hearing and heeding the 'feedback signals' from nature; it is largely passive, though it is a role that no doubt requires attentiveness and acquaintance. Essentially unidirectional like others, Dryzek's analysis closes down the object-referent gap and implies that nature largely determines what the subject-listener hears. Interestingly, the maker is a voice outside the text, too. The theorist here adopts the classic silent stance of the author, setting to one side his role as maker of the representation involving the listener and nature. This is understandable – it is a deep convention of academic and other writing – but it is worth noting that it has the effect of reinforcing the objectifying character of the claims being made. That is not to denigrate his efforts; as I shall try to argue below, this analysis can prompt a clearer view of the political role of (in this case green) political theory.

Dryzek's account moves on to the political institutional corollary of all this – the idea that the state, as we know it, is so constrained by anti-ecological imperatives that it is not likely to be a good 'listener' in the present sense. Elected representatives within the state are no different from other state personnel in this respect. Accordingly, Dryzek adopts the bioregional paradigm, where 'redesigned political units should promote, and in turn be promoted by, awareness on the part of their human inhabitants of the biological surroundings that sustain them' (2000: 157). The connection between listening to nature and living close to it in reconfigured units is explicit: people who are close to nature are 'in day-to-day contact with particular aspects of the ecosystem, and therefore in a much better position than distant managers or politicians to hear news from it' (2000: 157).

In essence, the listening in Dryzek's account is presented as an unmediated relation between listener and nature. Literally, those closer to particular places can 'hear' them better. Dryzek explicitly separates the 'listening' aspect of democracy from its representative aspect (2000: 154), and makes it clear that 'unlike the situation in aggregative liberal democracy, this communication does not have to be mediated by the material interests of particular actors' (2000: 154). Interestingly, Dryzek suggests that we ought to be careful not to 'anthropomorphise' (2000: 151). He is keen to avoid aesthetic representations, which would require and emphasise a gap between nature and listener. But one can argue (and I would) that to anthropomorphise is one mode of using metaphors as coded subjects to 'get at' (to make audible, as a parallel to making visible) nature's messages. It is one example of a move that is essential or unavoidable if one is to even attempt 'readings' of nature. Such metaphors, or representations, far from distorting messages from nature, make 'listening' possible. Dryzek of course uses his own metaphors – notably that of the 'feedback signal', an electronic metaphor for nature which, precisely because it belongs to a different realm, brings into view a conception of the object we wish to understand.

Like Rousseau, Dryzek is suspicious of representation in two of its aspects, aesthetic and conventional-political, and he would like to transcend both. His prescription is radical indeed, favouring a highly decentralised, bioregional politics. In essence, Dryzek has a dream of political authenticity, of direct politics, more or less spontaneous and unmediated. Ultimately, it seems to me, this sort of work taps into deep-seated Garden of Eden metaphors – back to nature means back to a simpler, more authentic, more tuned-in human nature, of something roughly analogous to humanity before the Fall. The Rousseauian links are evident enough: a vision full of politics, but of spontaneous orders of politics, relatively free from the corrupting artifice of aggregative representative institutions as we know them.

Representation, metaphor and institutional design

Let me try to take stock of these selective comments on green writings on representation and offer some observations on some key characteristics of the green thinking identified with respect to representation: unidirectional approaches, objectivity and authenticity claims.

The first major criticism was that of *unidirectionality*, the problem of seeing representation as a one-way process, where the representative is a mere receptor or reflection of some primary object or person or group. Representation, I have argued, is best seen as bi- or multidirectional: representative and represented are in a shifting and mutually constitutive relationship. Real things, people, animals and species exist. To be sure, there are limited sets of ways in which these referents could be described or accounted for. But that leaves plenty of scope for competing representations or constructions of them as objects. Making these representations or constructions is what politicians, artists and political theorists do. Representation works in two directions: the referent's material reality conditions the range of what can be said about it, and makers and subjects create representations within that range.

Overlapping with that point, I criticised some greens for assuming that an *authentic* presence of 'nature' or its interests was 'out there', if only we could listen carefully enough, or get close enough to it. By contrast, my preferred approach holds that identity in representation is authored rather than authentic, that it is necessarily partial and selective. I was also critical of a further closely related green tendency to see nature or the environment as possessing '*objective* interests'.

Do these criticisms amount to a rejection of green political thinking? Not at all. But they might point to a different approach, one more in tune with a broader and thicker conception of political representation. I turn now to how we might deal with metaphors of nature as representations, and subsequently comment on the politics of green thinking.

Stressing the constructedness of our representations or conceptions of nature does carry some tricky judgements. I do think that the 'epistemic' dimension of representing non-humans and other species is sometimes overemphasised. There is more to be said for an alternative, 'interpretive' approach, which allows more space for accepting and exploring a plurality of competing representations (reading in possibilities rather than reading off certainties). However, it makes little sense to press this point to the bottom. Raising the epistemic questions does at least have the virtue of leading us to ask 'how do you know?' and invites critical discussion of different forms of knowledge generation. This, for example, can lead us to key issues about the status of scientific knowledge.

Clearly, natural phenomena (like volcanoes) exist and have an impact beyond cultural representations of them. As I have indicated, I do not argue that there is no referent, or extra-discursive reality. Certain forms of knowledge of them in this respect can have a particular, if contingent, validity. A 'more valid' representation of nature in this respect means one that is more efficacious, gains more purchase on the phenomenon in question when applied or assumed. I would go so far as to say that a strong consensus in the broader scientific community regarding validity is a strong indicator of validity. Producing broad and deep consensus among specialists with expertise is a powerful thing. The scientific, causal debates about global warming have largely been settled recently by the sheer degree of scientific consensus on causes and likely consequences of climate change.

Which representations of 'nature'/nature we may rely upon more is a relative and difficult matter, though. As suggested, the claims of scientific knowledge rest upon assumptions about the social dimension of creating scientific knowledge and on the Popperian fallibilist view that science proves nothing but offers 'conjectures and refutations'. There is no escaping representations, then – we cannot 'see' nature *without* metaphors or mediating representations which characterise it and bring it into focus – and no *non-contingent* means to judge relative validities, even if we agree with Soper's excellent account of these issues when she observes that, even if there is a lot of culture in nature, there is some nature which is also not just culture (Soper 1996).

Having said that, some metaphorical representations of nature have had great material consequences because people have acted upon them. Other ways of seeing nature have had less impact, including until recent times metaphors favoured by greens (such as the idea of 'partnership' discussed by Plumwood in this volume). There are many and varied ways in which 'nature' can be, and has been, represented. The power of metaphors of nature often grows from a sliding from one meaning of 'nature' – nature as 'the essential quality or character of something' – to another, namely 'the external, material world itself' (Demeritt 2002: 777–8). Sliding from the first to the second meaning can lead us to believe that when we gaze into the external world we are accessing some sort of essence. This is a powerful tool, and one of course that has been exploited by classic political theorists such as Hobbes and Rousseau, and continues today in arguments that, for instance, the free market is a 'natural' way for people to interact and to meet their needs.

Dominant metaphors can tell us a great deal about the societies that hold to them. They can also tell us a great deal about what can or should be done to the 'nature' which the metaphors make visible. We can look at these on a grand historical scale. Three main metaphors – 'the book of nature, man as the microcosm, and the world as machine' – have informed Western views of nature, according to Mills (Mills 1982: 237). In terms of the preferred model of representation, these metaphors are subjects which are put up by those who use them (makers) to signify their object (nature). In the Middle Ages, the dominant metaphor of the book of nature implied, for example, that nature had an author, that its meanings could be read, that it had varied levels of meaning, and that physical nature bore legible marks of the authorial hand or presence. This theocratic view gave way in the Renaissance to a more anthropomorphic view in which humanity rather than God provided the dominant metaphor. Man, or more specifically the human body, was the measure of all things. Mills invites us to

consider how much of the language we still habitually employ derives from just such an anthropomorphic view of the world. We speak of mountains as possessing 'brows', 'shoulders', 'backs', and 'feet', and rivers have 'heads' and flow through 'gorges' out into 'mouths'. We refer to a 'neck' of land, an 'arm' of the sea, a 'vein' of mineral ore, and the 'bowels' of the earth. (1982: 242)

Finally, into the modern era, the metaphor shifted to that of the 'earth machine'. Clocks and later computers became the source of concepts for nature. Viewing nature through mechanistic metaphors implies that nature is made and can be remade, and that it can be controlled and tinkered with.

By looking at dominant metaphors we can learn a great deal about the societies which harboured and developed and lived by the metaphors: 'Nature is no more a book or a giant human being than it is an extraordinarily complex machine. That certain societies should find such views of it convincing, however, is highly informative and provides us with a direct means of knowing their central needs and aspirations' (Mills 1982: 249). Without assuming that these metaphors were unchallenged or unambiguous, we can also learn what might, and often did, follow from their prominence. A machine, for example, can be owned and used and dismantled and changed and sold and controlled – a machine metaphor determines nothing in itself, but it carries the potential to facilitate domination and commercialisation of nature. A machine implies a maker of the machine and a purpose, so religious views of nature might be at home with the machine metaphor, too. My point is that metaphors underpin belief, and belief underpins actions. The metaphors of nature we have and use condition what we can do with and to nature.

That is probably too much the grand sweep of history approach. From a more modest but probably a more fruitful perspective, we inhabit a messier and dynamic world of competing and overlapping metaphors. Among the ones that green political theorists and others often address critically are:

– economic metaphors, concerned with nature's 'richness' and involving 'producers' and 'consumers'

- pyramidal metaphors with 'humans as the pinnacle of evolution'
- sex-typing metaphors such as 'mother nature', carried over into ideas of, for example, 'virgin nature'
- mechanistic and cybernetic metaphors
- wild nature as an agricultural crop ('harvesting the fish crops') (Meisner 1992: 2)

The green temptation is to find better, alternative metaphors, such as Nature as home, Nature as musical ('harmony in diversity'), Nature as a living being, and so on (Meisner 1992: 2). Metaphors are nothing if not suggestive and multifaceted, and any one metaphor will outrun attempts to characterise it or interpret its implications in one direction. Thus there is no single, unambiguous good or bad, helpful or dangerous metaphor from a political ecological point of view. It is just not that simple. Meisner, in his thoughtful account of the issue, seeks new metaphors which are 'both evocatively powerful and cognitively practical; they must evoke positive feelings about nature, and suggest a conception that leads to humility, respect, and non-exploitative ways of living' (1992: 9). He recognises how elusive such metaphors are likely to prove, though he favours, for example, ones which see nature as alive, as process rather than as thing, as partner rather than as possession (1992: 8) (see Plumwood, this volume).

We have seen how powerful the temptation is for all of us – green political theorists are hardly the exception – to seek to break the boundaries of representation, to find directness, engagement, contact, authenticity, as I have suggested Dryzek does. The desire to escape from, or to fix upon 'better', metaphors is a recognition of the power of the material consequences of metaphor or representations, and at the same time a tilt towards overcoming the undesirable contingencies of the play of representations in political life.

Because we cannot escape representations in a larger sense, it is a positive thing from a green point of view that radical political efficacy does not require such an escape. Representation is a rich concept, and it can readily encompass the mutual constituting and indeterminacy present in all relations between one who represents and one who is represented. At the same time, the concept is rich enough to point us to claims and practices well beyond traditional parliamentary representation, as I indicated at the outset. Animals can be engaged with, looked for, traced, understood and appreciated in new ways by humans opening up themselves to new ways of 'reading' and 'writing' them (see, for example, Hinchliffe et al. 2004). But to do this is to tap into new ideas of what it means to represent, and to make representations, in the senses of both what it can involve and who can do it. We live in and by representations, and representation making is a necessary human activity, not one that diminishes in importance just through physical proximity to or familiarity with 'nature' or anything else. The desire to move beyond a politics of representation to a direct engagement with nature is understandable enough, but it is misconceived. Our need to 'make up nature' does not go away just because we are close to it (or even because we *are* it).

Politics brings varied representations into play. Perhaps, instead of 'enfranchising constituencies that are affected' – the traditional, parliamentary way of looking at representation – we could look to multiple representations or constructions of the affected (nature), putting new interpretations and perspectives 'into play', politically. Perhaps, too, this is the real task of green parties and pressure groups – makers of provocative new metaphors of nature, creators of portrayals that can win hearts, minds, votes and actions (see also Eckersley 2003).

It is here that the point about politics and theory, which I mentioned in the context of the green critique, comes into its own. Looked at from a particular angle, one can say that what Eckersley, Dobson, Goodin and Dryzek variously offer is a compelling set of metaphors or representations of nature: mysterious constructions about nature alive, pervaded with meanings, speaking to us if only we can listen, replete with interests that are comparable to our own, a set of forces demanding our attention and deserving our respect. In short, what we have gained from these writers are metaphors which link conceptions of nature with political prescription. These are potentially powerful *political* arguments, aesthetically compelling and culturally resonant representations of nature. That will not be news to anyone, but I mean the claim in a strong way: dressed and presented and published as political theory, they are in fact a highly sophisticated form of political argument, the home for which ultimately (in a well-functioning democracy) ought to be the cut and thrust of daily political life, in the parliamentary politics of representation to be sure, but well beyond there to the local and international, formal and informal political spaces where representation happens, representations are made and power is generated.

From a green perspective, forging and refining and arguing for metaphors of nature which prompt pro-ecological actions is the right approach. I am engaged in something much less than that task here. A prerequisite to the success of such efforts is an open society which allows a richer variety of representations to become available. A dynamic process of making and remaking representations of nature – on a crude level, this overlaps with a 'the more, the better' view – is a positive thing for various reasons. We might adapt J. S. Mill's argument, that we can only know the rightness of one argument by testing it against others, to say that the efficacy of making nature visible through one metaphorical representation can be teased out and tested by way of contrast with another or others. We could say that unmasking metaphors which facilitate environmental destruction is all the more easy when alternatives can be evoked or created or deployed in argument (it is fortunate, for example, that by the time the former premier of the Australian state of Tasmania described the Franklin River, the proposed damming of which provoked a major environmental dispute in the early 1980s, as a 'brown, leech-ridden ditch', there was a strong environmental movement to argue for alternative images and portrayals of the wild river and Tasmanian wilderness more generally). We might cite the imaginative power of metaphor as a contributor to processes of 'reflective democracy' (Goodin 2003), where citizens and politicians are invited or induced to reflect upon the interests and needs of human and non-human others by exposure to provocative depictions and accounts. In my limited way here, I have pointed out how green political theorists themselves offer potent metaphors with real political resonance.

I suggested at the outset that questions of democratic institutional design lurk within my comments. If democratic representation happens in but also well beyond elective and parliamentary domains, then our thinking about innovative democratic designs can and should follow suit. We might start, for example, from the premise that institutionalising multiple modes of representing a range of shifting human and non-human interests is perfectly democratic, and that seeking means to test openly in argument varied representations of nature requires new democratic thinking. This is a complex topic indeed, and these are very brief comments – I have written elsewhere how varied devices, placed in sequences, might evoke and draw in to democratic processes more interests and needs and phenomena than merely living human constituencies, and indeed alternative representations of the latter too (Saward 2003). Alongside a representative parliament, why not a citizens' jury to evoke statistical representation, local forums to evoke representation-in-place, a parliament of Dobsonian proxies of nature and future generations, and the precautionary principle to capture assumed needs and interests whose character at present eludes the reach of our understanding? Representative politics is much more about portrayal and image making in argument than it is often assumed. Green political theorists, I have suggested, are engaged precisely in these political debates more than conventional readings of their work might indicate. Their work on political ecology might pose one major challenge in particular to mainstream political theory – how to imagine in detail a democracy that revels in representative politics in the broader and deeper sense, since the metaphors and representations we invoke are critical to shaping political outcomes, for 'nature' and for us as a part of it.

References

Alcoff, L. (1991). 'The Problem of Speaking for Others', *Cultural Critique* (Winter): 5–32.

Ankersmit, F. R. (1996). *Aesthetic Politics*. Stanford, Calif.: Stanford University Press.

(2002). *Political Representation*. Stanford, Calif.: Stanford University Press.

Barry, J. (1999). *Rethinking Green Politics*. London: Sage.

Becker, H. S. (1986). 'Telling About Society', in *Doing Things Together*. Evanston, Ill.: Northwestern University Press.

Bourdieu, P. (1991). *Language and Symbolic Power*, trans. J. B. Thompson. Cambridge, Mass.: Harvard University Press.

Cohen, J. (1968). 'Commentary: Representation and the Problem of Identity', in J. R. Pennock and J. W. Chapman (eds.), *Nomos X: Representation*. New York: Atherton Press.

Demeritt, D. (2002). 'What Is the "Social Construction of Nature"? A Typology and Sympathetic Critique', *Progress in Human Geography* **26**: 766–89.

Derrida, J. (1982). 'Sending: On Representation', *Social Research* **49**.2 (Summer): 294–326.

Dobson, A. (1996). 'Representative Democracy and the Environment', in W. M. Lafferty and J. Meadowcroft (eds.), *Democracy and the Environment*. Cheltenham: Edward Elgar.

Dryzek, J. S. (2000). *Deliberative Democracy and Beyond*. Oxford: Oxford University Press.

Eckersley, R. (2000). 'Deliberative Democracy, Representation and Risk', in M. Saward (ed.), *Democratic Innovation*. London: Routledge.

(2003). 'Ecocentric Discourses: Problems and Future Prospects for Nature Advocacy', paper presented to the Second Tamkang International Conference on Ecological Discourse, Tamsui, Taiwan.

Goodin, R. E. (1996). 'Enfranchising the Earth, and Its Alternatives', *Political Studies* **44**: 835–49.

(2003). 'Democratic Deliberation Within', in J. S. Fishkin and P. Laslett (eds.), *Debating Deliberative Democracy*. Oxford: Blackwell.

Hall, S. (1997). 'The Work of Representation', in S. Hall (ed.), *Representation: Cultural Representations and Signifying Practices*. London: Sage and The Open University.

Hinchliffe, S., Kearnes, M. B., Degen, M., and Whatmore, S. (2004). 'Urban Wild Things: A Cosmopolitical Experiment', *Environment and Planning D: Society and Space* **23**.5 (October): 643–58.

Latour, B. (2003). 'What if We Talked Politics a Little?', *Contemporary Political Theory* **2**.2 (July): 143–64.

Mansbridge, J. (2003). 'Rethinking Representation', *American Political Science Review* **97**.4: 515–28.

Marin, L. (2001). *On Representation*, trans. C. Porter. Stanford, Calif.: Stanford University Press.

Meisner, M. (1992). 'Metaphors of Nature: Old Vinegar in New Bottles?', http://trumpeter.athabascau.ca/content/v9.4/meisner.html (accessed 11 December 2003).

Mills, W. J. (1982). 'Metaphorical Vision: Changes in Western Attitudes to the Environment', *Annals of the Association of American Geographers* **72**: 237–53.

Pitkin, H. F. (1967). *The Concept of Representation*. Berkeley: University of California Press.

Przeworski, A., Stokes, S. C., and Manin, B. (1999). *Democracy, Accountability, and Representation*. Cambridge: Cambridge University Press.

Saward, M. (1998). *The Terms of Democracy*. Cambridge: Polity Press.

—— (2003). 'Enacting Democracy', *Political Studies* **51**: 161–79.

Seitz, B. (1995). *The Trace of Political Representation*. New York: State University of New York Press.

Soper, K. (1996). 'Nature/"nature"', in G. Robertson et al. (eds.), *FutureNatural*. London: Routledge.

Spivak, G. C. (1988). 'Can the Subaltern Speak?', in C. Nelson and L. Grossberg (eds.), *Marxism and the Interpretation of Culture*. London: Macmillan.

Thompson, D. (1988). 'Representatives in the Welfare State', in A. Gutmann (ed.), *Democracy in the Welfare State*. Princeton: Princeton University Press.

Young, I. M. (2000). *Inclusion and Democracy*. Oxford: Oxford University Press.

12   Freedom and rights

Richard Dagger

'[T]hat ill deserves the Name of confinement that hedges us in only from Bogs and Precipices.' These words, from §57 of John Locke's *Second Treatise of Government*, have long posed a challenge to those who hold that a firm commitment to negative liberty – that is, to liberty understood as the absence of interference, impediment or restraint – is one of the defining features of liberalism. To be sure, Locke goes on to acknowledge that '*Liberty* is to be free from restraint and violence from others'; but this liberty, he insists, 'cannot be, where there is no law' (Locke 1965 [1689–90]: 348). The challenge, then, is to show either that Locke is wrong, because the laws and hedges that keep us from falling into bogs or over precipices really do deprive us of liberty, or that he is not the arch-liberal he is so often taken to be.

Locke's words also pose a second challenge, however, one which is more pertinent to the concerns of the present volume. To put it simply, does Locke gives bogs and precipices their due? Is it not possible that bogs and precipices, as parts of nature, have interests and perhaps even rights of their own – rights that require the hedging in or confining of human beings, not so that we may live freely, but so that bogs and precipices may? Or might it not be possible that we diminish our own freedom or violate somebody's rights when we drain a bog or turn a precipice into a gentle slope? Questions of this sort could hardly have occurred to Locke and his contemporaries, but they are inescapable in our time of ecological challenge.

What follows, then, is an attempt to rethink freedom and rights in the light of this ecological challenge. This attempt, I should note, will proceed largely within the liberal tradition, at least if liberalism is understood as a theory that has much in common with civic republicanism (see Dobson's chapter in this book). I proceed in this way for two reasons. First, liberalism in one form or another now seems to be

For their comments, discussion, and assistance, I am grateful to Terence Ball, Mark Brown, Angela Grimwood, Elizabeth Willott, and the editors.

the dominant position among political theorists, and a book of this sort will have to speak to liberal concerns if it is to have any practical effect. Within political theory, moreover, the most influential analyses of the concepts of freedom and rights have been the work of liberal philosophers. If we are to consider how political theorists should conceive of rights and freedom in the light of the ecological challenge, we shall have to attend to these analyses.

Liberalism, of course, is quite a capacious theory, with room for liberals to debate quite vigorously among themselves, as well as with others, the meaning and significance of freedom, rights and other concepts. It is also capacious enough to allow for a rethinking of these concepts at a time of pressing environmental problems. Such a rethinking, I shall argue, should lead us to conceive of freedom and rights less as barriers or shields that protect individuals against interference – as forms of *independence* – and more as matters of organic growth and connection, or *interdependence*. Indeed, we must conceive of freedom and rights in this organic, interdependent way if we are to respond adequately to the ecological challenge. If Garrett Hardin is right, we shall have to rely upon 'mutual coercion, mutually agreed upon' if we are to avoid environmental tragedy (Hardin 1968). But it will be easier to agree to this mutual coercion if we see our rights not as inviolable barriers against others but as forms of relations that entail responsibilities to others. I shall argue, therefore, for a move away from the negative conceptions of rights and freedom and toward an understanding that relates both concepts to autonomy. If this seems to be a self-defeating leap from one negative, atomistic way of thinking to another, I can only ask the reader to bear with me until I explain what I mean by 'autonomy'.

The nature of freedom and rights

Philosophers frequently frame their discussions of rights and freedom in terms of the negative/positive distinction. In the case of liberty, Thomas Hobbes and Jeremy Bentham are two of the most influential to conceive of it negatively – that is, as the *absence* of impediment or restraint. T. H. Green later argued that freedom, 'rightly understood', is 'a positive power or capacity of doing or enjoying something worth doing or enjoying ... in common with others' (Green 1991 [1880]: 21). But Green's notion of positive liberty includes an evaluative element that strikes many scholars as misplaced. Can't we be just as free, they ask, when we do or enjoy something that is not especially worthwhile as when we do or enjoy something that is? For that matter, can't we freely do something reprehensible or vicious? These objections may not be altogether fair to Green, whose concern was not so much with whether individuals act freely when they do this or that as with 'the ideal of true freedom', understood as 'the maximum of power for all members of human society to make the best of themselves' (Green 1991 [1880]: 23). But this emphasis on 'true freedom' as making the best of oneself only heightens the problems of positive liberty, according to a line of argument made famous by Isaiah Berlin's 'Two Concepts of Liberty'.

Positive freedom is a worrisome notion, Berlin charges, partly because it confuses freedom with ability – '[m]ere incapacity to attain a goal is not lack of political freedom' (Berlin 1969: 122) – but even more because of its implicit reliance on a distinction between two selves: the lower or empirical self and the true, real or higher self with which it is often at odds. Once we draw this distinction, Berlin says, we are

in a position to ignore the actual wishes of men or societies, to bully, oppress, torture them in the name, and on behalf, of their 'real' selves, in the secure knowledge that whatever is the true goal of man (happiness, performance of duty, wisdom, a just society, self-fulfilment) must be identical with his freedom – the free choice of his 'true', albeit often submerged and inarticulate, self. (Berlin 1969: 133)

Thus does positive liberty open the door to tyranny. Better, then, to cleave to the negative conception of liberty as, in Berlin's terms, the absence of interference.

Reinforcing this view is the tendency to draw a distinction between negative and positive rights. In this case the distinction rests on the understanding of rights as valid claims that impose correlative duties or responsibilities on the part of others. There is some controversy on this point, but there is also general agreement that the kind of right with which we are most often concerned in moral, political and legal philosophy is the *claim-right*, and claim-rights – for example, the rights you acquire when I sign a contract to work for you – entail correlative duties. A negative right thus is one that imposes only a duty of non-interference on others, such as the right to speak freely, whereas a positive right requires someone's active assistance or compliance, as in the putative right to medical care. As 'putative' here suggests, scholars and jurists often assume that negative rights are the principal or primary form of rights – the real rights, as it were – because they protect the individual from interference and thereby preserve his or her liberty. Negative rights are thus conceptual kin to negative liberty.

In neither case, however, is the negative view of rights or liberty entirely persuasive. With regard to rights, the distinction between negative and positive proves to be difficult, at best, to sustain (Shue 1980: 35–64).

Negative rights supposedly require only forbearance on the part of those who may be tempted to interfere with us, as in the case of the person who has no duty to hear me out but does have a duty *not* to shut me up when I exercise my right to free speech. Yet many supposedly negative rights make no sense unless there is a system of social co-operation and supporting institutions that demand more than merely leaving one another alone. Your right to vote, for example, imposes a duty of non-interference on others, but it also requires them to support the registrar's office, the board of election commissioners, and other institutions that make voting possible (Waldron 1993: 580). If we are to be reasonably secure in the enjoyment of our supposedly negative rights, moreover, we must be able to rely on the police, the courts, the county recorder's office and other instruments of the legal system, all of which impose more costs on others than the cost of mere forbearance (Holmes and Sunstein 1999).

The difficulty here is especially evident if we consider rights that are linked to the physical environment. At first glance, someone who claims a right to experience wilderness or to enjoy a healthy environment is claiming a negative right. That is, she is telling us not that we should provide her with an all-expense-paid trip to the nearest wilderness or healthy environment, but that we should not interfere with her experience or enjoyment of them. The problem, however, is that one cannot experience wilderness or enjoy a healthy environment when these things are not available, and their continued existence, or restoration, requires more than non-interference on the part of others; it requires at least that we impose rules that restrict access and use lest there be no wilderness left to experience. If we want to make a case for environmental rights of this sort, then we are necessarily making a case for the active assistance and compliance, as well as forbearance, of other persons.

A similar problem arises with regard to negative liberty. There is little dispute that freedom is in part a matter of being free from impediment or restraint, but Locke and others have supplied ample reason to think that there is more to freedom than that. According to one well-known analysis, freedom is always a matter of some agent's being *free from* some obstacle in order to be *free to* do something (MacCallum 1967), and Charles Taylor and others have gone on to argue that what one is free to do is at least as important as what one is free from. Taylor's striking contrast between London and Tirana, the capital of communist Albania in the 1970s, illustrates the difference between freedom as an *opportunity*-concept and an *exercise*-concept. Religion had been abolished in Albania, Taylor observes, but 'there are probably far fewer traffic lights per head in Tirana than in London', where people are free to worship in public places even if only a minority do so. As the 'number of acts restricted by traffic lights must be greater than that restricted by a ban on public religious practice', it follows that the residents of Tirana are less restricted, and have more opportunities to move through town, than Londoners (Taylor 1979: 183). Yet few people would conclude that Tirana's residents are therefore freer than Londoners. All opportunities are not equal. Once this is admitted, however, it becomes necessary to find some way of discriminating between important and insignificant opportunities, which is to say that evaluative judgements about what is worth doing or enjoying cannot be divorced from assessments of freedom in the way that advocates of negative liberty have claimed. On Taylor's account, these judgements implicitly appeal to the positive conception of freedom as 'the exercising of control over one's life' – hence, freedom as an exercise-concept (Taylor 1979: 177).

Philip Pettit has recently employed a related distinction between *option-freedom* and *agency-freedom* as part of his argument for the 'republican' conception of freedom as non-domination. When we speak of freedom, he says, we sometimes have in mind how plentiful or scarce someone's options are; the more choices available to someone, the freer she is. In other cases, though, we have the person's status as a 'free agent' in mind – as someone who does not have 'to depend on the grace or mercy of others, being able to do one's own thing without asking their leave or permission' (Pettit 2003: 394). That is why we regard a non-arbitrary law that deprives us of some options as something very different from criminal interference that has the same effect. Pettit does not refer to §57 of Locke's *Second Treatise* in this context, but he could well have done so when he explains how a law may at the same time be 'inimical to one variety of freedom while being friendly to the other' (Pettit 2003: 398). Other things being equal, of course, we will want to have as much option-freedom as possible while maintaining our agency-freedom. What we should not want, according to Pettit, is to extend our option-freedom if it means sacrificing our status as free agents. We should also be wary, to give a green cast to Pettit's argument, of extending the option-freedom of people today in ways that threaten the sustainability of the environment and reduce the options – and perhaps even the agency – of future generations (Holland 1999; Norton 1999).

To be a free agent, for Pettit, is to be free from domination. That is why he regards republican freedom as a form of negative liberty – as the *absence* of domination. Like Taylor, however, he clearly believes that freedom is more than the absence of interference, impediment or restraint. To hold the status of free agent is to be recognised as someone who is capable of acting and of taking responsibility for those actions.[1] But as 'status' and 'recognised' imply, one cannot be a free agent entirely on one's own. Others must see and treat me as a free agent, and laws, police and courts are necessary to protect me against those who would not. Nor do my options always increase when others simply leave me alone, for their indifference or distance will deprive me of the opportunity to do all of those things, such as the tango, that require two or more people. As with negative rights, in sum, so with negative liberty: attempts to protect our independence against interference founder on our inescapable *inter*dependence.

The freedom and rights of nature

But what has this to do with bogs and precipices? Do they, or other parts of nature, or nature as a whole, have rights – negative, positive or otherwise – that impose duties on human beings? Should they be free from our interference, or liberated from our domination, to go their own way? Or does it make no sense to speak of bogs, precipices and other parts of non-human nature as free agents with rights against us? These are much-discussed questions, and I cannot hope to rehearse the debates adequately here, much less resolve them. Nevertheless, I shall state my position – one that is nearer to social than to deep ecology – and sketch my reasons for taking it.

With regard to the possible freedom of nature or its elements, there are two reasons for resisting this way of thinking that seem to me decisive. The first has to do with agency and the second with what Christopher Stone has called the 'ontological problem' (Stone 1974: 34 and passim). Agency is an important consideration because, following Pettit and Taylor, there is more to freedom than having options or being free from impediments. If we ask whether nature is capable of freedom, the answer should begin by noting not only that 'nature' is notoriously difficult to define, but that it seems to fall into three broad categories. At one extreme are those natural objects and animals to which we cannot reasonably attribute free action; at the other are human beings, who typically have the potential for agency. In the middle category are those animals that give enough evidence of preferring and choosing to warrant the belief that they act freely, in Pettit's sense of option-freedom, but not that they are agents. Thus we speak of lions being 'born free' or of deer 'ranging freely', even though neither lions nor deer are agents

---

[1] On agency, see Pettit 2001, esp. ch. 1. For a less stringent conception of agency that allows for 'agency in nature', see Dryzek 2000: 148–52; but cf. Dobson 1996: 142–44.

responsible for their deeds. Bogs, precipices, trees, rocks and other natural objects do not exercise option-freedom, however, nor is it anything more than metaphor to write, as Dave Foreman does, of 'freeing shackled rivers' from the dams that confine them (Foreman 1991: 407). We do occasionally personify rivers and other forces of nature, as when we call the Mississippi 'Old Man River', and we may even talk of tearing down a dam so that a river may be 'free to follow its course'. But this is on a par with saying that untying a ribbon or pulling out some pins 'freed' someone's hair. We know that the river will flow once the dam is out of the way because it cannot choose to remain cooped up in a lake or reservoir. In Pettit's terms, it has neither agency-freedom nor option-freedom. There may be good reasons to tear down dams that block rivers, to be sure, or to leave bogs, precipices and other natural 'objects' as they are, but promoting or respecting their freedom is not one of them.

The example of the river also illustrates the ontological problem that Christopher Stone struggles to overcome in his brief for the legal standing of nature and natural objects. The problem is that there is no obvious or certain way of identifying just what it is that should be freed when someone sets out to free *the natural*. Is it the river, or the molecules of water that compose it, or the atoms that compose them? Or is it the river valley, or the hydrologic cycle? Or the bioregion, or the whole of nature? Stone's answer is to say, first, that it depends on what one is concerned with: 'from time to time one will wish to speak of that portion of a river that runs through a recognized jurisdiction; at other times, one may be concerned with the entire river, or the hydrologic cycle – or the whole of nature' (Stone 1974: 9, n. 26). The 'one' who wishes to speak, however, and the 'one' who has the concern is not a river or valley or cycle but a person – an agent that is capable of giving voice to his or her concerns. This leaves us with Stone's second answer, which is to say that this ontological problem applies to persons as much as to natural forces and objects. And it is true that we talk not only of a person's being free but also, at times, of a people's or a country's freedom. In the latter case, though, we know that the elements that compose the people or country differ from the elements that compose the river by being themselves, at least potentially, free agents. We know this, in particular, because individual persons sometimes make it clear that those who claim to speak for their country do not speak for them – something that we can hardly expect of a tree in the forest or a drop of water in the pond. Stone's second response to the ontological problem is thus no more successful than his first.

To be fair, Stone's concern is to make a case for the legal *rights* of nature, not for its freedom. But his arguments fare no better when applied to rights. Indeed, the ontological problem is perhaps even more vexing in the case of rights than in that of freedom. Is it the tree that has rights or the forest? Does the tree have rights or the river that is uprooting it, or – to bring animal nature into the discussion – the bark beetle that is killing it? Or do all of these entities have rights that, like the rights of persons, sometimes come into conflict with one another? And if they do, how are these conflicts to be adjudicated?

These and similar questions have prompted Roderick Nash to observe that the 'use of "rights" in this connection has created considerable confusion. Suffice it to say ... that while some use the term in a technical philosophical or legal sense, others take it to mean that nature, or parts of it, has intrinsic worth which humans ought to respect' (Nash 1989: 4). I am less willing than Nash to excuse the confusion, and not only because of a professional interest in being as clear as possible in the use of important concepts. Another concern is the risk of an 'escalation of rights rhetoric' that threatens either to overwhelm other concepts and considerations or, by a process of conceptual inflation, to rob the appeal to rights of much of its power.[2] If we can make a case for the worth of nature without appealing to the rights of nature, then we should do so.[3]

To say that, however, is to assume that we cannot make, in Nash's words, 'technical philosophical or legal sense' of the rights of nature, and I should explain why I think that assumption is warranted. In my view, the only entities that have rights are those that are able to respect the rights of others. Arsonists have rights, for example, but bolts of lightning do not. Both may destroy my house, but only the arsonist violates my rights in doing so, and only the arsonist, not the lightning bolt or the forest fire, can enjoy various legal rights when brought to justice – including, on some views, a right to be punished. In other words, rights presuppose agency.

This is not, I should note, a view universally accepted among those who analyse rights in the 'technical philosophical or legal sense'. In Joel Feinberg's oft-cited analysis, it is not agency but interests that make something a bearer of rights (Feinberg 1980). On the agency account, after all, we should refuse to attribute rights not only to rocks, plants and non-human animals, but also to babies and other human beings – victims of stroke, for example, or various forms of dementia – who plainly lack agency. Yet we commonly hold that these people have rights, so it must be that their rights follow from their interests, such as their interest

---

[2] The quoted phrase is from Sumner 1987: I. See also Golding 1990: 60–4, and Wellman 1999: ch. 5.

[3] Goodin 1992 is exemplary in this regard, but I do not endorse his consequentialism.

in life, nutrition and escaping cruelty. And if we recognise these rights in humans incapable of agency, then we must also recognise them in other beings that have these interests – not in plants, bogs or precipices, according to Feinberg, but at least in the higher animals. If one protests that rights are claims, and we ought not to predicate rights of something or someone that cannot press a claim, Feinberg's response is to agree with the first assertion but not the second. Rights are indeed claims, in his view, but all that is necessary is that someone be able to press the claim in behalf of the rights-bearer, not that this someone be the rights-bearer him-, her- or itself.

Given Feinberg's analysis, why cling to the view that rights pre-suppose agency? The answer is that Feinberg fails to take account of the two senses in which someone or something has an interest. Here I follow S. I. Benn, who pointed out a telling difference between what one is *interested in* and what is *in one's interests* (Benn 1977: 405–11). Babies and non-human animals surely have an interest in food, shelter and whatever is conducive to their wellbeing. But that requires no activity on their part, no sense of giving a direction to one's life that happens when one *takes an interest in* something. Rights are important here as claims because they are

normative resources that enable [a person], by controlling the actions of others, to manipulate his social environment for his own ends – whatever those ends may be. Having rights enables him to pursue *what he is interested in*; and this may be very different from what is *in* his interests. (Benn 1977: 407; emphasis in original)

Following Benn rather than Feinberg, however, still leaves us with the problem of babies and the demented. Don't they have rights despite their lack of agency? They do, in my judgement, by virtue of their potential in the one case and their past in the other. In the normal course of affairs, a human infant will gradually take an interest in giving a shape to his or her life and become someone capable of respecting the rights of others; and it is our recognition of this potential that warrants our attributing rights to infants. In the case of the irretrievably demented, we are justified in according them rights in recognition of what they would have done or would do were they still agents. And what of those unfortunate infants who apparently lack the potential ever to become agents? These children have no rights, in my view, but that is not to say that they may be disposed of or treated however we see fit. Some things are wrong even when done to entities that have no rights.

If I am correct, then, about rights presupposing agency, it follows that bogs, precipices and non-human nature have no rights. If I am wrong and Feinberg is correct, all that follows is that the category of rights-bearer extends to many, but not all, non-human animals. Bogs and precipices are still excluded. But that is most emphatically not to say that they are of no account or no worth. It is to say, instead, that we must look for other ways to make the case for the value of nature. We must also look for ways to rethink our rights and freedom, as persons, in light of the ecological challenge.

Ecology and autonomy

As Nash observes in *The Rights of Nature* (Nash 1989), Stone and Foreman and others who want to accord rights to nature or to liberate it from human domination typically take Aldo Leopold's 'land ethic' as their point of departure. They do so with good reason, for Leopold's account of the evolution of ethics offers some hope to those who want to bring about a shift in consciousness. There was a time, Leopold remarks, when many people were regarded simply as property and not, therefore, as worthy of ethical consideration; hence Odysseus' hanging twelve slave girls all on one rope was a matter of expedience rather than ethics. We would condemn such an action now, and properly so, but that is because our sense of who counts has expanded to embrace more and more people as full members of the ethical community. In light of our increasing understanding of our interdependence with the natural world, moreover, we now have good reason to expand the ethical community even more dramatically by adopting a land ethic that 'enlarges the boundaries of the community to include soils, waters, plants, and animals, or collectively, the land' (Leopold 2004 [1949]: 417).

Like Stone, Foreman and many others, I find this a powerful argument. Its power, however, does not reside in appeals to the rights of nature or pleas for its freedom, for Leopold does not press his case in those terms. Instead, its power lies in leading people to see themselves as parts of nature who both depend on it and have a special responsibility for its care. The land ethic is not addressed to the land, or even to the higher animals, but to persons, the only beings capable of reading and acting on Leopold's words.[4] I take it, then, that it is our freedom and rights as persons that must be reconsidered if we are to adopt a land ethic that will enable us to address the ecological challenge brought on

---

[4] Gerald Gaus (1998: 252–3) reaches a similar conclusion by a very different route.

by people who have been acting freely and, for the most part, within their rights as ordinarily understood.

This reconsideration must begin, as Leopold insisted, with an appreciation of the extent to which we are bound up with nature – or, properly speaking, with the rest of nature. Ecology, the science of the interrelationship of organisms and their environment, teaches this lesson, and part of the ecological challenge consists in helping people to see, as a familiar distinction puts it, that they are not *apart from* nature so much as *a part of* it. Freedom is not something to be wrested from nature, on this view, nor rights simply a way of dividing nature into what is properly mine and thine. They are, instead, to be exercised and enjoyed within the bounds of nature. What an ecological or land ethic does, in other words, is to encourage us to think of our relationship to nature as a matter of *autonomy*.

This statement is likely to strike many readers as implausible, as I noted earlier, and perhaps altogether wrongheaded. That is because autonomy is often understood as a kind of global or summary condition attributed to those who enjoy extensive negative freedom, as in the 'personal autonomy' of the individual who is generally free from inter-ference to do and say as he wishes whenever and wherever he wishes to do or say it. Or it might refer to the condition of one who is not only free from interference by other people, but free also in the sense of having considerable power over nature – free to cross rivers on bridges, to water her lawn when she pleases, to fly across oceans and continents on aeroplanes, and so on. Such a person is autonomous, self-governing, in large part because of her ability, in co-operation with others, to govern nature. So understood, autonomy is an attractive ideal to many people. Yet it is difficult to see how it comports with a land or ecological ethic.

The difficulty will not seem so great, however, once we notice that autonomous people may also govern themselves with an eye to the effects of their actions on the physical environment. Autonomy is self-government, not licence, and it is a condition that we can properly attribute only to those who have a sufficient degree of self-awareness to be capable of governing themselves.[5] Nor is there any reason to think that such people cannot also see themselves as being interdependent both with other people and with nature as such. The question, then, is not whether autonomy is compatible with the land ethic, but whether

---

[5] Cf. Eckersley (1996: 223) for a 'more inclusive notion of autonomy' as 'the freedom of human and non-human beings to unfold in their own ways and live according to their "species life".' But this seems to conflate autonomy with flourishing.

the pursuit of autonomy, properly understood, leads to an endorsement of the land ethic.

Pettit's distinction between option-freedom and agency-freedom provides a helpful way to begin to answer this question. As Pettit says, the more options we have, the freer we are; but 'number alone may not be that important' (Pettit 2003: 392). Having a choice among '20 barely discernible beers', to borrow his example, will mean little to the wine-fancier and the teetotaller, who would no doubt think themselves freer if there were something besides beer on offer. Even the beer drinker is likely to think that a choice of twenty beers does not make her twice as free as a choice of ten would do – especially if her favourite is among the ten. And the recovering alcoholic who has only one beer set before him may think that one is enough to challenge his *agency*-freedom, as turning down twenty varieties would not show him to be more of a free agent – more autonomous, more self-governing – than turning down any one of them. What counts is the value of the options, not merely the number.

How, then, should we evaluate our options? One way is to ask what taking this option may mean for other options we may want to pursue, or leave open for others, at some time. To take an option is to act, and actions have consequences, one of which quite often is the foreclosing of other options. Having the option to drive one's motorcycle without wearing a helmet is only one of the most familiar of many such examples. Other examples speak more directly to civic and environmental concerns. Wal-Mart and other 'big-box' stores offer a vast array of consumer goods that promise option after option. When these stores move into town, however, they reduce the options of those who might want to be a main-street merchant. Such stores also contribute to metropolitan sprawl, the urban heat-island effect, and other environmental problems as they convert farm land and open country into acres of car parks – lots that themselves grow larger to accommodate the gasoline-guzzling 'Sport Utility Vehicles' that Americans, at least, seem to need to haul away the big-screen televisions and other goods they buy at these stores.[6] For all its celebration of choice, the consumer culture manifest in these stores makes some options much more available than others.

From the ecological standpoint, furthermore, the options that consumer culture makes most readily available are those that offer short-term benefits to individuals at the cost of long-term damage to the environment. In the United States, for instance, time spent in traffic continues to increase along with car ownership and the distance people

---

[6] For further remarks on (sub)urban sprawl, see Dagger 2003.

live from their workplaces. Frustration with traffic congestion has led to increased funding for mass transit, but it has also produced two less wholesome results: the addition of many miles of roads and highways, with the resulting urban sprawl, and increasingly comfortable cars. Rather than give up their cars, in other words, people want new and improved roads, which seem to fill up and become congested almost as soon as they are opened; and so as long as they are going to be stuck in traffic, people want cars with air conditioning, entertainment systems and plenty of head, leg and hip room. Meanwhile, as they wait comfortably if not contentedly in traffic, their cars continue to burn petroleum, spew carbon dioxide-laden fumes into the air, and drip pollutants on to the ground (Kay 1997).

When evaluating our options, then, we should do what we can to take those that truly preserve or extend our freedom rather than those that sooner or later will deprive us of it. We should also evaluate these options with an eye to their implications for autonomy. As the examples of Taylor's Tirana and the recovering alcoholic demonstrate, multiplying options does not always enhance autonomy, understood as the ability to lead a self-governed life: someone who is able to turn down twenty kinds of beer is not twenty times as self-governing as someone who has only one to refuse. What matters is that we have options that promote the ability to be self-governing. This means that we must be able to enjoy a reasonably secure sense of the self as something that is not simply the plaything of external forces or the creature of ungovernable impulses. Autonomy in this sense is sometimes taken to be a kind of self-creation, as if the self were capable of sitting in judgement on all of one's traits and desires, rejecting those that do not conform to one's self-conception and forging a unit out of those that do. There is some truth to this conception of autonomy, I think, as anyone who appreciates the distinction between first- and second-order desires – that is, the second-order desire *not* to have the first-order desire for, say, alcohol or sweets – will recognise. But that is not to say autonomy is the ability to create oneself entirely as one sees fit, from the ground up. On the contrary, self-*discovery* is at least as important to autonomy as self-*creation*. We must know our aptitudes and inclinations, our motives and limitations, in order to have the self-awareness that makes autonomy possible. This, apparently, is the kind of knowledge that the alcoholic must acquire if he or she is to overcome a debilitating appetite for alcohol.

Self-knowledge is also what we need if we are to respond properly to the ecological challenge. That may seem to be an extraordinary claim, especially as we quite clearly need to know much more about the nature of this challenge and about the effects of human actions on the physical environment. As I see it, however, the attempt to gain self-knowledge is part of these wider enquiries. To know ourselves is to know that we are parts of nature – not independent of but interdependent with it. If we are to be self-governing, then we must have some grasp of how we as human beings fit into the larger scheme of things. Like the alcoholic, we must learn that some of our habits and tendencies are self-destructive because they threaten, as Leopold warned, the food chain, the land pyramid, and the biotic community of which we are inescapably members. If we are to be autonomous, in sum, we must come to understand ourselves not only as *free* but also as *natural* agents.

Ecology and the right of autonomy

My conclusion, then, is that people need not surrender their freedom in order to respond effectively to the ecological challenge. To be sure, they must surrender some of their options, or option-freedom, but that is not the same as surrendering their agency or their autonomy. But what of their rights? Must these be lost if nature is to be saved?

If rights presuppose agency, as I have followed Benn in holding, then the answer is surely no. Some particular rights will be lost, of course, when laws limit people's options. For example, laws that create a green belt around a metropolitan area may deny farmers the right to sell their farms to those who would build housing estates on the land. But green-belt laws would also give others the right to open countryside within a reasonable distance of their homes, and it is not obvious that there would be a net loss of rights once the gains are set against the losses. In general, the contraction or reinterpretation of property rights would be offset or outweighed by the expansion of both substantive and procedural environmental rights (Eckersley 1996: 228–33; Nickel and Viola 1994).

The more important point, though, is that facing up to the ecological challenge is entirely consistent with the right of autonomy, which I have elsewhere elaborated as the right on which all others rest: the right to the promotion and protection of the ability to lead a self-governed life.[7] We are both individuals and members of communities, on this view. We owe our individuality and whatever degree of autonomy we attain in large part to the other members of our communities, but they also owe us respect for our autonomy, whether potential or actual. They owe us respect for our *right* of autonomy, that is, just as we owe them respect for

[7] In Dagger 1997, esp. ch. 3. For criticism, see Knowles 2001: 161–5.

theirs; for only an agent who is capable of respecting the rights of others can be the bearer of rights. As members of communities, of course, we cannot always have things our own way. What counts, however, is that we have a chance to make ourselves heard and to be accounted an equal in public deliberations. When these conditions hold, we need not worry about losing the fundamental right of autonomy.

What the ecological challenge teaches us is that we are not only individuals who are members of communities with other people; we are also members of biotic communities that are themselves parts of nature as a whole. We must grasp this fact, and come to understand its implications, if we are to be autonomous. This does not mean, again, that bogs and precipices have rights against us. But it does mean that we should think of rights not simply as barriers or shields that protect us against others, but as forms of relationship that enable us to pursue peacefully our private and public endeavours. Of all these, the greatest may be the endeavour to meet the ecological challenge.

References

Benn, S. I. (1977). 'Personal Freedom and Environmental Ethics: The Moral Inequality of Species', in Gray Dorsey (ed.), *Equality and Freedom*. Dobbs Ferry, N.Y.: Oceana Publications, 401–24.

Berlin, I. (1969). *Four Essays on Liberty*. Oxford: Oxford University Press.

Dagger, R. (1997). *Civic Virtues: Rights, Citizenship, and Republican Liberalism*. New York: Oxford University Press.

—— (2003). 'Stopping Sprawl for the Good of All: The Case for Civic Environmentalism', *Journal of Social Philosophy* **34** (Spring): 28–43.

Dobson, A. (1996). 'Democratising Green Theory: Preconditions and Principles', in Brian Doherty and Marius De Geus (eds.), *Democracy and Green Political Thought: Sustainability, Rights and Citizenship*. London: Routledge, 132–48.

Dryzek, J. (2000). *Deliberative Democracy and Beyond: Liberals, Critics, Contestations*. Oxford: Oxford University Press.

Eckersley, R. (1996). 'Greening Liberal Democracy: The Rights Discourse Revisited', in Brian Doherty and Marius De Geus (eds.), *Democracy and Green Political Thought: Sustainability, Rights and Citizenship*. London: Routledge, 212–36.

Feinberg, J. (1980). 'The Rights of Animals and Unborn Generations', in *Rights, Justice, and the Bounds of Liberty*. Princeton: Princeton University Press.

Foreman, D. (1991). 'Earth First!', in Terence Ball and Richard Dagger (eds.), *Ideals and Ideologies: A Reader*. New York: HarperCollins.

Gaus, G. (1998). 'Respect for Persons and Environmental Values', in Jane Kneller and Sidney Axinn (eds.), *Autonomy and Community: Readings in Contemporary Kantian Social Philosophy*. Albany: State University of New York Press.

Golding, M. (1990). 'The Significance of Rights Language', *Philosophical Topics* **18** (Spring): 60–4.

Goodin, R. (1992). *Green Political Theory*. Cambridge: Polity Press.

Green, T. H. (1991 [1880]). 'Liberal Legislation and Freedom of Contract', in David Miller (ed.), *Liberty*. Oxford: Oxford University Press.

Hardin, G. (1968). 'The Tragedy of the Commons', *Science* **162** (13 December): 1243–8.

Holland, A. (1999). 'Sustainability: Should We Start from Here?', in Andrew Dobson (ed.) *Fairness and Futurity: Essays on Environmental Sustainability and Social Justice*. Oxford: Oxford University Press.

Holmes, S., and Sunstein, C. (1999). *The Cost of Rights: Why Liberty Depends on Taxes*. New York: W. W. Norton.

Kay, J. H. (1997). *Asphalt Nation: How the Automobile Took Over America, and How We Can Take It Back*. New York: Crown Books.

Knowles, D. (2001). *Political Philosophy*. London: Routledge.

Leopold, A. (2004 [1949]). 'The Land Ethic', in Terence Ball and Richard Dagger (eds.), *Ideals and Ideologies: A Reader*, 5th ed. New York: Pearson Longman.

Locke, J. (1965 [1689–90]). *Two Treatises of Government*, ed. P. Laslett. Cambridge: Cambridge University Press.

MacCallum, G. C., Jr. (1967). 'Negative and Positive Freedom', *Philosophical Review* **76**: 312–34.

Nash, R. (1989). *The Rights of Nature: A History of Environmental Ethics*. Madison: University of Wisconsin Press.

Nickel, J., and Viola, E. (1994). 'Integrating Environmentalism and Human Rights', *Environmental Ethics* **16** (Fall): 265–73.

Norton, B. (1999). 'Ecology and Opportunity: Intergenerational Equity and Sustainable Options', in Andrew Dobson (ed.), *Fairness and Futurity: Essays on Environmental Sustainability and Social Justice*. Oxford: Oxford University Press.

Pettit, P. (2001). *A Theory of Freedom: From the Psychology to the Politics of Agency*. New York: Oxford University Press.

(2003). 'Agency-Freedom and Option-Freedom', *Journal of Theoretical Politics* **15**.4: 387–403.

Shue, H. (1980). *Basic Rights: Subsistence, Affluence, and U.S. Foreign Policy*. Princeton: Princeton University Press.

Stone, C. (1974). *Should Trees Have Standing? Toward Legal Rights for Natural Objects*. Los Altos, Calif.: William Kaufmann.

Sumner, L. W. (1987). *The Moral Foundations of Rights*. Oxford: Clarendon Press.

Taylor, C. (1979). 'What's Wrong with Negative Liberty?', in Alan Ryan (ed.), *The Idea of Freedom: Essays in Honour of Isaiah Berlin*. Oxford: Oxford University Press.

Waldron, J. (1993). 'Rights', in Robert Goodin and Philip Pettit (eds.), *A Companion to Contemporary Political Philosophy*. Oxford: Basil Blackwell.

Wellman, C. (1999). *The Proliferation of Rights: Moral Progress or Empty Rhetoric?* Boulder, Colo.: Westview Press.

13   Citizenship

Andrew Dobson

Just who is throwing down the gauntlet here? Is political ecology a challenge for citizenship, or is citizenship a challenge for political ecology? Let's take the first possibility. Challenging citizenship could mean a number of things, but in the first instance it is a discursive challenge. Citizenship occupies a disputed yet established discursive space in modern politics and there are four broadly accepted reference points. First, citizenship provides an account of political relationships – sometimes between members of a political entity, and sometimes between those members and the political entity itself. Second, the stress on *political* relationships is important, because if citizenship is to continue to mean anything after its encounter with political ecology, we must be able to distinguish it from other types of relationship such as friendship or family. Third, the political entity most often associated with contemporary citizenship is the nation state, and – fourth – the relationships in question are usually talked about in terms of rights and responsibilities. So the 'ecological challenge' to citizenship could relate to any of these items of the architecture of citizenship: who or what are to be members, what counts as 'political', the nature of the space within which citizenship relations take place, and the kinds of rights and responsibilities that citizenship might entail.

The citizenship tent: inside and outside

Even without a specifically ecological challenge, there is plenty of wriggle room in the citizenship tent for debate to take place. We have become accustomed to think in terms of at least two types of citizenship – liberal and civic republican. These differ principally in the way they think about the nature and balance of citizenship rights and responsibilities. It is generally agreed that civic republican citizenship taps into the classical tradition in which the individual's allegiance to the political community is regarded as in tension with the individual's allegiance to him- or herself. This tradition, therefore, stresses responsibility – to the wellbeing of the political community – ahead of the rights of the individual. In contrast, the citizenship we have come to associate with liberal democracy is much more a matter of rights claiming than responsibility exercising. The idea of the contribution that the individual might make to the community gives rise in republican theory to a language of citizenship virtue. Traditionally these virtues are thought of in 'masculine' terms – courage, strength, sacrifice – although it turns out these are better understood as masculinist interpretations of what these virtues might entail. Liberal citizenship is by no means a virtue-free zone (the virtues of tolerance and open-mindedness are often referred to in this context), but such citizenship does not trumpet its virtues in the same way as its republican cousin. So liberal and republican citizenship have historically vied with one another over the meaning and balance of the rights and responsibilities of the citizen, and over the role that virtue might play in citizens' political behaviour.

But these disagreements relate to only one of the four elements of the architecture of citizenship that I outlined above – the rights and responsibilities element. In the other three respects, liberal and republican citizenship are broadly in agreement. So they agree that the political arena is constituted by public rather than private spaces; they agree that the nation state is the basic model for the 'container' of citizenship; and they agree that membership of the citizen community is related to membership of the nation state.

Looked at in this way, we see the apparently fundamental disagreements between liberal and republican citizenships for what they really are: a rather comfortable accommodation characterised by skirmishes in one corner of the big tent they've constructed, rather than by challenges that might change the shape of the tent itself. This is not to say that challenges of a more fundamental type have not been offered. Feminist critiques of citizenship, for example, have pointed out how the supposedly universal representation of the citizen present in both republican and – especially – liberal citizenship is in fact a gendered creature whose descriptive and aspirational features make citizenship either inappropriate for many women or even positively hostile to their interests. One key element of this critique is to call into question the exclusion of the private sphere from citizenship conversation and practice. For feminist critics of masculinist citizenship, the private sphere is as much a site of citizenship activity as the public sphere, and the virtues of life properly lived in the private sphere should be considered, prima facie, as potential political virtues. By calling into question received opinion concerning an element of citizenship architecture about which the two principal disputants in fact agree, feminist citizenship constitutes a fundamental challenge to received models of citizenship – more outside the tent than in it, as it were.

Another challenge of a fundamental type comes from cosmopolitanism (see Linklater in this volume). This challenge relates to the issue of the 'container' of citizenship, and to the liberal and republican agreement that citizenship is only meaningful as status and as activity within the nation state, or in contexts modelled on the nation state, such as the European Union. Cosmopolitan citizenship focuses on the political claims made upon us as members of a common humanity, and thus the political space of cosmopolitanism – in contrast to both liberal and republican citizenship – is in principle the universal cosmopolis rather than this or that nation state. In calling into question an agreed tenet of both liberal and republican citizenship, cosmopolitanism, like feminism, constitutes a considerable challenge to received opinions regarding the shape of citizenship.

The ecological challenge

So we have shuffled 'challenges' to citizenship into scuffles inside the tent, on the one hand, and tugs at the guy ropes from outside, on the other. Liberal and civic republican debates take place in an established discursive space, while feminism and cosmopolitanism challenge the very shape of that space. Now what of the ecological challenge? One way into this is to refer back to the second question at the start of this chapter: is citizenship a challenge for political ecology? I take it that this question refers to the issue of whether political ecology can be spoken in the language of citizenship; the challenge in question is that of translating the descriptive and prescriptive elements of political ecology into citizenship-speak. The answer to whether this can be done is by no means obvious. Feminist critiques of liberal and republican determination to reserve citizenship for the public sphere have led some to say that 'feminist citizenship' is a contradiction in terms because citizenship is *by definition* a phenomenon of public political space. Similarly, whatever cosmopolitanism is, it is certainly not a theory of citizenship, to some of its critics, because citizenship only makes sense *by definition* in the context of the nation state or analogous political formations. In both these cases, according to their citizenship critics, feminism and cosmopolitanism fail the challenge of citizenship: to speak in its language. So, once again, what of the ecological challenge?

In my estimation this challenge comes in two guises – one inside the tent and one outside it. Let's take it as read, to begin with, that liberal and civic republican citizenships pretty much exhaust the alternatives available to us. From this point of view, the ecological challenge to citizenship consists in adapting the liberal and civic republican forms to the environmental case: taking account of the environmental dimension to political life in the context of these two alternative forms of citizenship. I believe that liberal and civic republican citizenship can meet this challenge relatively comfortably, and that in doing so, political ecology proves itself reciprocally capable of expressing itself in the language of these citizenships. Let me spend a little time now describing and assessing this encounter before going on to reflect on what I see as a more profound form of the ecological challenge to citizenship – one with its origins outside rather than inside the tent, as it were. I'll begin with liberal citizenship.

Inside the tent (1): liberal citizenship and political ecology

I established earlier that one of the key tropes in liberal citizenship is expressed in the language of rights. The liberal citizen is characterised as a bearer of rights of various sorts – political, civic and perhaps even social rights. Membership of a regime in which liberal citizenship is established confers entitlements upon citizens – entitlements that citizens claim against the established political authority. Thus liberal citizenship involves, for example, the right to vote, the right to associate freely and the right – perhaps – to a minimum level of social security. To the degree that environmental politics can be expressed in the language of rights, it can also be incorporated into the canon of liberal citizenship. There are a number of ways in which this might happen, one of which is in itself more challenging than the others. First, the list of human rights might be extended to include the right to a liveable and sustainable environment. According to Tim Hayward, this is increasingly a part of states' constitutional repertoire: 'more than 70 countries have constitutional environmental provisions of some kind, and in at least 30 cases these take the form of environmental rights ... No recently promulgated constitution has omitted reference to environmental principles, and many older constitutions are being amended to include them' (Hayward 2000: 558). Relatedly but more profoundly, this right to a sustainable environment might be regarded as the precondition for the enjoyment of other political, civic and social rights. Just as socialists have traditionally argued that the right to free association means little without the material preconditions that make this right a real and daily possibility, so political ecologists suggest that without a liveable environment other formal rights cannot be substantively enjoyed.

Finally there is the possibility of rights *of* the environment. This is a notoriously rocky road to travel (see Dagger and Sterba in this book), but I can illustrate some of the consequences for citizenship of taking it. This is more of a challenge than either of the other approaches to rights talk because it calls into question an otherwise utterly invisible and unremarked point of agreement between liberal and civic republican citizenship, which is that citizenship is for humans only. Most of the debate in liberal citizenship has been about *what* the entitlements of citizens should be; the ecological challenge to this consensus is to ask *who or what* should have these entitlements, whatever they may be. Of course there are debates within both liberal and civic republican citizenship about qualifications for membership of the citizen body, and these debates have become increasingly acute – even a matter of life and death – as the rates of movement of peoples across the world have increased, and as 'entitlement-rich' countries try to control the flow of immigrants from 'entitlement-poor' countries. But these debates have no 'ontological' dimension – yet this is what the ecological challenge involves.

The animal rights movement has long traded on the 'argument from similarity'. All those who subscribe to the Universal Declaration of Human Rights simultaneously subscribe to the view that all humans have those rights. Article 2 of the 1948 Declaration states, in fact, that: 'Everyone is entitled to all the rights and freedoms set forth in this Declaration, without distinction of any kind, such as race, colour, sex, language, religion, political or other opinion, national or social origin, property, birth or other status' (http://www.un.org/Overview/rights.html). Animal rightists will claim, though, that Article 2 – the 'anti-discrimination' article – speaks with forked tongue, and that there is a considerable sting in its tail. What is the 'other status' to which it refers so darkly? To the extent that non-human animals are excluded from the charmed circle of rights holders (it is, after all, a declaration of *human* rights), some kind of discrimination is taking place. The basis for this discrimination is made clear in Article 1 which reads, in part, as follows: 'All human beings are born free and equal in dignity and rights. They are endowed with reason and conscience and should act towards one another in a spirit of brotherhood.' The key words are 'endowed with reason and conscience': only those beings so endowed are entitled to whatever protection the declaration of human rights might afford, and therefore to any citizenship rights that might flow from them.

But, animal rightists ask, why should these particular qualities determine the shape of the community of rights holders? There are alternatives. Jeremy Bentham famously wrote that 'the question is not,

Can they *reason?* nor, Can they *talk?* but, Can they *suffer?*' (Bentham 1970[1823]: 311). The capacity to suffer is shared by more creatures than the capacity to reason or to talk. So if *this* is the capacity that determines the holding of rights, the charmed circle is widened at a stroke. In sum, the animal rights movement argues that rights should be conferred on animals other than human ones. We could argue forever about *what* rights and *which* animals, but let's take a relatively simple case and see what impact it might have on liberal citizenship.

If any group of animals has a claim to be similar to humans in relevant respects it's the great apes. This thought has given rise to the Great Ape Project (GAP) (http://www.greatapeproject.org/), and for the purposes of the project the great apes comprise 'human beings, chimpanzees, bonobos, gorillas and orang-utans' (see the boundary crossing in action in the gathering of human beings under the umbrella term 'great apes'). GAP works 'for the removal of the non-human great apes from the category of property, and for their immediate inclusion within the category of *persons*' (my emphasis), and its political aim is 'to include the non-human great apes within the community of equals by granting them the basic moral and legal protection that only human beings currently enjoy'. If and when the non-human great apes are categorised as 'persons', it will be hard to deny them some of the rights that liberal conceptions of citizenship bestow. Quite what liberal *political* rights (e.g. the right to vote) might mean in this context is hard to see, but non-human great ape versions of civil rights (e.g. the right to associate freely) and social rights (e.g. the right to social security) are by no means impossible to conceive.

In this context, then, the ecological challenge to liberal citizenship is a considerable one. We saw earlier that adding environmental rights for humans to the liberal citizenship list was relatively uncontroversial in principle, if tricky in detail. We also saw that while both liberal and republican citizenship debate the issue of qualifications for membership of the citizen body, this debate always takes place in the human context. But attempts to keep humans human are usually tautologous rather than convincing, say animal rightists (among others). Consider the following, from Francis Fukuyama. The human essence, he says, cannot be 'reduced to the possession of moral choice, or reason, or language, or sociability, or sentience, or emotions, or consciousness, or any other quality that has been put forth as a ground for human dignity. It is all of these qualities coming together in a human whole that make up Factor X' (Fukuyama 2002: 171). This is, to say the least, a mildly disappointing conclusion, as it comes close to saying that what makes humans human and therefore special is – well, their humanity.

Thus the ecological challenge to liberal citizenship – as far as membership is concerned – takes the form of an immanent critique, if you will. Liberals are asked to adjust their ontological sights, in line with their professed commitment to seek out inappropriate discrimination wherever it lies, and to see that some non-human animals (at least) should be admitted to the realm of potential citizens. While this can just about be characterised as a scuffle inside the citizenship tent to which I referred earlier, it is likely to be a pretty prolonged and intense one that might make the tent sway a little. I wondered earlier whether political ecology would be able to meet the challenge laid down by (in this case) liberal citizenship: the challenge to speak itself in the language of this citizenship. The answer seems to be affirmative – and perhaps uncomfortably so, for liberals. Not only can political ecology talk in terms of the rights of liberal citizenship, but in insisting on an enquiry into the nature of the qualifications for rights holding, it suggests that denying citizenship rights to at least some non-human animals is inconsistent with liberal principles themselves.

Inside the tent (2): civic republican citizenship and political ecology

If liberal citizenship is amenable yet peculiarly vulnerable to the challenge of political ecology, the civic republican model seems to be a less equivocally robust ally. Three features of civic republicanism resonate loudly with the impulses of political ecology: the focus on the common good and the related elevation of responsibility over rights, the stress on political virtue, and the idea of the active citizen.

First, then, 'the environment' is a public good on which we all depend for the production and reproduction of daily life. There has been plenty of debate, of course, about whether environmental protection is more effectively brought about through private rather than public ownership, but too close a focus on the detail of this debate can obscure the basic agreement that motivates it: that it is in all our interests as embodied creatures, dependent on our environment for the resources that sustain life, to ensure a healthy and sustainable non-human natural context for our endeavours. Even those who argue for private ownership of (parts of) the natural environment do so on the basis (they say) that this is the best way to ensure sustainability for us all. This squares with a key idea in civic republican citizenship: that the citizen has a duty to promote the common good. Where the citizen's own interests clash with the common good, the latter should take precedence. Indeed, it is the duty of the citizen to think in terms of the common good when making decisions.

Jean-Jacques Rousseau famously distinguished between the Will of All and the General Will on the basis that the former is what is produced when people deliberate on the basis of their own interests, and the latter is what emerges when people decide what to do in the light of what is in the common interest. The civic republican impulse squares with the latter, and can thus provide a source of inspiration for political ecology.

Earlier I characterised the debate between liberal and civic republican citizenship as a tussle over the stress to be placed on the rights and responsibilities of citizens. In caricature: the liberal citizen claims rights and the civic republican citizen exercises responsibility. The civic republican's responsibility is to work towards the common good – and it is not hard to see how this might provide a powerful resource for political ecologists. The stress on the quotidian, personal nature of green politics is one of the strongest currents in political ecology. We are constantly enjoined to link the facts of the form of our daily behaviour with the state of the environment we find around us. Green politics urges us to connect the way we live our lives with the impact we make upon the natural world. We are made to feel responsible for the state of the environment, and simultaneously encouraged to see that we can do something about it. Sometimes this feels like zealotry – and in this, again, our instinct to link civic republicanism and political ecology does not betray us, for zealotry is indeed a pathological feature of them both. And both of them often invoke sacrifice – in the case of civic republicanism, the sacrifice of the individual to the cause of the republic, and in the case of political ecology, the sacrifice of individual wants and desires to the requirement of environmental sustainability. There is a common ascetic moment too. Civic republicans have their minds on the high and abstract goal of improving the fortunes of the republic, while political ecologists are urged to forgo the pleasures of materialist satisfaction in the cause of sustainability.

This links to the second element of common cause between civic republicans and political ecologists: the importance of the exercise of virtue. In neither case are virtues exercised for their own sake, but as a means to an end. For civic republicans, virtues are connected with improving the condition of the republic, while for political ecologists they are a means to the end of environmental sustainability. These differing objectives colour the virtues themselves. Civic republicanism is replete with tales of courage, sacrifice, manliness, while developing theories of ecological citizenship speak of care, concern and compassion. In both cases there are calls to educate citizens in the exercise of these virtues, and so both forms of citizenship place great stress on young people as proto-citizens – to the extent, in the ecological case, where hopes for sustainability are sometimes almost wholly invested in the younger generation. Liberals will typically criticise civic republicans and political ecologists on these grounds: that education becomes inculcation, and that education *about* sustainability becomes education *for* sustainability. So whatever the similarities and differences between civic republicanism and political ecology as far as the content of virtue is concerned, they share common cause in their determination to see virtue as a key component of citizenship.

Finally, tying all this together is the vision of the citizen as an active political animal. The standard view of the liberal citizen is that of the passive recipient of entitlements. This is not an entirely accurate picture, as anyone who has spent time chasing down deficiencies in the provision of entitlements in liberal democratic states will know, but it is a powerful one which civic republicans systematically criticise. Civic republicanism is connected to the idea of politics as participation, and is heir to the classical Aristotelian view that those who do not participate in the political life of their community are not fulfilling their human potential. To this 'intrinsic' reason for participation is added the idea that participation improves the quality of political life. All this is, in turn, taken on board in the ecological conception of how political lives should be led. Green politics has a strong 'localist' impulse – even if we 'think globally' we are urged to 'act locally'. The ideological links between the 'city' of civic republicanism and the 'village' of green folklore are strong: they are the places where politics should be done, and both the source and the destination of the virtues that animate their respective politics. These localised forms of politics enable 'genuine' participation rather than the stunted forms available in the nation state context of liberal representative democracies. Finally, there is the idea that the aims of neither civic republicanism nor political ecology will be achievable without citizen participation. Sustainability requires a framework of rules and regulations, of course, say political ecologists, and in the most effective cases those subject to them will regard these rules and regulations as legitimate. But sustainability, it is said, also requires daily vigilance by citizens themselves in regard to their impact on the environment. The form of citizens' daily lives – their 'participation' in the widest sense – is what shapes the contours of sustainability itself.

So in the light of these three issues – the focus on the common good and the related elevation of responsibility over rights, the stress on political virtue, and the idea of the active citizen – civic republicanism seems easily to absorb the ecological challenge. So comfortable is this accommodation, indeed, that political ecological might be seen as drawing considerable strength from the impulses of civic republicanism.

In sum, the encounter between political ecology and liberal and civic republican forms of citizenship inside the tent seems a fairly friendly one. But what of conditions outside?

Outside the tent

At the beginning of the chapter I referred to four features of the general architecture of citizenship: the debate over rights and responsibilities, the issue of membership, what counts as 'citizenly activity', and the determination of the political space within which citizenship takes place. I have suggested that while liberal and civic republican citizenship differ in respect of the rights and responsibilities question, they are in broad agreement as far as the other three features are concerned. So they agree that membership is related in some way to the nation state, that citizenly activity takes place in the public realm, and that the archetypal contemporary citizenship space is the nation state. I pointed to two challenges to the consensus surrounding these three points: one from feminism and one from cosmopolitanism. The former points to the possibility of regarding the private realm as a site of bona fide citizenly activity, and the latter to the way in which citizenship might transcend the boundaries of the nation state. Finally, I have characterised the disputes between liberal and civic republican citizenship as taking place within the citizenship tent, while feminism and cosmopolitanism offer critiques from outside.

The political-ecological critique from outside builds on feminist and cosmopolitan insights. In particular it takes seriously the idea that citizenship can properly be linked to the private realm, and that the virtues associated with citizenship may need to be rethought along lines normally associated with feminism. Ecological citizenship follows cosmopolitanism in its determination to ask whether the nation state – and its homologues – are an exhaustive expression of the political space of citizenship. In this context, and as I have argued elsewhere (Dobson 2003), ecological citizenship perhaps offers a novel account of the political space of citizenship in the guise of the 'ecological footprint'. More of this later; let me deal first with the private realm as a potential site of citizenship activity.

I have already suggested that the ecological citizen, like her or his civic republican counterpart, is enjoined to work towards a common good. In the ecological case, let's call this 'environmental sustainability'. This objective will inevitably entail working out the causes and sources of environmental *un*sustainability and trying to do something about them. Some of these causes and sources will be beyond the immediate influence of individual citizens, and in any case many of the candidates for causing unsustainability are disputed. Is the environment under strain because of population growth? Is poverty a cause of unsustainability? Is wealth? Is it our attitudes towards the non-human natural world that are at fault? Is it a combination of these factors, or some others entirely? This debate takes place in the public arena, and to the extent that our impact on the environment is transmitted through and mediated by our social forms of life, the 'sustainability question' has an ineluctably public moment. It is therefore right and proper to think of ecological citizenship in traditional 'public' terms: arguments and activities that might influence institutions, corporations, movements, parties, bureaucracies, schools, departments, to move in a sustainable direction.

But in line with a remark I made earlier, ecological politics is a quotidian politics – a politics that embraces and entails the everyday metabolistic relationship between individuals and the non-human natural world, as well as that relationship mediated by our presence and participation in 'public' bodies. And we cannot and do not turn that relationship on and off when we cross some putative public-private divide. In a term borrowed from postmodernism, we are 'always already' consumers of environmental services and producers of waste, from the moment we are born to the moment we die, in public and in private, in sickness and in health. From this point of view it is perverse to regard campaigning for a recycling centre as an act of citizenship, and deny the accolade to the act of separating biodegradable and other materials just because you do it in the privacy of your own home. The ecological challenge is to regard both of these as acts of citizenship. I take it that this challenge prods the citizenship tent from the outside, for those who are inside take it as read that citizenship has a definitional and univocal connection with the public sphere.

There is one further way in which feminist and ecological critiques of traditional conceptions of citizenship have common cause: in connection with the idea of virtue. Earlier I discussed the way in which civic republicanism and political ecology share a language of virtue, but left hanging the question of what *counts* as citizenship virtue. I contrasted the traditional virtues of civic republicanism – courage, strength and sacrifice – with those sometimes canvassed in the ecological context: care, concern, compassion. Feminism (or some strands of it) has come to be associated with these virtues, particularly in the context of the 'justice vs. care' debate. But can these latter be regarded as citizenship virtues, properly speaking? At the beginning of the chapter I made it clear that after its encounter with political ecology, citizenship must still be regarded as denoting a different kind of relationship to those we encounter in other areas of life, such as friendship and family. If we embrace care and compassion as citizenship virtues, are we not in danger of confounding citizenship with the relationships where these virtues are supposed more typically to be on display? Some certainly think so. Take Michael Ignatieff: 'The pell-mell retreat from the language of justice to the language of caring is perhaps the most worrying sign of the decadence of the language of citizenship among all parties to the left of Mrs Thatcher' (in Rees 1995: 321); and, 'the language of citizenship is not properly about compassion at all' (Ignatieff 1991: 34). Why not?

It should be clear by now that the boundary between the inside and the outside of the citizenship tent is patrolled by the Definition Secretariat (DS). The private realm is outside the tent because citizenship is *by definition* a status and activity associated with the public arena; cosmopolitan citizenship is a contradiction in terms because citizenship *by definition* denotes rights and responsibilities within the nation state or its homologues. And, here, care and compassion are not citizenship virtues – apparently, according to Ignatieff, *by definition*. We should be wary, I think, of the DS. It is one thing to say that political concepts occupy a discursive territory, and quite another to reduce that territory to a small office containing the DS's desks and filing cabinets. There are at least three reasons to think that political concepts are more like living and breathing creatures than insects preserved in amber. First, they are historical. From this point of view it would be very peculiar if citizenship were to mean the same thing now as it did to the ancient Greeks. Take an issue with which I am about to deal in more detail: the 'container' within which citizenship is said to make sense. In contemporary political life there is really only one candidate for containership: the nation state. But a glance at the historical record reveals an array of alternatives: the ancient city state, the municipality, early modern republican cities. No doubt future theorists will look back at the development of the European Union and the nascent transnational positive rights – such as the right to vote in 'foreign' local elections – that go along with being a citizen of one of the member countries, and argue that this is one more instance of citizenship at work in contexts other than the nation state.

The DS will immediately point out, though, that each of these examples has a structural feature in common: they are all constituted political formations with the authority to grant and withdraw citizenship, and against which citizens can claim their rights and in respect of which they are expected to exercise their responsibilities. This structural feature is absent from other putative candidates for 'spaces of citizenship', such as the private sphere of feminists and the cosmopolis of cosmopolitans, says the DS, so we cannot predicate 'citizenship' of the kinds of relations we find there. As far as it goes, this is if course true, and if we regard citizenship as being univocally about *status*, then feminism (of the type on which I have been focusing here), cosmopolitanism and, quite possibly, political ecology will all fail the challenge laid down by citizenship: to speak in its language. But – and this is the second reason we should be wary of the DS – as we saw earlier when discussing civic republicanism, citizenship is also about *activity*. If we think of citizenship as activity aimed towards achieving the common good (a move that the DS might have something to say about, of course, even if this is as venerable a strand of the historical experience of citizenship as any), then cosmopolitan and ecological citizenship snap into focus *as citizenships*. In other words, complex concepts like citizenship offer their own *internal* space within which to live, breathe and grow.

Finally, as well as being historical and internally malleable, political concepts are *political*. This is as much as to say that definitions cannot stand outside the relationships of political power they are intended to describe. They stand in a complex relationship to this power: neither simply reflecting it nor uncomplicatedly calling it into question. To this degree, citizenship is a site of political struggle, and feminist, cosmopolitan and ecological challenges to it amount to the challenge to incorporate these new politics in it. If the personal is political, can citizenship really turn its back on private space? In a globalising world, has citizenship really got nothing to say about transnational obligation? Must citizenship remain silent about environmental sustainability in its infra- and extra-state contexts just because status-citizenship begins and ends with nation states and their homologues?

Let me pick up this last question as a way of completing this section. At the head of the section I said that political ecology's challenge from outside the citizenship tent builds upon aspects of feminism and cosmopolitanism: 'the former points to the possibility of regarding the private realm as a site of bona fide citizenly activity, and the latter to the way in which citizenship might transcend the boundaries of the nation state.' We have dealt with the private realm, and now it is time to turn our attention to other aspects of the political space of citizenship.

One self-evident aspect of environmental problems is that they do not respect national boundaries. We typically think of transnational environmental problems in this context, such as global warming and depletion of the ozone layer. To the extent that these problems have a political dimension, it seems perverse to deny a critical comment on them from such a fundamentally political notion as citizenship simply because citizenship is (said to be) a creature of the contemporary nation state. Although global warming and ozone depletion are the *causes célèbres* of transnational environmentalism, we should also remember that environmental problems are manifest at local and regional level. Are we to say, once again, that citizenship must remain silent at these levels because it is only and definitionally about relations between individuals and nation states and their homologues?

Since the Stoics, cosmopolitanism has offered an alternative imaginary for political space to bounded containers such as municipalities, cities and states. Prima facie, it seems an ideal source of inspiration for a phenomenon with transnational characteristics such as political ecology. The global cosmopolis of cosmopolitans and the planet-wide theatre of political ecology seem happily coincidental. Likewise, there is no doubt that the cosmopolitan harm conventions discussed in Andrew Linklater's chapter in this volume are of massive environmental relevance. Elsewhere I have commented in detail on the prospects of enlisting cosmopolitanism in the ecological cause (Dobson 2003). One difficulty, as the reference to local and regional environmental problems suggests, is that such problems reach down into states as well as beyond them, and, given its focus on the transnational rather than the intranational aspects of politics, the political imaginary of cosmopolitanism struggles to deal with this dimension. Secondly, cosmopolitan obligations on individuals are generated by membership of a 'common humanity'. The language of symmetry, reciprocity and interdependence is key to cosmopolitanism, yet some interpretations of the drivers and dynamics of environmental problems suggest that these problems are asymmetrically caused and experienced (poor people usually live in poor environments, rich people usually live in rich ones), and that this should be reflected in the nature and direction of citizenship obligations.

In this chapter it has become clear that one of the most disputed aspects of citizenship is over the nature of the political space within which citizen relations take place. Liberal, civic republican, feminist and cosmopolitan citizenships each have an account that squares with and is inspired by their political intentions. Liberal accounts of individual freedom give rise to liberal citizenship rights against the state; the civic republican focus on the active citizen inspires smaller-scale, more local forms of municipal citizenship; and the feminist insistence that the personal is political leads to the conclusion that 'private' citizenship has public implications. Given all this, we would expect a properly ecological challenge to citizenship to offer an account of citizenship space in accord with the intentions of political ecology. This space might be the 'bioregion' of some greens' inspiration, according to which our ecological understanding and political commitment is given not by artificial, human-historical constructs such as the nation state, but by configurations of ecosystems whose potential determines the possibilities for life for those who live within them. Bioregionalism is an anticipation of a future form of green living, and commitments to localised practices of conservation are often recognisably bioregional in inspiration. But until and unless we live fully bioregional lives, we are confronted with the fact that globalisation, not bioregionalism, is the ruling idea and practice. If cosmopolitanism cannot provide a complete ecological response to the challenge of globalisation, what can? Here the 'ecological footprint' comes into its own.

This idea has been developed to illustrate the varying impacts of individuals' and communities' social practices on the environment. It is assumed that the earth has a limited productive and waste-absorbing capacity, and a notional and equal 'land allowance' – or footprint – is allocated to each person on the planet, given these limits. The footprint size is arrived at by dividing the total land available, and its productive capacity, by the number of people on the planet, and the figure usually arrived at is somewhere between 1.5 and 1.7 hectares. Inevitably, some people have a bigger impact – a bigger footprint – than others (median consumers in 'advanced industrial countries' are generally reckoned to occupy about five hectares of ecological space), and this is taken to be unjust, in the sense of a departure from a nominal equality of ecological space.

The relevance of the ecological footprint to us is that it contains the key spatial and obligation-generating relationships that give rise to the exercise of specifically citizenly virtues. The *nature* of the obligation is to reduce the occupation of ecological space, where appropriate, and the *source* of this obligation lies in remedying the potential and actual injustice of appropriating an unjust share of such space. Importantly, it explains and reflects the asymmetrical and non-reciprocal nature of ecological citizenship obligations. Obligations are owed by those in ecological space debt, and these obligations are the corollary of a putative environmental right to an equal share of ecological space for everyone. Liberal harm-avoidance principles are often accused of being far too tame and of not requiring enough of those who subscribe to them. But in the context of a phenomenon such as global warming, it is clear that harm avoidance can involve perpetrators of harm in quite significant commitments – up to and including wholesale changes in lifestyle. The ecological footprint argument advanced above bears a family relationship to liberal harm avoidance, and is a good illustration of how the principle can lead to actions rooted in justice rather than a broader humanitarianism.

In sum, every political project implicitly or explicitly contains an account of political space, and the quest for environmental sustainability is no exception. This, I believe, is where the most significant ecological challenge to citizenship resides. The sub- and supra-national arenas of political action are crucial for environmentalists. The recent history of citizenship, and its now-dominant articulation as the claiming of rights within the nation state, suggests that citizenship can neither be talked of nor used in these contexts. But I have suggested that there are environmental resources (so to speak) in the burgeoning idea of cosmopolitan citizenship, and that these resources are best deployed by identifying what is peculiarly citizenly – as opposed to broadly humanitarian – about the source and nature of obligations in an asymmetrically globalising world. Environmentalism offers the earthy footprint – in addition to the state, the supra-state or cosmopolitan citizenship's dialogic community – as the spatial imaginary within which citizenship and its obligations are best conceived.

References

Bentham, J. (1970[1823]). *The Principles of Morals and Legislation*. Darien, Conn.: Hafner Publishing.

Dobson, A. (2003). *Citizenship and the Environment*. Oxford: Oxford University Press.

Fukuyama, F. (2002). *Our Posthuman Future: Consequences of the Biotechnology Revolution*. London: Profile Books.

Great Ape Project. http://www.greatapeproject.org/ (accessed 23 February 2005).

Hayward, T. (2000). 'Constitutional Environmental Rights: A Case for Political Analysis', *Political Studies* **48**.3: 558–72.

Ignatieff, M. (1991). 'Citizenship and Moral Narcissism', in Geoff Andrews (ed.), *Citizenship*. London: Lawrence and Wishart, 26–36.

Rees, A. M. (1995). 'The Promise of Social Citizenship', *Policy and Politics* **23**.4: 313–25.

14 Security

Daniel Deudney

What is the relationship between environment and security? Will environmental change produce violent conflict and thus insecurity? What is the relationship between 'national security' and the environment? Over the last thirty years, and particularly the last fifteen years, there has been a lively interest in these and related questions, under the rubric of 'environmental security'.

Beginning in the 1970s, environmental advocates began proposing redefined 'security' to encompass a wide array of threats, ranging from earthquakes to environmental degradation. Others pointed to the destruction of the environment caused by war, and hypothesised that interstate war and other forms of violence would result from resource scarcity and environmental degradation. Yet others proposed to 'reconceptualise sovereignty' in order to focus on 'ecological security'. Most of the pioneering conceptual work on environmental security was done by advocates of greater environmental awareness. Such concepts were advanced in the context of the renewed Cold War tensions in the late 1970s and early 1980s, and were extrapolations from the fears of resource wars in the wake of the oil crises of 1973 and 1979.

By the late 1980s, and early 1990s, 'environmental security' was a broad movement, had generated an empirical research agenda and had begun to shape policy. As the Cold War waned, such ideas began to attract the interest and support of military organisations who saw possibilities for new 'missions'. Others saw environmental deterioration, particularly in Third World countries, as part of an ominous new threat to Western interest and world order partly catalysed by Robert Kaplan's horrific travelogues and visions of 'the coming anarchy', and his proclamation that 'the environment is *the* national security issue of the 21st century' (Kaplan 1996). With apocalyptic visions about 'chaos' in the Third World, 'environmental security' became a contender in the United States effort to formulate a new post-Cold War foreign policy.

Initially the 'environmental security' paradigm and agenda seemed straightforward and non-controversial. But in the early 1990s, a range of objections and doubts were raised by scholars (including this author) who were all strongly sympathetic to environmental concerns.

Overall, scepticism is not only still warranted, but confirmed and strengthened for three reasons. First, environmental degradation is not very likely to cause interstate wars. Second, it is analytically misleading to think of environmental degradation as a national security threat, because the traditional focus of national security – interstate violence – has little in common with either environmental problems or solutions. Third, the effort to harness the emotive power of nationalism to help mobilise environmental awareness and action may prove counter-productive by undermining globalist political sensibility (see Scruton, chapter 1; de-Shalit, chapter 5; and Linklater, chapter 7).

Before looking at these points at length, I make two more general background points about the antiquity of theorising about environment (as 'nature' and 'material context') and security, and about some features of the contemporary world order which make violent environmental conflicts relatively unlikely.

Geopolitics

The widely assumed view that thinking about environment and security is a new enterprise could not be further from the truth. From its inception in Greek antiquity, through early modernity and then again in the global industrial era of the last two centuries, 'nature' understood as a range of variables (climate, soil fertility, topography) played a prominent role in Western political science, particularly concerning violence and security (Glacken 1967; Arnold 1986). Such 'physiopolitical' arguments appear prominently in Aristotle and Monestquieu, widely viewed as founders of empirical political science.

One of the most common ideas in use here is that of interdependence, particularly concerning violence and wealth generation. In the widely used heuristic of the 'state of nature', the crucial relationships between government and anarchy and security hinged on the degree of interdependence present. Out of this empirical and 'naturalist' investigation comes a morphology of species of regimes shaped in the first instance by the contours and variations of 'nature'.

With the advent of the industrial revolution and consequent changes in the size of spaces within which varying degrees of interdependence developed, there emerged an industrial and globalist version of this contextual-materialist theorising, present in diverse nineteenth-and early twentieth-century schools, ranging from the Scottish Enlightenment political economists to progressive internationalists and 'global geopoliticans'. The key new ingredient was human technology, which interacted with nature to compose a material context with immense influence on wide ranges of human affairs. One major substantive argument (now associated with 'realism' and particularly 'nuclear deterrence') was that 'war would kill war', as technology produced capacities for violence of such magnitude as to be transparently irrational to use.

'Geopolitics', a word of early twentieth-century origins, was once used to refer to the 'naturalist' and material-contextual influences on politics, but has recently come to be used as a loose synonym for interstate relations (Kristof 1960; Hepple 1986). A quick glance at the larger features of contemporary world order that relate to the use and management of violence will underpin the specific sceptical arguments about environmental conflict. There are six key relevant features of contemporary world politics: (1) the extent of international trade; (2) the security practices and institutions of international society such as international organisations, alliances and balancing; (3) the 'liberal hegemony' of capitalist, democratic industrial states' world military, economic, ideological and cultural realms; (4) the existence of dense and thickening networks of transnational sub-state actors; (5) the existence of nuclear weapons; and (6) the diffusion of conventional arms.

First, the extent of international trade has made it possible for states to grow rich through production rather than conquest. It is no longer necessary for a state to have all resources in its territory. At the same time, the fragility and value of physical globalised capital creates great disincentives for the use of large-scale violence. Second, international politics still has a great many anarchical features, but international institutions, norms and organisations are more extensive and influential than ever before in history. These arrangements provide the international order with a range of conflict mitigation and resolution mechanisms.

The hegemony of liberal democratic states, unprecedented in history, gives the overall fabric of world political life a relatively peaceful composition. People are better educated, better connected to the larger world, more inclined to consumption and wealthy enough to be concerned with 'intangible' quality-of-life issues and to be politically concerned about long-term and distant problems as well as the realisation of 'humanitarian' agendas. Dense transnational networks of NGOs, and professional associations and extensive international educational activities, in combination with the flow of business people across the globe, create a context within which large-scale violence is increasingly inhibited.

The invention of nuclear explosives has made it easy and cheap to annihilate humans and infrastructure in extensive areas, and this greatly dampens the incentives for states to engage in territorial aggression

(Luard 1989; Mueller 1989). At the same time, the spread of conventional weaponry and national consciousness has made it very costly for an invader, even one equipped with advanced technology, to subdue a resisting population, as France discovered in Indo-China and Algeria, the United States in Vietnam and the Soviet Union in Afghanistan. At the lower levels of violence capability that matter most for conquering and subduing territory, the great powers have lost effective military superiority and are unlikely soon to regain it.

These deeply rooted material and institutional features of the contemporary world order greatly reduce the likelihood that environmental scarcities and change will lead to interstate violence. All this does not add up to utopia, and many conflicts emerge from regions of poverty, ignorance and oppression, but compared to any previous time in history there are now more people that are free, prosperous and secure, and human capabilities of organisation and technology are at an unprecedented high point. The far-flung actors of the liberal democratic capitalist world have their own severe limitations in competence and purpose, are cumbersomely self-interested, and are subject to various venalities and ideological and cultural blindnesses and manias. Nor does their influence always prevail. Yet any analysis of tendencies in the contemporary world order toward large-scale violence that ignores these pacifying developments is missing a major set of forces and influences.

Violent conflict

One of the major themes of the 'environmental security' literature is that environmental scarcities and change will stimulate conflict, violence and interstate war. People often fight over what they value, particularly if related to 'security'. In emphasising such outcomes, environmental security analysts join realist international relations theorists in characterising political life, both domestic and international, as particularly prone to conflict and violence.

Given the diversity and complexity of environmental problems and the large and diverse array of possible conflicting parties, starting with nearly two hundred sovereign states, generalisations are hazardous and are likely to have important exceptions. To assess the prospects for resource and pollution wars, we need to consider several overall features of contemporary world politics that make such conflict unlikely, and then examine more closely the six major scenarios for environmental conflict most discussed by environmental security analysts. In general I argue that important features of world politics make interstate violence and war much less likely than environmental security analysts suggest.

Much of the recent work on environmental conflict and violent change suffers from two methodological problems. Many studies on environmental conflict purport to have found trends in the frequency with which environmental scarcities produce conflict, yet few compare frequency of current conflict with the possible cases of environmental scarcities, or compare present with past frequency. Nor do analysts of environmental conflict systematically consider the ways in which environmental scarcity or change can stimulate co-operation. This lacuna is particularly glaring because analysts typically advocate more co-operation as a response to the scarcities and changes they identify or foresee.

Most studies on environmental conflict rarely consider the character of the overall international system in assessing the prospects for conflict and violence. The frequency with which environmental scarcity and conflict will produce violent conflict, particularly interstate wars, is profoundly shaped by the features of the contemporary world order described earlier.

Resource wars

The hypothesis that states will begin fighting each other as natural resources decline has intuitive and historical appeal. As resource supplies diminish, there will be fewer opportunities for positive-sum gains between actors. Fears of resource war partly derive from the cataclysmic world wars of the first half of the twentieth century, when Germany and Japan sought land and resources to sustain their wavering great power status (the United States had a richer resource endowment than the Axis powers). During the Cold War, fears of shortages and industrial strangulation and the presence of important natural resources in the Third World helped turn the latter into an arena for East–West conflict.

There are, however, three reasons for concluding that resource war scenarios are of diminishing plausibility for the foreseeable future. First, the prospects for resource wars are lessened by the growing difficulty that states face in obtaining resources through territorial conquest. Second, the robust character of the world trading system means that states no longer experience resource dependency as a major threat to their military security and political autonomy. During the 1930s, the collapse of a much weaker version of this system drove states to pursue economic autarky, but contemporary resource needs are routinely met without territorial control of the resource source (Lipschutz 1989). Third, non-renewable resources are, contrary to popular belief, becoming less scarce. The most striking manifestation of this trend is that prices for virtually every raw material have been stagnant or falling for the last several decades despite the continued growth in world economic output, and despite the cartelisation of Third World raw material suppliers.

Water and oil

General features of contemporary world politics suggest that resource war scenarios are generally implausible, but two difficult cases – water and oil – warrant more specific reflection. 'Water wars' have been one of the most frequently hypothesised forms of resource wars, particularly in the Middle East, a water-scarce region with particularly volatile and violent political relations. In desert and semi-arid regions, making up over a third of the earth's land area, water scarcities clearly exert an overwhelming influence, because without fresh water these lands are unable to support much life, human or otherwise, and violent conflicts over fresh water access have occurred since the beginning of recorded history. The potential for conflict seems further exacerbated by the fact that many important rivers and aquifers flow across the territory of many countries. Some researchers claim a disturbing trend toward the use of force in resource-related disputes. But in the overall register of contemporary violence conflicts, violent water disputes are negligible, despite the great importance riparian states attach to water resources.

Proponents of the 'water war' scenario also fail to consider the ways in which water scarcity has stimulated co-operation and provided disincentives to violent conflict. Precisely because so many rivers are international, their development requires interstate co-operation. There are many important examples of such co-operation that have already occurred, perhaps most notably the Parana River in South America, which Brazil, Paraguay and Argentina have co-operatively developed. Furthermore, once dams and other extensive infrastructure have been built, interstate violence becomes an increasingly costly option. By the same token, using the 'water weapon' by impeding flows to the detriment of downstream users is less appealing due to the vulnerability of dams to military attack. Also, because the political relations of the Middle East are so volatile and violent, it is unwise to extrapolate a global trend from largely hypothetical developments in this one region.

Finally, much of the scarcity of water projected in many parts of the world presumes the continued existence of highly inefficient use of water and of large subsidies that hide the real economic cost of water usage. As many analysts have pointed out, the introduction of economically rational pricing for water would eliminate much of the projected water 'scarcity' with far less social disruption and cost than military aggression to acquire additional supplies (Beaumont 1994).

The second 'hard case' – oil – clearly appears to be significantly implicated in the recent wars in Kuwait and Iraq. War over oil remains a real possibility, because the Persian Gulf region contains two-thirds of the world's proven oil reserves, and because many of the states in this region are so domestically unstable and militarily weak relative to their neighbours. But this region is exceptional. With the possible exception of the tiny country of Brunei in South-East Asia, it is difficult to locate other examples of states that are as oil rich, population poor and militarily weak in such proximity to militarily powerful states as the Persian Gulf emirates are vis-à-vis Iraq and Iran. Furthermore, the swift and decisive response of nearly the entire international community to Iraqi aggression in the first Gulf war is likely to deter similar aggressions.

Power imbalances

Environmental degradation could also possibly cause war by altering the relative power capacities of states. Changes in relative power position can contribute to wars either by tempting a rising state to aggress upon a declining state, or by inducing a declining state to attack a rising state before their relative power declines any further. However, alterations in the relative power of states are unlikely to lead to war as readily as the lessons of history suggest, because economic power and military power are perhaps not as tightly coupled as in the past. The relative economic power position of major states such as Germany and Japan has changed greatly since the end of World War II, but has not been accompanied by war or the threat of war. In the contemporary world, whole industries rise, fall and relocate, often causing quite substantial fluctuations in the economic wellbeing of regions and peoples, without producing wars. There is no reason to believe that changes in relative wealth and power positions caused by the uneven impact of environmental degradation would be different in their effects.

Part of the reason for this loosening of the link between economic and military power has been the nuclear revolution, which has made it relatively cheap for the leading states to display a staggering capacity for violence. Given that the major states field massively oversufficient nuclear forces without major economic strain, environmentally induced economic decline would have to be extreme before their ability to field a minimum nuclear deterrent were jeopardised. A stark example of this new pattern is the fact that the severe decline in Russia's economy and defence spending in the 1990s did not diminish Russia's ability to deter great power attack.

Spillover wars

A third possible route from environmental degradation to interstate conflict and violence is pollution across interstate borders. It is easy to imagine situations in which one country upstream and upwind of another dumps an intolerable amount of pollution on a neighbouring country, causing the injured country to attempt to pressure and coerce the source country to eliminate its offending pollution. Fortunately for interstate peace, strongly asymmetrical and significant environmental degradation between neighbouring countries is relatively rare. The more typical situation involves the activities of groups in neighbouring countries as well as other groups in their own countries. This creates complex sets of winners and losers, and thus a complex array of potential intrastate and interstate coalitions. In general, the more such interactions occur, the less likely it is that a persistent, significant and highly asymmetrical pollution 'exchange' will occur. The very multitude of interdependencies in the contemporary world, particularly among the industrialised countries, makes it unlikely that intense cleavages of environmental harm will match interstate borders, and at the same time not be compensated for and complicated by other military, economic or cultural interactions. Resolving such conflicts will be a complex and messy affair, but they are unlikely to lead to war.

Global commons conflicts

There are also conflict potentials related to the global commons. Many countries contribute to environmental degradation of the global commons, and many countries are harmed, but because the impacts are widely distributed, no one country has an incentive to act alone to solve the problem. Solutions require collective action, and with collective action comes the possibility of the 'free rider'. In the case of a global agreement to reduce carbon dioxide emissions to reduce the threat of global warming, if one significant polluter were to resist joining the agreement, with the expectation that the other states would act to reduce environmental harms to a tolerable level, the possibility arises that the states sacrificing to reduce emissions would attempt to coerce the free rider into making a more significant contribution to the effort.

It is difficult to judge this scenario because we lack examples of this phenomenon on a large scale. Free-rider problems may generate severe conflict, but it is doubtful that states would find military instruments useful for coercion and compliance. For example, if China or Russia decided not to join an agreement to reduce carbon dioxide emissions, it seems unlikely that the other major states would really go to war with such powerful states. Overall, any state sufficiently industrialised to be a major contributor to the carbon dioxide problem is likely to present a very poor target for military coercion.

Impoverishment, authoritarianism and war

In the fifth environmental conflict scenario, increased interstate violence results from internal turmoil caused by declining living standards. In this 'neo-Malthusian' scenario, the consequences of economic stagnation for politics and society are likely to be significant and largely undesirable. Peoples could live peacefully at lower standards of living, but reductions of expectations to conform to these new realities will not come easily. Faced with declining living standards, groups at all levels of affluence are likely to resist reductions in their standard of living by pushing the deprivation upon other groups, thus giving class relations a 'zero-sum' character. Faced with these pressures, liberal democratic and free market systems would increasingly be replaced by authoritarian governments capable of maintaining minimum order (Heilbroner 1974; Ophuls 1976). The international consequences of these domestic changes might be increased conflict and war. If authoritarian regimes are more war prone because of their lack of democratic control, and if revolutionary regimes are war prone because of their ideological fervour and lack of socialisation into international norms and processes, then a world political system containing more such states is likely to be more violent.

Although initially compelling, this scenario has flaws as well. First, the pessimistic interpretation of the relationship between environmental sustainability and economic growth may be based on flawed economic theory. Wealth formation is not so much a product of cheap natural resource availability as of capital formation from savings and greater efficiencies. Many resource-poor countries, like Japan, are very wealthy, while many countries with more extensive resource endowments are poor, suggesting the absence of a direct relationship between resource abundance and economic wellbeing. Environmental constraints require an end to economic growth based on increasing raw material through-puts, rather than an end to growth in the output of goods and services.

Second, even if economic decline does occur, interstate conflict may be dampened, not stoked. Of course, how societies respond to economic decline may in large measure depend upon the rate at which such declines occur. It may also be the case that as people get poorer, they will be less willing to spend increasingly scarce resources on military capabilities. The experience of economic depressions over the last two centuries may be misleading, because they were marked by under-utilised production capacity and falling resource prices. In the 1930s, increased military spending had a stimulative effect, but if economic growth is retarded by environmental constraints, then military spending would exacerbate not ameliorate this economic slowdown.

State collapse and internal conflict

The sixth, and most plausible, scenario for environmental conflict centres upon internal political conflict arising from environmental scarcities and change, particularly degraded or depleted renewable resources of forests, fisheries and soils (Homer-Dixon 1999). Such analysis has tended to suffer from an absence of historical comparison and a failure to examine cases of environmental change that either did not lead to violent conflict, or that stimulated co-operative arrangements.

Even assuming that environmental degradation can lead to internal turmoil and state collapse, what are the international ramifications if some areas of the world suffer this fate? The impact of this outcome on international order may not be very great. If a particular country, even a large one like India or Brazil, were to disintegrate, among the first casualties would be the complex organisational skills, specialised industrial products and surplus wealth needed to wage interstate conventional war. In the modern era, 'the predisposing factors to military aggression are full bellies, not empty ones' (Brodie 1972, 14). The 'wretched of the earth' may be able to deny an outside aggressor an easy conquest, but they are themselves a minimal threat to outside states.

In the contemporary world connectivity is high, but not tightly coupled. Regional disasters, such as the rule of Idi Amin in Uganda, the Khmer Rouge Cambodian rampage and the spread of the Sahel, produce great human misery, but do not much affect the economies and political systems of the West. Indeed, many of the world's citizens did not even notice.

Overall, the prospects of environmental degradation causing interstate violence are much weaker than is widely thought. In part, this is because of features of the international system that have little to do directly with environmental issues. Conflict scenarios drawing analogies from historical experience fail to register the important ways in which the contemporary interstate system differs from earlier ones, particularly regarding incentives for aggression. Interstate violence seems poorly suited to resolve many of the conflicts that might arise from environmental degradation. The international trading system and complex interdependence also militate against violent interstate outcomes. Overall, the world system appears to have the resilience needed to weather significant environmental disruption without large-scale violent interstate conflict.

National security

A second strand of 'environmental security' thinking has sought to redefine 'national security' or more broadly 'security' to encompass threats to societal welfare that have traditionally been outside their domain. Historically, such conceptual shifts have often accompanied important changes in politics, as new phrases are coined and old terms take on new meanings. The wide-ranging contemporary conceptual ferment in the language used to understand and act upon environmental problems is both expected and desirable.

But not all neologisms and linkages are equally plausible or useful. Before either expanding the concept of national security to encompass both environmental and violence threats, or redefining 'national security' or 'security' to refer mainly to environmental threats, it is worth examining just how much the nation state pursuit of security from violence has in common with environmental problems and their solutions.

National security (as opposed to national interest or wellbeing) has been centred upon *organised violence*. Security from violence is a fundamental human need, because loss of life prevents the enjoyment of all other goods. Resource factors traditionally were understood as contributing to state capacities to wage war and achieve security from violence, but they were 'security' issues because of their links to state war-making capability rather than intrinsically seen as security threats in their own right.

Wars, militaries and the environment

Military violence and environmental degradation are linked directly in at least three ways. First, the pursuit of national security from violence through military means consumes resources (fiscal, organisational and leadership) that could be spent on environmental restoration. However, this relationship is hardly unique to environmental concerns. There is no guarantee that money saved from military expenditures would be spent on environmental restoration.

Second, preparation for war poses a significant environmental burden, through the consumption of metal and fuel, and the generation of toxic and radioactive waste.

Third, war is directly destructive of the environment. Most of this destruction is an unintentional effect of war, while some of it is the intentional destruction of the natural environment, or 'environmental warfare'. History is replete with examples, from the ancient destruction of olive groves to defoliants in Indo-China and oil fires in Kuwait. Advanced conventional war could produce catastrophic releases of radiation from civilian nuclear power plants. Most ominously, extensive nuclear detonations and fires could have significant impacts on the global environment, producing a 'nuclear winter'. Awareness of these potentials played a role in mobilising popular resistance to the arms race and in de-legitimising nuclear weapons.

In summary, war and the preparation for war clearly contribute to environmental problems. These impacts mean that the use and threat of large-scale violence to resolve conflicts have costs beyond the intentional loss of life and destruction. Despite this, most environmental degradation is not caused by war and preparation for war. Most environmental degradation would remain even if the direct environmental effects of preparing for and waging war were completely eliminated. The main sources and solutions must be found outside the domain of the traditional national security system related to violence.

Threats and national security

The war system is a significant but limited source of environmental destruction, but in what ways is environmental degradation a threat to national security? One answer is to broaden the definition of national security to encompass environmental harms. The appeal of this move hinges on the differences and similarities of security from violence and environmental threats. Upon examination, we see great differences with regard to the *type* of threat, the *source* of threat, the degree of *intentionality* and the types of organisations involved.

First, environmental degradation and interstate violence both entail threats to life and property, but in very different ways. Both may kill people and may reduce human wellbeing, but not all threats to life and property are threats to security. Disease, ageing, crime and accidents routinely destroy life and property, but we do not think of them as 'national security' threats or even threats to 'security'. (Crime is a partial exception, but crime is a 'security' threat at the individual level because crime involves violence.) Regarding earthquake or hurricane damage, we speak of 'natural disasters', not 'national security threats'. If everything that causes a reduction in human wellbeing is labelled a 'security' threat, the term loses any analytical usefulness and becomes a loose synonym of 'bad'.

Second, the scope and source of threats to environmental wellbeing and national security from violence are very different. Not many environmental problems are particularly national in character; few environmental problems afflict just one nation state. They often spill across international borders, or affect the global commons beyond state jurisdiction. But most environmental problems are not international, because many perpetrators and victims are within the borders of one nation state. Individuals, families, communities, other species and future generations are harmed. A complete collapse of the biosphere would surely destroy nation states as well as everything else, but there is nothing distinctively national about the causes, the harms or the solutions that warrants us giving such privileged billing to the national grouping.

A third dissimilarity between environmental wellbeing and national security from violence is in the level of intention involved. Interstate violence typically involves a high degree of intentional behaviour manifest in organisational mobilisation, weapons procurement and war waging. In contrast, environmental degradation is largely the unintentional side effect of many other very mundane activities.

Fourth, organisations that provide protection from violence differ greatly from those in environmental protection. National security from violence is pursued by organisations that are secretive, hierarchical and centralised. They typically deploy expensive, specialised and advanced technologies. Citizens typically delegate national security to remote and highly specialised organisations that are far removed from civil society. Professional groups staffing national security organisations are specialised and trained in the arts of killing and destroying.

In contrast, environmental restoration requires changes in aspects of virtually all mundane activities such as house construction, farming techniques, sewage treatment, factory design and land use. The routine behaviour of virtually everyone must be altered. And the professional ethos of environmental restoration is stewardship – more respectful cultivation and protection of animals, plants and land.

In sum, national security from violence and environmental habitability are far more dissimilar than similar. Given these differences, linking them via redefinition risks creating a conceptual muddle rather than a paradigm or worldview shift. If all the forces and events that threaten life, property and wellbeing are understood as threats to national security, the term will come to be drained of useful meaning. This is even more of a problem for 'comprehensive security' images that add together all possible threats. If all large-scale evils become threats to national security, the result will be a *de-definition* rather than a *redefinition* of security. In the unlikely event this were to happen, it would be necessary to invent new or redefine old words to serve the role performed by the old, spoiled ones.

'Moral equivalents of war'

A third contemporary 'environmental security' move is to link security and environment in order to mobilise and motivate. When national security is at stake, people are willing to bear heavy costs in lives, wealth and lost liberty. Therefore, if people reacted as urgently and effectively to environmental problems as to the national security from violence problem, then much more effort and resources would be mobilised. This form of 'environmental security' is a rhetorical and psychological strategy to redirect social energies now devoted to war and interstate violence toward environmental amelioration.

This mobilisation strategy is neither original nor unique to the environmental cause. Social reformers have long sought a 'moral equivalent to war'. In the United States, 'war on poverty', 'war on crime' and 'war on drugs' have not been particularly successful despite their rhetorical linkages. The discourse of national security has a set of powerful associations that cannot simply be redirected to intractable social problems, like the environment, with little in common with the pursuit of national security from violence.

Aside from its ineffectiveness, this strategy might alter environmental politics in very negative ways. National security claims are politically potent because they are connected to state institutions, national identities and international war. Tapping these potent forces risks making environmental politics more conflictual and parochial, producing a 'militarised environment' rather than 'green security' (Kakonen 1994). It is instructive to compare the specific interrelated assumptions, norms, ideologies, identities and institutions associated with the national war state and those associated with environmental sustainability.

States, wars and nations

At the centre of attention must be the powerful trinity of the state, nation and war that largely defines 'national security' in contemporary world politics. State institutions, national identities and interstate war have such salience and persistence in world politics because they powerfully reinforce one another. The sad truth is that it is very difficult to create national self-consciousness without war. The dominant view of political scientists and historians is that 'states make war and war makes states' (Tilly 1985). States build and sustain national political identities by using memories of war in educational systems, public ceremonies and direct indoctrination.

An apparently attractive feature of treating environmental problems as national security threats is the urgency created, and the corresponding willingness to accept great sacrifice. If the basic sustainability of the planet is being undermined, then surely some crisis mentality is warranted. But it is difficult to sustain urgency and sacrifice for extended periods. Crises call for resolution, and the patience of a mobilised populace is rarely long. Wars demand victory and a return to normality, producing a cycle of passivity and arousal that is not likely to make much of a contribution to establishing enduring patterns of environmentally sound behaviour. Furthermore, crisis solutions are often 'crash' projects, more expensive, more centralised and poorly designed.

Another seemingly appealing fit between national security and environmental problem solving is the tendency to use worse-case scenarios as the basis for planning. However, military organisations are not unique in this regard. The insurance industry routinely prepares for the worst possibilities, and many fields of engineering, such as aeronautical design and nuclear power plant regulation, also employ extremely conservative planning assumptions. However, it is not necessary for environmental policy to be modelled after national security and military organisations to achieve risk-averse planning.

Conventional national security organisations are geared to zero-sum approaches: 'our' gain is 'their' loss. Trust is low, as everyone is a potential enemy, and agreements mean little unless congruent with immediate interests. If the Pentagon had been put in charge of negotiating an ozone protocol, we might still be racing to stockpile chlorofluorocarbons as 'bargaining chips'. National security organisations discount the future and pursue very near-term objectives, a clear mismatch with the needs of environmental sustainability.

Coercive conservation and ecototalitarianism

Framing the environmental problem as a national security threat may also entail the expansion of state capabilities to regulate and manage the environment, and this may engender oppression and conflict in the many countries where states are weak and repressive, and political identities are not national. Many states in the developing world are already practising 'coercive conservation', the use of state power to dispossess rural populations, particularly indigenous peoples, of their traditional natural resources in order to benefit state elites and multi-national corporations (Peluso and Watts 2001).

Expanding the security state also puts individual freedom at risk. State action to secure against a threat often involves erosion of individual liberty. In the wake of the murderous and genocidal authoritarian and totalitarian states of the twentieth century, the language of 'comprehensive security' and 'ultimate security' feed into fears of 'eco-totalitarianism' (Stern 1995; Myers 1993). Because almost all human activities affect the environment in some way or another, assigning states the task of environmental security suggests total control.

Lack of attention to these 'liberty fall-outs' in environmental security thinking may in part derive from more general left and socialist blindness toward the perils of 'big government'. But this inattention may also derive from the exceptional American experience. The original American Constitutional order, an elaborate system of constraints on the accumulation of centralised state power and collective problem solving, impeded responses to the problems of industrialism domestically and globalisation internationally. External military threats have been catalysts to state building in the United States, and progressives seeking stronger governmental institutions have often found it expedient to frame their social welfare agendas in terms of national security. Similarly, American nationalism has centred upon liberal and civic identities, which have countered fractious ethnicities and moderated conflicts. Thus, evoking national security in the United States perhaps has different and more innocent implications than it does in much of the rest of the world, where too much rather than too little state power threatens public safety and liberty.

Enemies in the global village?

Perhaps most importantly, privileging national identity and security collides directly with worldviews and identities supportive of sustainable environmental practices. The nation is not an empty vessel or blank slate waiting to be filled or scripted, but is instead profoundly linked to 'us versus them' thinking, of the insider versus the outsider, of the compatriot versus the alien. The stronger the nationalism, the stronger this cleavage and the weaker transnational bonds. Nationalism reinforces militarism, fosters prejudice and discrimination and feeds the quest for sovereign autonomy (see de-Shalit, chapter 5).

In contrast, with environmental problems, 'we have met the enemy and they are us', as the comic strip figure Pogo aptly observed. Given that existing 'us versus them' groupings in world politics poorly match causal patterns of environmental problems, we need to redefine who 'we' are and who 'us' encompasses. A central theme of environmental political thought is that ecological interdependence requires replacing or supplementing national with other forms of group identity. Privileging the nation directly conflicts with the 'one world', the 'whole earth', the 'global village', and the 'common fate' understanding of our situation, and the 'world community' and 'international co-operation' needed to solve many environmental problems. Taken to an absurd extreme – as 'national security' threats sometimes are – seeing environmental degradation in a neighbouring country as a national security threat could evoke interventions and armed conflicts.

Contemporary national security is also closely connected to the institution of state sovereignty. In the international society of states, sovereignty has come to mean the existence in a polity of a final and undivided authority over a particular territory, which only states can possess, and the reciprocal recognition of this authority which states extend to one another. This system of legitimate authority marginalises the autonomy and authority of other actors both within states and outside them. When issues of national security are at stake, states tend to be particularly jealous of their sovereign prerogatives. Enhanced state concern for sovereign prerogatives could greatly impede environmental co-operation, because responding to international and global environmental problems often requires arrangements that divide and pool authority.

Toward terrapolitan civilisation

Fortunately, environmental awareness need not depend upon co-opted 'national security' thinking. Integrally woven into ecological concerns are a powerful set of interests and values – most notably human health and property values, religions and ethics, and natural beauty and concern for future generations. Efforts to raise awareness of environmental problems can thus connect directly with these strong, basic and diverse human interests and values as sources of motivation and mobilisation. Far from needing to be bolstered by national security mind sets, a green sensibility can make strong claims to being the master metaphor for an emerging post-industrial civilization.

Fully grasping the ramifications of the emerging environmental problems requires a radical rethinking and reconstitution of many of the major institutions of industrial modernity, including the nation. The nation and the national are complex composites of different components, most notably ethnicity, religion, language, war memories and place. This last dimension of the national – identification with place, which geographers refer to as 'geopiety' and 'topophilia' (Tuan 1994), opens avenues for reconstructing identity in ecologically appropriate ways (see also Eckersley, this volume). Identification with a particular physical place has been an important component of national identity.

With the growth of ecological problems, this sense of place, and threat to place, take on a new character. Environmentalists positing the 'bioregion' as the appropriate unit for political identity subvert the state-constructed and state-supporting nation. Even more subversively, the globalist assertion that the entire planet is the only naturally autonomous bioregion evokes 'earth nationalism'. Such an earth nationalism is radical in the sense of returning to fundamental roots, and in posing a fundamental challenge to the hegemonic state sponsored concept of nation. In contrast to the traditional opposition between abstract and de-contextualised cosmopolitanism and the rooted and contextualized nation, the 'earth national' sensibility might be usefully termed 'terrapolitan' (Deudney 1995).

Conclusion

The degradation of the natural environment upon which human well-being depends is a problem with far-reaching significance for all human societies. But this problem has little to do with the problem of national security from violence that continues to afflict politics. Not only is there little in common between the causes and solutions to these two problems, but the nationalist and militarist mind sets closely associated with national security thinking directly conflict with the core of the emerging environmentalist worldview. Harnessing these sentiments for a 'war on pollution' is a dangerous and probably self-defeating enterprise. And, fortunately, the prospects for resource and pollution wars are not as great as often conjured by environmentalists.

Overall, the pervasive recourse to national security paradigms to conceptualise the environmental problem represents a profound and disturbing failure of political imagination. If the nation state enjoys a more prominent status in world politics than its competence and accomplishments warrant, then it makes little sense to emphasise the links between it and the emerging problem of global habitability. Nationalist sentiment and the war system have a long-established logic and staying power that are likely to defy any rhetorically conjured 'redirection' toward benign ends. The movement to preserve the habitability of the planet for future generations must directly challenge the power of state-centric nationalism and the chronic militarisation of public discourse. Environmental degradation is not a threat to national security. Rather, environmentalism is a threat to the conceptual hegemony of state-centred national security discourses and institutions. For environmentalists to dress their programmes in the blood-soaked garments of the war system betrays their core values and creates confusion about the real tasks at hand.

References

Arnold, David (1986). *The Problem of Nature: Environment, Culture and European Expansion*. Oxford: Blackwell.

Beaumont, Peter (1994). 'The Myth of Water Wars and the Future of Irrigated Agriculture in the Middle East', *International Journal of Water Resources Development* **10**: 9–22.

Brodie, Bernard (1972). 'The Impact of Technological Change on the International System', in David Sullivan and Martin Sattler (eds.), *Change and the Future of the International System*. New York: Columbia University Press.

Conca, Ken, and Dabelko D. Geoffrey (eds.) 2002. *Environmental Peacemaking*. Baltimore, Md.: Johns Hopkins University Press.

Deudney, Daniel (1990). 'The Case Against Linking Environmental Degradation and National Security', *Millennium* **19**: 461–76.

—— (1995). 'Ground Identity: Nature, Place, and Space in the National', in David Sullivan and Martin Sattler (eds.), *The Return of Culture and Identity to International Relations Theory*. Boulder, Colo.: Lynne Reinner, 129–45.

Glacken, Clarence (1967). *Traces on the Rhodian Shore: Nature and Culture in Western Thought from Ancient Times to the End of the Eighteenth Century*. Berkeley: University of California Press.

Heilbroner, Robert (1974). *An Enquiry Into the Human Prospect*. New York: Norton.

Hepple, L. W. (1986). 'The Revival of Geopolitics', *Political Geography Quarterly* **5**.4: 521–36.

Homer-Dixon, Thomas F. (1999). *Environment, Scarcity, and Violence*. Princeton: Princeton University Press.

Kakonen, Jyrki (eds.) (1994). *Green Security or Militarized Environment*. Aldershot, Hampshire: Dartmouth.

Kaplan, Robert (1996). *The Ends of the Earth: A Journey to the Frontiers of Anarchy*. New York: Vintage Books

Kristof, Ladis (1960). 'The Origin and Evolution of Geopolitics', *Journal of Conflict Resolution* **4** (March): 15–51.

Lipschutz, Ronnie D. (1989). *When Nations Clash: Raw Materials, Ideology and Foreign Policy*. Cambridge, Mass.: Ballinger.

Luard, Evan (1989). *The Blunted Sword: The Erosion of Military Power in Modern World Politics*. New York: New Amsterdam Books.

Mueller, John (1989). *Retreat from Doomsday: The Obsolescence of Major War*. New York: Basic Books.

Myers, Norman (1993). *Ultimate Security: The Environmental Basis of Political Stability*. New York: Norton.

Ophuls, William (1976). *Ecology and the Politics of Scarcity*. San Francisco: Freeman.

Peluso, Nancy, and Watts, Michael (eds.) (2001). *Violent Environments*. Ithaca, N.Y.: Cornell University Press.

Stern, Eric K. (1995). 'Bringing the Environment In: The Case for Comprehensive Security', *Co-Operation and Conflict* **30**.3: 211–37.

Tilly, Charles (1985). 'War Making and State Making as Organized Crime'. in Peter Evans, Dietrich Rueschemeyer and Theda Skocpol (eds.), *Bringing the State Back In*. Cambridge: Cambridge University Press, 169–91.

Tuan, Yi-Fu (1994). *Topophilia: A Study of Environmental Perception, Attitudes, and Values*. Bloomington: University of Indiana Press.

Index

accountability 18, 106, 111, 122–5, 145, 177
  of corporations 19, 119
  democracy and 139, 145
  mutual 124
  of NGOs 17, 18, 19
Achterberg, W. 25
acting locally and thinking globally 39,
  81–2, 96, 224
activism: *see also* environmental
  activism, cosmopolitanism 104
  local 96–7, 102
  motivation for 70
  political 9
affectedness 105, 107
affluence 169
agency 19, 68, 174, 204, 213
  green theory of 143
  human 95
  moral 149
  of nature 68–9, 205
  rights and 207–9, 213
aggression 151, 155–6
Alaska 134
Alliance of Small Island States 123
Allier, J.M. 176
Anderson, Benedict 98
Anderson, T. 30
androcentricism 53, 58, 67
animal liberation 159, 160
animal rights movement 220, 221
animals 87, 159, 205, 220
  interests of 137–9, 141, 143, 159–61
  moral concern owed to 27, 28, 57
anthropocentrism 52, 59–60, 62, 148–9,
  161–3
  environmental activism and 64
  feminism and 56–8, 67
  liberalism and 21, 23, 26–9, 31
  nationalism and 87–8
  socialism and 41
Aristotle 123, 233
  pity 121

Arnold, D. 233
attachments 104, 106, 112
authoritarianism 132, 139, 145, 240–1
authority, political 180
autonomy 29, 86, 180
  ecology and 209, 213–14
  illusion of 64–5, 72

balance 40
Balfour, Lady Eve 7
Ball, Terence 131–45
Bangladesh 46
Barnett, A. 17
Barry, B. 27, 122
Barry, J. 21, 29
Basic Income 48
Batty, H. 86
Beaumont, P. 238
Beauvoir, Simone de 53
belief 194
Bell, D. 22, 25
belonging 105–6
Benn, S.I. 208, 213
Bennholdt-Thomsen, V. 46
Bentham, Jeremy 27, 135, 201, 220
Beran, H. 76
Berlin, Isaiah 202
Bernstein, S. 176
Berry, Wendell 143
Bhopal, gas explosion at 118–19
biocracy 134, 139–44
bioregionalism 20, 97–8, 103, 190–1, 229,
  249
borders 82–7
Brazil 170
Brennan, A. 87
Brodie, B. 241
Bull, H. 166
Burke, E. 2, 10, 12, 18
  hereditary principle 13–14
Bush administration 82
bystander phenomenon 122

Callicott, Baird 159
capital 8, 13, 36
capitalism 23, 35, 37, 41–4, 66, 170
 allocation of resources 41
 exploitative nature of 45
 globalised 35–6
 green challenge to 38
 role of money 43–6
Carson, Rachel 62–3
Carter, A. 27
Catton, W.R. 133
China 170
Christianity 62
citizen, active 222, 224–5, 228–9
citizenship 101, 104, 112, 216–231
 architecture of 216–18, 225–31, 227
 concept of 107, 226
 cosmopolitan 101, 231
 ecological 225–6, 230
 ecological challenges to 218–19
 feminist critique of 217–18
 forms of 106
 global environmental 120
 liberal 216–23, 229
 nationalism and 76
 qualifications for 221
 relations comprising 216
 republican 216–18, 221–5, 229
 rights and 216, 227
citizen's income 48
civil society 81, 177–80
Cohen, S. 110
collective action 103, 175, 239
command economies 48
common experience 121–2, 125, 166, 229
common good 47, 222–5
communication 67, 142, 190–1
communitarianism 77, 91–106
 and cosmopolitanism 102–5, 112
 ecological potential and limitations
  100–1
 green perspective on 95–100
 identity and community 105–7
communities 28, 179
 ecologically sustainable 92
 epistemic 178, 180
 of fate 110, 187
 imagined 104, 114
community 39, 98–100, 103, 181, 213
 bioregional 97–8
 biotic 138
 boundedness of 92–5, 171
 and cosmopolitan 112–13
 extending the sense of 105, 125, 136–7
 local 96–7, 107

moral 138, 141
 national 98–100
 of nations 109, 110
 political 141
compassion 103, 115, 123, 227
compromise 133
concepts, political 2
conceptual change and conceptual history
  135
conflict 235–42
conflict resolution principles 67, 150–8,
  162–3
 principle of disproportionality 153–5
 principle of human defence 155–7
 principle of human preservation 150–3
 principle of rectification 157
connectedness 112, 121, 124, 210,
  226, 241
conservation 78, 79, 246–7
conservatism 7–12
constructivism 58
consultation, right to 123
consumerism 11, 12, 30, 36, 76, 211–12
consumption 71, 119, 170, 211–12
co-operation 67, 168, 174, 203
 interstate 166, 168–9, 174–5, 237, 248
co-operatives 47–8
corporations 19, 84, 119
cosmopolitanism 109–21, 125, 179, 229,
  249
 challenge to citizenship 218, 225, 228
 citizenship 227–9, 231
 and communitarianism 91, 93–4, 99,
  101, 102–5
 and political practice 125
coverture 65–9
Crawford, N.C. 114
credit 44–5
culture 53–4, 56, 72, 124
 environmental 72
 local 95
 and nature 58
 shared 105

Dagger, Richard 200–14, 220
Daly, H. 44
Darwin, Charles 62
Davis, W. 120
Dearing, R.L. 113
deep ecology 26, 32, 61–5
 anthropocentrism 60
 unity interpretation of 65–7
De Gues, M. 25
de-Shalit, Avner 27, 75–89, 99
Demeritt, D. 193

democracy 9, 21–2, 49, 71, 105–7, 131–45, 240
  and accountability 145
  cosmopolitan 105
  credit and 45
  decentralised 134, 140
  deliberative 21, 142, 144, 197
  democratic deficit 177
  economic 44–8
  and environmentalism 132–4
  green 136
  history of 132
  indirect 140
  liberal 217
  protectionist theory of 144
  shortcomings of 131
  social 72
  socialism and 47–9
  and sustenance 47–9
Derrida, J. 184
Descartes, Rene 20
deservingness 148–50
Deudney, Daniel 232–50
Devall, B. 28
developing countries 177, 232, 247
dialogue 67, 72, 123
dignity, equal 93
diversity 91, 145, 166, 172, 176, 181
DiZerega, G. 29
Dobson, Andrew 1–4
  citizenship 200, 216–231
  cosmopolitanism 123
  democracy 21
  ecological footprint 102, 105, 120
  justice 77, 122
  liberalism 22, 29
  participation 133
  political representation 144, 183, 186–7, 196
  property 30
Dodge, J. 97
dominance, gender, class and species 68
domination 154; *see also* freedom, non-domination
Douglas, M. 124
Dower, N. 112
Downs, Anthony 135
Dryzek, J. 21, 135, 142, 167
  representation, political 186, 190–1, 195, 196
dualisms 61, 64
Dunlap, R. 82
duties 22, 106, 112, 114, 116–17, 202, 222

Earth First! 133, 162–3

Eckersley, Robyn 1–4, 91–107, 123–4, 143
  democracy 137, 187–8
  environmental management 110, 119, 172
  identity 249
  liberalism 21
  nature's interests 144
  political theory 167–81
  representation, political 186, 196
  rights 213
ecoanarchism 99
ecocentrism 137, 143
ecocommunitarianism 103
ecofeminism 51, 52, 55–6
  vegan 56–7
ecological footprint 102, 105, 120, 230
ecological impulse 60
ecologism 1, 30
ecology 55, 83–7
  and autonomy 209, 213–14
  and nationalism 76–88
econationalism 99
economic growth 9, 21, 36, 42, 240
  economic good 71
economics 39, 42, 73
ecosystems 98, 138–9, 141
ecototalitarianism 246–7
education 143–5, 223, 234, 248
egoism 154, 175
Elgin 46
Elias 113
emotions 111, 113–15
empowerment 71, 172
Engels, F. 41
Enlightenment 20–1, 91, 94–5, 233
entropy 8–9, 16
environment
  national 99
  responsibility for 223
  rights linked to 203, 220
environmental activism 17–18, 40, 71, 101, 196
  acting locally and thinking globally 39, 81, 224
  local solutions 39
  motivation 60
  political theory 38–41, 58–61, 64, 71
  responsibility 120
environmental harm 37, 111, 174, 233
  causes of 11, 118–19
  costs of 176
  effects of 115
  nationalism and 88
  prevention of 75
  security and 250

environmental harm (*cont.*)
  types of 111, 118–121
  violence and 242–3, 249
  and war 238–41
environmentalism 11, 30, 51, 132–4
environmental issues 228
  complexity of 133, 235
  global character of 168–9, 228
  as national security threats 246
  scale of 168
environmental management 169
environmental protection 14, 84, 176, 244
environmental regulation 175, 177–9, 180
environmental restoration 244
environmental theory 51–2, 58, 77, 140
  political 1, 3–4, 95–100, 176, 186–7, 219
equality 11, 37, 41–2, 46–7, 71, 156
equilibrium 9, 10
ethics 65–7, 151, 156
  communitarian 95
  cosmopolitan 113
  environmental 113
  feminist 60, 72, 112
  solidarity 70
externalities 43

fairness 156 *see also* justice
Farr, J. 136
Feinberg, Joel 117, 207–9
feminism 3, 51–73, 112
  anthropocentric 56–8
  Artemisian 53
  critique of capitalism 42
  critiques of citizenship 217–18, 225–9
  dualisms 61
  ecological 52–6
  gynocentric 54
  hybrid ecological 54
  partnership 67–9
  project of 54
  socialist 55
  solidarity 70
Ferry, L. 132
Fisher, W.F. 36
foreign policy 82
Foreman, Dave 134, 206, 209
freedom 32, 200–13, 229
  agency-freedom 204, 206, 211
  economic 8, 29–31
  individual 7, 247
  of nature 205–9
  nature of 201–5
  negative 200–4, 210
  as opportunity 203
  option-freedom 204, 206, 211–13

positive 201–2, 204
  republican 204
free market 7, 8, 20, 23, 29, 38, 44, 240
free market environmentalism 30
free riders 84, 239
free trade 23, 87
Fukuyama, Francis 35, 221
future generations 26, 131
  duty to 79–80, 138
  interests of 137–9, 141, 143
  needs of 156
  representation of 187, 197

Gallie, W.B. 134
Gardiner, Rolf 7
Garner, R. 25
geopolitics 233–5
Geras, N. 117
Gilligan, G. 113
Glacken, C. 233
global conscience 115, 121
global economic system 72, 169, 175, 181
global governance 167, 171, 177–8, 180, 182
globalisation 109, 169, 230
  citizenship and 106
  and cosmopolitanism 101–2
global village 86, 247–8
global warming 86, 119, 122, 123
Goldhagen, D.J. 117
good 24, 71
Goodin, Robert 112, 133, 143
  democracy 134, 197
  representation, political 137, 140, 144,
    186, 188–90, 196
Good Samaritanism 117
Gopal-Jayal, N. 83
Graham, Kenneth 100
Gray, T. 86
Great Ape Project 221
Great Britain, political decision-making
    15–16
Green, T.H. 201–2
Greenpeace 18
green political theory 1
guilt 113–15, 117, 125
gynocentrism 54

Haas, P.M. 173, 174
Hage, G. 99
Hailwood, Simon 29
Hall, Stuart 186
Halliday, F. 121
Hardin, Garrett 201
Harding, Sandra 70
Hardt, M. 48

harm, responsibility for 102, 111
Harmon Doctrine 119
harmony 40
harm principle 103, 113, 115–18, 120, 124, 138, 229, 230
Hay, Peter 60, 65
Hayward, Tim 87, 219
Hegel, G.W.F. 13, 99, 110
hegemony 234, 250
Heilbroner, R. 133, 240
Held, David 99, 102, 105–7
Hepple, L.W. 234
hereditary principle 13–14
heritage 78–9, 79
Himmler, Heinrich 132
Hinchliffe, S. 195
Hitler, Adolf 132
Hobbes, Thomas 2, 201
holism, and individualism 157–63
Holland, A. 204
Holmes, S. 21, 203
Homer-Dixon, T.F. 241
homo clausus 113, 116, 120
human and non-human issues 59–61, 64–5, 71
human embeddedness 40–1, 62, 64, 112
humanity 53–4, 176
human/nature dualism 56–7, 63–4
human rights 110, 115, 220
Hume, David 121–2
Hurrell, Andrew 165–82
Hutchinson, F. 43–4
hybridity 51–2, 54–6
hyperseparation 62–5

identity 70, 91–5, 112
ideologies, political 1–3
Ignatieff, Michael 227
immanent realism 40
imperialism 176
independence 201
individualism 28, 157–63
institutional design 191–8
institutions 12, 16, 139–44, 171
  coverture 66
  international 111, 174, 176, 234
instrumentalism 59, 66, 77–8, 166
interdependence 201, 210, 229, 233
  and security 248
  and war 239, 242
interest, national 81, 82
interests 137–41, 144, 190, 248
  conflict of 158
  of future generations 138–9, 141, 144
  of humans 149

internalisation of 188–9
  of nature 138–40, 188
  of non-human living things 138–41, 144, 149, 152
  objective 192
  and rights 207
  of voters 183
international agreements 84–5, 172
International Criminal Court 118–19
international law 166, 167, 172–3, 179
  criminal 110, 118
  environmental 118, 119
  of war 114, 115
international organisations 81, 84, 125, 234
international relations 171, 234
international society 172
intervention, international 85–7
Iraq 118
Islamic societies 10

Johnson, H. 81
Jouvenel, Bertrand de 141
justice 25, 37, 67, 95, 148–62, 227
  abstract principles of 99
  anthropocentrism and 148–50
  empowerment and 71
  environmental 148
  global 94, 102, 111, 122–5, 125
  restorative 123
  social 11, 15
  socialist 156
  socioeconomic 38
  welfare liberal 156

Kakonen, J. 245
Kant, Immanuel 25, 27, 109, 121, 143
Kaplan, Robert 232
Kay, J.H. 212
Kemball-Cook, D. 81
Keynes, J.M. 9
Kingsnorth, Paul 97
knowledge 40, 62, 192, 193
Konstan, D. 121
Kovel, Joel 49
Krasner, I.S.D. 85
Kristof, L. 234
Kummer, K. 124
Kymlicka, W. 105
Kyoto protocol 82, 84, 174

Lamb, R. 81
land ethic 136–7, 209–10
Lane, Robert 142
Leal, D. 30

legitimacy, political 177
Leopold, Aldo 63, 136, 209–10, 213
liberalism 20–32, 66, 174–6, 200–1
    anthropocentrism 26–9, 31
    classical 20, 29–30
    conception of the good 24
    and concern for animals 28
    and economic freedom 29–31
    green theory 23, 23–32
    limits to neutrality 24–5, 31
    neoliberalism 72
    neutrality 23–6
    ontological assumptions 24–5
    as a political theory 21, 23
    self 92
    social 29, 31–2
    welfare 154
libertarianism 154
liberty: *see* freedom
Light, A. 77
Linklater, Andrew 91, 102, 109–21, 218, 229
Lipschutz, R.D. 236
listening 142, 190, 191
Litfin, K.T. 167
living standards 240
Local Employment and Trading Schemes 47
Locke, John 2, 29–30, 66, 200, 203–4
Lomborg, Bjørn 18, 19
loyalty 92–3, 100, 103
    ecological 100
    hybrid 51
    local 14, 103–4
    and motivation 96
    national 15–16, 98, 165
Luard, E. 235
Lupton, D. 113

MacCallum, G.C. 203–4
MacCormick, N. 165
MacIntyre, Alastair 94
Mackie, J.L. 116
Mandragon co-operatives 48
market economy 8, 11, 40–4, 46, 48, 92 *see also* capitalism free market efficiency of 37
    and the poor 43
market failure 38
Marx, Karl 2, 40–1, 44, 47
    money 43–4
    origin of capitalism 43
    trading of commodities 42
Mason, M. 124
Massingham, H.J. 7

Matthews, F. 96, 135
McCright, A. 82
McLean, I. 82
Meadows, D. 37
Meisner, M. 194–5
Mellor, Mary 35–49, 93
metaphor 191–8
Midgley, Mary 62
militarism 247, 249
military violence 242–3
Mill, James 135
Mill, John Stuart 21, 25, 135, 145, 197
    harm principle 26, 116–17, 138
Miller 76, 78, 105
Mills, Mike 136
Mills, W.J. 193–4, 194
Moeller, S.D. 122
Monbiot, George 15, 19
money 41–6, 48
    capitalisation of 43
    investment through money systems 44–5
    monopoly 86–7
Montesquieu, Baron de 233
moral concern, hierarchy of 27–8
moral intuition 176
moral recognition, extension of 139
moral status 87, 148, 154, 158, 187, 204
motivation 13–14, 17, 60, 70, 92
    attachment and 105
    and loyalty 96
Mueller, J. 235
Myers, N. 247
myth 79, 83

Naess, A. 28, 77
Nash, Roderick 207, 209
national interest 81, 82
nationalism 75–88, 233, 247, 249
    anthropocentrism and 87–8
    definition of 75–6
    econationalism 99, 249
    and ecology 76–88
    egalitarian 76
    heritage and 78–9
    solidarity and 76–8
nation states 12, 110, 165, 216, 249
    boundaries 82
    citizenship 217–18, 225, 227–28
    co-operation between 166
    and war 245–6, 249
natural resources 30, 38, 98
    limits of 37, 45
    private ownership of 30, 38
    scarcity of 26, 229, 236
nature 31, 40, 54, 56, 58, 66, 104, 142

agency of 66, 68–9
boundaries and 84
concept of 68, 176, 192, 205, 233
interests of 188–9, 192
legal standing of 206
maintenance role of 68, 72
metaphorical representations of 193–5,
  196–7
nature/culture dualism 54–5
political representation of 186–7, 189,
  196–7
rights of 205–9, 209–10
solidarity with 71
value of 28–9, 66
Nayakrishi, Andolon 46
Nazi attitude to nature 99, 132, 145
needs 46
  basic 150–1, 153, 155–6, 158, 162
  non-basic 154–6
negotiation, culture of 70–3
Negri, A. 48
Nelson 46
neo-liberalism 72
Nepal 153
New Agricultural Movement, Bangladesh
  46
NGOs 81, 84–5, 180
  accountability 17, 19
  environmental 18, 95
  role of 177–8, 180, 239
Nickel, J. 213
NIMBY 81, 97
non-domination 154, 204
non-humans, moral concern for 52, 59,
  63
norms 172–3, 178–9, 234
Norton, Bryan 28, 204
Nozick, Robert 27, 29–30
nuclear power 243
nuclear weapons 234, 238
Nussbaum, Martha 103, 111
Nylen, W.R. 48

O'Connor, J. 43
oil, conflict over 238
Oksanen, M. 31
Olsen, W. 43–4
O'Neill, J. 77
O'Neill, O. 124
Ophuls, W. 21, 133, 240
opportunity, equality of 32
oppression 53, 67
'ought' implies 'can' principle 151–2, 162

participation 133, 224

partnership 67–9, 72, 193, 195
Pearce, J. 47
Peluso, N. 247
Perelman, M. 46
permissibility 152
  strong 152, 153, 162
  weak 152
Pettit, Philip 204–6, 211
Pitkin, Hannah 141, 183–4
pity 121–2
place, sense of 82–3, 97, 100–1, 249
Plumwood, Val 51–73, 193, 195
pluralism 166–7, 173–4
  moral 22
  norms and 166, 173, 177, 179
Pois, R.A. 132
policy, environmental 80
political ecology 219–25, 228–9
political order 165
political theory
  classical 2
  green 143, 170, 186–7, 197
politics 8, 17, 65–7, 83–7, 124, 219, 234
  communitarian 95
  geopolitics 233–5
  global 15
  green 167, 224
  partnership 67–9
  solidarity 70, 70–3
pollution 87, 120, 239
Ponniah, T. 36
population policy 27
poverty 43, 169, 240–1
power 67, 180, 182, 228, 238
  balance of 166, 172, 238–9
  unequal 121, 166, 176, 177
precautionary principle 120, 197
preferences 25, 141
  individual 25
  time preference 80
preservation 78–9
pressure groups 17
principle of disproportionality 153–7, 163
principle of human defense 155–7, 162–3
principle of human preservation 150–3, 155,
  158, 162–3
principle of rectification 157–8, 163
production 36, 41–2, 45–6, 48, 119
  feminist critique of 56
property, private 14, 22–3, 29, 32, 46, 66,
  68–9, 72
  distribution of 32, 156
property rights 23, 25, 29, 31, 119
provisioning 46–9
public goods 174, 222–3

Raddon, M.-B. 47
rationalism 175
rationality 149
  instrumental 77–8
Rawls, John 24–5, 27, 167, 171
  just savings principle 25
  theory of justice 25
realism, immanent 40
reason 91, 94, 95, 114
representation, political 139–41, 144, 177,
    183, 192
  aesthetic aspect of 186
  bi-directionality 188, 192
  claims to 185
  concept of 184, 195
  cultural aspect of 186
  green political theory and 186–7
  institutional design and 191–8
  metaphor and 191–8
  process approach to 184–6
  unidirectionality 188–9, 190, 192
reproduction 56, 68, 69
republicanism 110, 200, 204, 222, 224
rescue 117
respect 56, 69, 99, 102, 143, 190
responsibility 173, 202, 222–4
  of citizens 223, 230
  simple and complex 120
restoration 79, 244
rights 22, 59, 106, 200–13, 207
  and agency 208–9, 213
  of autonomy 213–14
  citizenship and 216, 219, 223, 229
  economic 38
  environmental 219, 221
  human rights 110
  of nations 84
  of nature 205–9
  nature of 201–5
  negative 201–2, 205
  political 221
  positive 202, 227
  property 23, 25, 29, 31, 119
  qualifications for 222
  respect for 207
  right to be consulted 123
Rolston, W. Holmes III 153
Rorty, Richard 95, 103, 114–15
Ross, W.D. 116–17
Rousseau, J.-J. 10, 223
Rowbotham, M. 45
Royal Chitwan National Park, Nepal 153
Ruether, Rosemary 62

Sagoff, M. 20, 159

Salisbury, Lord 9
Sandel, M. 92
Saward, Michael 107, 134, 183–98
Scheff, T. 113
Schlosberg, D. 21
Schopenhauer, A. 113
Schumpeter, Joseph 135
science 62
Scott, James 165
Scruton, Roger 7–19
Searle, D. 81
security 181, 232–50
  comprehensive 245, 247
  ecological 232
  environmental 232, 235, 242, 245
  geopolitics and 233–5
  national 233, 242–5, 248–9
  national organisations 246
  threats to 243–5
self 95, 104, 111
  homo clausus 113, 116, 120
self-awareness 210, 212
self-determination 88, 94–5, 99, 105, 107
self-interest 13, 121
self/other dualism 61, 64–5, 67
self-regard 116
self-sufficiency 39, 44
self-transcendence 80
Sessions, G. 28
settled land 14 *see also* property
shame 113–15, 117, 125
Shapiro, J. 170
Shell Oil 18
Shiva, V. 119
Shrivastava, P. 119
Shue, H. 119, 202
Singer, B. 25
Singer, P. 59, 159
Slaughter, A.-M. 179
Smith, Adam 122
Smith, D.M. 110
Smith, G. 21
social bonds 92, 98, 103, 106
social contract 10, 13
socialism 7, 11, 35–7, 36, 46–7, 154
  anthropocentrism 41
  democracy and 47–9
  green 46
  limits of 36–8
  sufficiency and 46–7
social order 165, 166
social wage 48
solidarism 172–4, 177, 181, 182
solidarity 70–3, 71, 76–9, 104–5, 177
Soper, K. 40, 193

sovereignty 83–4, 110, 124, 167–8, 177, 179
    concept of 173, 232
    external and internal 83, 85–6
    greening of 181
    limits to 85–6
    local 15
    national 16, 83
    and nationalism 247
    over natural resources 98
    recognition of 166
    and security 248
Soviet Union 170
species 28
    anti-speciesism 87
state, the 37, 110, 143, 165–82
    autonomy of 179
    collapse of 241–2
    domestic weakness of 169
    ecological responsibility 124
    responses to the ecological challenge
        171–80, 180–1
    role of 178, 180, 190
    security apparatus 247
    and war 245–6
Staub, E. 111
Stephens, P. 30
Sterba, James P. 148–63, 220
Stern, G.K. 247
stewardship 144, 244
Stiglitz, Joseph 35
Stockholm agreement 119, 173
Stone, Christopher 205, 206–7, 209
stories and myths 79, 83
subsistence 42, 46
suffering, capacity for 221
sustainability 15, 97–8, 103, 106, 169, 172,
        175, 247
    citizenship and 223–5, 228, 231
    concept of 10, 11, 176
    definitions of 176
    and economic growth 44, 240
    right to 219
sustainable development 80, 169
sustenance 47–9, 49
sympathy 114, 115, 122

Tamir, Y. 76
Tangney, J.P. 113
Tasmania 197
Taylor, Charles 92, 203–5, 212
terrapolitanism 248–9
territory 82
Thompson, Dennis 184
Tilly, C. 246
Time Banks 47

time preference 80
trade, international 234, 236, 242
Trail Smelter agreement 119
transnational specialist networks 173, 178
tribalism 93–4, 99
trust 105
trusteeship 9, 10, 14
Tuan, Y.-F. 249

uncertainty 41, 171
United States, Constitution of 247
Universal Declaration of Human Rights
    220
Universal Reason 91, 93, 95
utilitarianism 59

value 42, 104, 177, 248
    conflict of 175–6
    diversity of 175
    green theory of 143, 145
    instrumental 166
    intrinsic 28, 166
    objective 189
    production of 56
VandeVeer, Donald 25
vegetarianism 56–7, 159
Viola, E. 213
violence 234, 235–42
virtue 217, 222–4, 226
voluntary simplicity 46–7
voters, interests of 183

wage labour 41–3, 44
Waldron, J. 203
Wallack, M. 25
Walzer, Michael 93–5, 99, 167
war 17, 166, 233, 235–42, 245–6, 249
    civil war 241–2
    intention and 244
    law of 114, 115
    moral equivalents of 245–9
    over natural resources 236–7
    poverty and 240–1
Waring, M. 42
Warnock, G. 116, 117
Warren, Mary Ann 159
water, conflict over 237–8
Watts, M. 247
Weale, A. 30
weapons, conventional 235
weapons, nuclear 234, 238
welfare state 23, 35, 37, 43, 48
wellbeing 77, 131, 244
Wenz, P. 27

Wiesel, G. 117
Wight, Martin 170
Williams, Raymond 14
Wissenburg, Marcel 20–32, 77
women, work of 42, 46–7, 68
women's movement 69

world order 166–7, 171
Wright, Patrick 7, 17
WTO 16, 175

Young, Iris 135
Young, S. 79